John McDonald

THE ORIGINS OF ANGLING

THE ORIGINS OF ANGLING

by John McDonald

assisted by
Sherman Kuhn and Dwight Webster
and the editors of *Sports Illustrated*

WITH PAINTINGS BY JOHN LANGLEY HOWARD

AND A NEW PRINTING OF

The Treatise of Fishing with an Angle

ATTRIBUTED TO DAME JULIANA BERNERS

DOUBLEDAY & COMPANY, INC., GARDEN CITY, NEW YORK, 1963

Library of Congress Catalog Card Number 63–11120

Printed in the United States of America

Contents

Introduction

The principal justification for this book is that *The Treatise of Fishing with an Angle,* the first writing on modern sport fishing, has long been out of print. As it is the first, and as no better essay on fishing has been written, it should always be in print. For most of two centuries, the fifteenth and sixteenth, it was alone the standard work on the sport and put its stamp on all subsequent history. In the ages before the treatise almost nothing is known about the sport. Since the treatise is a dramatic historical event, seemingly coming from the blue, we have looked into a number of questions surrounding it: the origins and history of fishing and to some extent of hunting; the mystery of Dame Juliana Berners, the legendary nun and sportswoman to whom the treatise is attributed; the deciphering of the dressings for the first known modern trout flies; and other matters. Thus the treatise became the starting point for a wider review of the sport.

The treatise was first printed in the second *Book of St. Albans* in 1496. It was written about seventy-five years earlier, and one incomplete manuscript copy, made by a scribe around 1450, survives and is in possession of the Yale University Library—thanks to the late angling collector David Wagstaff, and Mrs. Wagstaff. We print both versions in facsimile, with notes on them. This is the first time that a facsimile of the manuscript has been printed. To assist in the reading of the facsimiles we have placed them on left-hand pages with the transcripts line for line on the right-hand pages. And for easy reading we have made modernized texts of each version. Here and there we have repeated a point or a fact for the convenience of the reader.

To serve a wide variety of interests, we have divided the book into two parts. Part One is for the reader who has a general interest in fishing and hunting and a curiosity about the origins of the style and state of mind of sport. Part Two is for addicts of a number of things: fishing, old manuscripts, comparative texts, minutiae of various kinds, and early modern English; it may also interest students in the medieval and Renaissance fields.

Part One contains the modernized versions of both texts; a history of writing about fishing, with some observations on a relationship with hunting; the unsolved mystery of the author, involving a kind of chronicle, over centuries, of eminent antiquaries at work on a legend; and a discussion of the first modern trout flies, illustrated.

Part Two contains the facsimiles and transcripts of the *Treatise of Fishing*, a description and history of the manuscript, and a comparison of the manuscript and the printed text. Having issued a warning about the technical intricacy of Part Two, we owe the reader the tip that whoever takes the trouble to read the texts in the original with the help of the transcripts will be rewarded with a charming experience that cannot be obtained any other way.

The Appendixes contain the prologues of two hunting treatises which had a significant influence, we think, on the *Treatise of Fishing* and on the sport. They also contain some documentary material on the origin of the legend of Dame Juliana Berners.

The art of writing about sport holds to a remarkably firm line of thought for twenty-five hundred years and comes down to the present through a clear tradition, marked by one great transformation when it passed from the ancient Greeks to the writers of the Middle Ages. If there is a thesis in this book, it is that the spirit of modern sport and the art of the sporting treatise—*The Treatise of Fishing with an Angle* in particular—grew out of an interaction of two basic elements of the medieval mind, chivalry and learning. The exercise of skill and knowledge was thereby given the meaning we call sport.

ACKNOWLEDGMENTS

This book is a collaboration. The transcripts and modernizations of *The Treatise of Fishing with an Angle* and the textual analysis and special notes on these are the work of Professor Sherman Kuhn, Editor of the *Middle English Dictionary,* University of Michigan. Professor Kuhn also contributed to the book as a whole. The trout-fly analysis for Chapter 5 and the tying of the flies for the illustrations were done by Dwight Webster, Professor of Fishery Biology at Cornell University; he also collaborated in writing that chapter. The rest of the book was written by me and the responsibility for the book as a whole is mine.

Parts of the book in somewhat different form appeared in *Sports Illustrated* in May and June, 1957. In the sense that it originated there and received the encouragement of the editors, it is a *Sports Illustrated* project. I wish especially to thank Sidney James, Richard W. Johnston, Percy Knauth, Virginia Kraft, and Richard Gangel of that magazine for their participation, and John Langley Howard for painting the treatise flies; also Don Moss for the painting on the jacket of this book.

I am indebted to the Yale University Library for making available its extraordinary resources in the field of angling, and for permission to reproduce the manuscript of *The Treatise of Fishing with an Angle,* and the first printed version in the 1496 edition of the *Book of St. Albans.* In particular I wish to thank Miss Marjorie Wynne, Librarian of the Yale Rare Book Room, for her expert assistance in the use of the collection and for her patient and willing response to many requests. The New York Public Library and The British Museum also kindly yielded their treasures. I wish to thank the Cambridge University Library (England) for its courtesy in finding and checking various things and for permission to reprint in facsimile the handwritten notes of William Burton in a copy of the *Book of St. Albans* which, it appears, once belonged to him; the Bodleian Library, Oxford, for its many willing favors and permission to print samples of William Burton's handwriting; and Columbia University Library for permission to reprint a Latin text by John Pits; also the Stanford University Press for permission to reprint the prologue to Frederick II's *The Art of Falconry.*

I owe a great debt to Warner G. Rice, Chairman of the English Department, University of Michigan, for assistance in arrangements and for valued comment in detail on a draft of a portion of the book. A. L. Binns, the University, Hull, England, kindly read the chapter on authorship, and made helpful notes in letters and in the draft, which, like a fifteenth-century compiler, I swept into that chapter. I wish to thank Jeannette Fellheimer for research in the work of John Leland and Sir Henry Chauncy, and for comments on Chapter 4; Walter Magnusson for assistance with translations from the Latin of John Pits and Thomas Hearne; John C. McPherson for various translations from the Latin and Greek, including Sappho, and discussions about them; Gerald Eades Bentley, Louis Finkelstein, Robert La Hotan, Jane Mull, R. D. Paine, Jr., Daniel Seligman, R. W. Southern, and Lionel Trilling for reading drafts of parts of the book; William Kienbusch for finding old and scarce fishing books; and Nancy Kwok for library assistance; Mary Wilde and Richard McKelvey of the *Middle English Dictionary* for assistance on the transcripts of the treatise; also Barbara Mullen, scribe and critic; and Peggy Sweet's corporation of scribes. Along the way I had helpful talks with my old friend and fishing companion Dan Bailey and the fishermen around his Fly Shop in Livingston, Montana; and also with Joe Brooks, Dorothy McDonald, Jim Deren, Sparse Grey Hackle, and the late Jack Atherton. I want to thank William Whipple, copy editor, Anne Wrotzlau, designer, and my editor at Doubleday, Pyke Johnson, and his assistant Lynda Spence, for their interest and care in forming the book; also Jason Epstein for his original interest.

The great work on the second *Book of St. Albans* is Joseph Haslewood's facsimile edition in 150 copies (1810). My debt to his notes will be apparent in the chapter on the authorship of the *Treatise of Fishing*. Before Haslewood there was the pioneering essay on the *Book of St. Albans* by William Oldys, in a note to his piece on Caxton in *Biographia Britannica* (1748). The *Treatise of Fishing* acknowledges a debt to the hunting treatise *Master of Game*, and the connection was noticed by writers in the nineteenth century, but the first to develop the thesis that *Master of Game* is the probable model of the fishing treatise appears to be John Waller Hills in his *A History of Fly Fishing for Trout* (1920). My debt to Hills is evident in the chapter on the origins of angling; in the chapter on trout flies we go sometimes with him, sometimes against, as noted. The late Charles H. Haskins, medievalist of Harvard, made a number of valuable excursions into the field of sports; I have attempted to note my debts to him where they occur. A transcript of the early manuscript version of the *Treatise of Fishing* was published in about four hundred copies by Thomas Satchell in London in 1883, under the title *An Older Form of the Treatyse of Fysshynge wyth an Angle*. Satchell, with the assistance of the eminent medieval scholar W. W. Skeat, produced a very good transcript which we consulted. We considered reprinting it but decided that Professor Kuhn should make a new one, owing to some advances in knowledge since Satchell's time. We made valued use of Alice Dryden's *The Art of Hunting* (1908); Wm. A. and F. Baillie-Grohman's edition of *The Master of Game* (1904 and 1909); and Casey A. Wood and F. Marjorie Fyfe's translation of Frederick II's *The Art of Falconry* (1943, reissued 1961).

Among the historians of fishing and fishing literature consulted were George Washington Bethune (the Introduction to his edition of *The Compleat Angler,* 1847); Robert Blakey (*Angling Literature,* 1856); Osmund Lambert (*Angling Literature in England,* 1881); W. J. Turrell (*Ancient Angling Authors,* 1910); H. M. Hall (*Idylls of Fisherman,* 1912); and William Radcliffe (*Fishing from the Earliest Times,* 1921). The significance of chivalry and learning in the medieval mind is developed by R. W. Southern in *The Making of the Middle Ages;* a debt to his work will be apparent. J. Huizinga's *The Waning of the Middle Ages* provided a useful study of the fourteenth and fifteenth centuries; H. S. Bennett's *Chaucer and the Fifteenth Century* a helpful survey of the period of the *Treatise of Fishing.*

John McDonald

Cranberry Island, Maine
August 1962

PART ONE

CHAPTER 1

The Treatise of Fishing with an Angle *in History*

The Angler must entice, not command his reward. . . .
GERVASE MARKHAM

The Treatise of Fishing with an Angle set forth the argument, new at the time, that among the four good sports, hunting, hawking, fowling, and fishing, the best is fishing. The novelty of the treatise was not simply that it gave fishing the highest rank among these outdoor sports—though more than one noble hunter must have blinked at the contention—but that in doing so it put fishing in the same class with hunting. Its doctrine is clear: the rule is rod, line, and hook—all other kinds of fishing are set aside—and the proper comparisons are with the hunting sports. With this definition the treatise began the first known codification of the practices of the sport of fishing.[1]

[1] A sport or game may be thought of as the set of rules that describes it. The rule of rod, line, and hook has been widely accepted since sport fishing was described in the *Treatise of Fishing*. Whoever has fished with a hand line will take exception, rightly. The sport is also divided into schools according to different forms of disguise, such as bait, spinning tackle, and artificial flies. The real objection today to the poacher with net, spear, or dynamite is not simply that he removes fish, but that he disturbs the morale of the angler who abides by the rule of the disguised hook. Professional fishing may be viewed as a game in which the rules are those of economics. But sport obviously suggests also a pastime rather than the purpose of making a living, though this concept needs modification to make room for the professional sportsman. The word *angling*, since the time of the treatise, has come to be a writer's word for the sport. In speech, at least in the United States, one goes fishing no matter what kind of fishing it is or what its purpose is.

Praising one's favorite sport at the expense of others is an ancient practice in writing, but those who wrote on the varieties of hunting in the Middle Ages had not troubled to mention fishing even negatively. Sport fishing was not recognized in writing until the fishing treatise suddenly appeared, very like a hunting treatise, but gently mocking the heroic sports. The hunter's lips blister from the horn; after laboring and sweating he finds his hare to be a hedgehog; the author does not even dare to report the hunter's griefs in full for fear of giving offense. The hawk ignores the hawker's shouting and whistling and is often sick from the diseases of birds. The fowler returns from his snares cold, wet, and empty-handed. But fishing with an angle rod brings good spirits and a fair old age. In its most celebrated passage the treatise tells what remains to the angler who catches no fish:

> And yet, at the very least, he will have his wholesome and merry walk at his own ease, and also many a sweet breath of various plants and flowers that will make him right hungry and put his body in good condition. He will hear the melodies of the harmony of birds. He will also see the young swans or cygnets following their brood swans, the ducks, the coots, the herons, and many other birds with their broods, which seems to me better than all the noise of hounds and blasts of horns. . . .

Sport fishing thus was introduced to a reading audience in the early fifteenth century on a cheerful, nonheroic note, which since then has been characteristic of the sport, except perhaps for big-game fishing. The humor of the treatise had a clear target. For medieval hunting and hawking were chivalric sports, held to be good pastimes for warriors and practiced by noblemen and others who aimed to be like noblemen. Indeed, hunting ranked with love, combat, and religion as a kind of branch of chivalry, and in the fifteenth century the language of hunting was still a sign of that tradition. Knights, real and fictional, were usually hunters, employing terms supposedly invented by the legendary Tristram, ideal hunter, lover, and warrior. Hawks were bred by rank according to the orders of society; first was an Emperor's hawk (gerfalcon) for an Emperor's wrist. King Arthur was often hunting while his knights engaged in more strenuous adventures. Such immortal tales as Chrétien de Troyes' *Eric and Enide,* and the anonymous *Sir Gawain and the Green Knight,* would lose important elements in their plots and backgrounds without falconry and the chase. But chivalry had become decadent and nostalgic by the time the fishing treatise was written. The special literature of hunting, essential to a noble education, had been refined to such an extent that a hunting treatise could be more a play on words than practical instruction. Other moods were rising in the fading Middle Ages, among them a feeling for individual, private serenities to be sought in nature. Angling meant retirement, in spirit far from the restless passion and triumphs of medieval hunting.

From hunting, however, the angler obtained the art of the sporting treatise. The medieval hunting treatise—derived, it appears, from the ancients—was constructed essentially in two parts, first, the argument and elevation of the subject, and then the instruction in technique. These two elements reflect respectively aspects of chivalry and learning, two forces of mind that have given a character to modern culture. Likewise the fishing treatise—out of hunting and so, indirectly, out of chivalry—is a manual of ideals and deportment as well as of the technique of fishing. It teaches a style of life. The aristocratic ideal was knightly. In fishing, the formalism of late chivalry was transformed into a code of good and quiet manners. The *Treatise of Fishing* is not addressed to noblemen but to all who are "virtuous, gentle, and freeborn." In a world then divided into conditions of serfdom, freedom, and nobility, the angler was something fairly new, a plain gentleman.

It is difficult to believe that the fishing treatise can be so novel as it appears. Cultural events do not usually happen suddenly. And as knowledge of the past is subject to interpretation and to future discoveries, a reservation is called for. The author of the treatise actually mentions the existence of "books of credence," a phrase which has suggested the possibility of earlier, now lost writings on the sport. The possibility is real but bare. Writers in the Middle Ages preferred to claim learning by books rather than by experience; and the treatise does not say its authorities were fishing books, let alone books on sport fishing. When the medieval scholar Charles H. Haskins made a special search for writing on sport in the Latin language,[2] he found no works on hunting or fishing by the Romans; if they read anything on sport they read it in Greek. Haskins found little record of any sport in the early Middle Ages, but in the twelfth and thirteenth centuries Latin writing on sport appears in considerable body.

This medieval "Latin period," preceding the early French and English vernacular periods, brings in the renaissance of writing on sport; we shall

[2] C. Haskins, *Studies in Medieval Literature,* Chapter V, "The Latin Literature of Sport" (Oxford: Clarendon Press, 1929).

later look at its prize piece of work—a treatise on falconry—for its bearing on the *Treatise of Fishing*. But Haskins found only one work in this period touching on fishing, a manual on country life by Petrus de Crescentiis (c. 1300) and that "hardly sporting." Medieval literature before the *Treatise of Fishing*, though abounding in scenes and symbols of hunting, ignores the fishing sport, so far as one can tell. The historian of fishing W. J. Turrell found no mention, except a few statutes, of fishing of any kind in English literature between the tenth and fifteenth centuries.[3] Some notices of fishing that was not just utilitarian may turn up in descriptions of rural life; but, as it is, to the testimony of Haskins on Latin and Turrell on English must be added the silent testimony of generations of medieval scholars who have reported nothing tangible on the sport from their reading of masses of medieval manuscripts in French and English.

It would be absurd, of course, to suppose that people have not fished for pleasure since the hook was invented in prehistoric times. Fishing is instinctive; you don't have to read to enjoy it. And so experienced is the *Treatise of Fishing* in the delights of making a rod, coloring a line, dressing a trout fly, and taking a fish, that there can be no doubt of the existence of an old oral tradition of the sport. But as the *Treatise of Fishing* has no known antecedent in fishing history and asserts for the first time distinctive sporting attitudes toward fishing, it serves as the point of origin of modern angling. For most of two centuries after it was written it was the sole authority on angling in England, along whose streams the sport was developed. Thereafter it shaped the general outline of the large body of writing about sport fishing which has come into existence.

Yet the *Treatise of Fishing* doubtless had literary antecedents of some kind, since writers learn from writers as well as from other experience. The basic tackle and technique of sport fishing clearly come down through the main line of professional fishing tradition, oral, pictorial, and written.[4] The literature of professional fishing, however, which has an old and fairly continuous tradition to which *Moby Dick* and Hemingway's *The Old Man and the Sea* belong, has not only no connection with sport but an incom-

[3] W. J. Turrell, *Ancient Angling Authors* (London: Gurney and Jackson, 1910), p. 3.

[4] The artificial fly, like the trained falcon, tempts one to imagine it was the invention of sport; but the falcon at one time was probably the most effective way of capturing certain game; and the fly in season will certainly outfish bait, when the object is trout, salmon, grayling, whitefish (Rocky Mountain), and other risers.

patibility with it. The *Treatise of Fishing* prescribes sport fishing for the avoidance of melancholy; for the ancient writers melancholy was the dominant mood of professional fishing.[5]

A funereal epigram of Sappho's (written about 600 B.C.) has long been accepted by fishing historians as the key to the old writing on fishing. The Greek epigram of this kind is a literary feat, telling a whole story in a couplet, and so can hardly be translated with the virtuosity of the original. Sappho says something like this: To the fisherman Pelagon, his father Meniscus has put upon the Altar [or on the wall or other place in a small, local Shrine] his son's wicker fish trap and single skulling oar as a memorial of a poor unhappy life.

This feeling appeared again in a famous sea idyl by Theocritus, Alexandrian Greek writer who is known as the first great pastoral poet. Turning from shepherds to fishermen, he told a spooky story that has influenced the entire poetic history of fishing. Asphalion (the fisherman) wakes up in the night in his lowly cabin and tells his friend a dream. Fishing from a rock with a rod, he had hooked a big fish and when he landed it, after a tremendous struggle, he found that its scales were made of gold. Fearing it might be the favorite of a sea god, he dragged it on shore and swore never to go to the sea again but to stay on land with his treasure. When he awoke, he was dismayed and immediately in terror for his rashness at having sworn the oath. His friend advised him that dreams are lies and that he should go back to work or he would starve.

The form of this poem, a conversation among professional fishermen called a "piscatory eclogue"—an approximation to the pastoral, in which fishermen rather than shepherds are the speakers—was used by poets for two thousand years. In the eighteenth century an English writer, Moses Browne, wrote on angling in this manner and his work had a vogue for a while, but the eclogue genre failed to convey the moods of the sportsman as it had those of the shepherd and the fisherman with his terror, toil, and dreams.

One might wonder whether the water poets imposed their melancholy theme on the ancient fishermen—certainly Italian fishermen today sing gaily with their families on Sunday boat picnics, and Maine fishermen are unable to speak without wit—but the old popular myth of the fisherman Glaucus

[5] Ovid cited fishing as a remedy for love. Plutarch, on the other hand, had Cleopatra angling for Antony. This playful tradition has come down through John Donne and Shakespeare to the present without having much to do with catching fish.

suggests that the poets were in touch with a peculiar reality of the minds of men at sea. Readers of Ovid and other old storytellers will recall how Glaucus upon seeing his catch of fish eat a magical herb on the ground and return to the sea, tasted the herb himself and followed them into the water, and became a sea god with eyebrows of bristle, seaweed hair on his chest, and a fish's tail; how he pursued the nymph Scylla, who eluded him, and on appealing to a divinity, Circe, to intercede in his favor, saw her instead in jealousy change Scylla into a sea monster, now, of course, the rock off the Italian coast. In Greek poetry Glaucus was the principal fisher hero, ranking with the shepherd hero Daphnis who, being mortal, for his elusive nymph, died of a broken heart.

There was, however, in Greek writing on fishing also a didactic branch, much of which is known to have been lost. The best surviving work of this kind is Oppian's *Halieutica* (A.D. 169), a Greek hexameter poem in five books, two describing many fishes of the sea, and three the art of fishing with a wide variety of "arms" (hooks, several kinds of nets, a trident, and other tackle). Oppian begins by comparing hunting and fishing. The hunter sits comfortably in a cave during a storm while the fisherman is out in a leaky boat braving the elements. The sea, however, has its charm and there are pleasures in fishing, but—curious argument for fishing—the hunter has more pleasure than toil. *Halieutica* is part sea pastoral and part manual of instruction, and as one of its readers has said, it has "the right spirit of enthusiasm." Oppian's dolphins are divine and his descriptions of the mysteries of the sea inviting, yet his fishing seems to be regarded as work. There are in *Halieutica* also elements of the art of the sporting treatise; its argument against hunting, for example, serves to provide an opposition between land and sea to the advantage of the latter. But since few medieval writers knew Greek literature before it was translated in quantity into Latin in the Middle Ages, and since, as we have seen, there is nothing on the sport in earlier Latin, it is unlikely that Oppian had any influence on the origins of modern writing on sport.[6]

The first English (Anglo-Saxon) text on fishing is the *Colloquy on the Occupations,* a late tenth-century book by Aelfric the Abbot, the great writer and teacher of his time. Aelfric mentions the use of nets, fishhooks,

[6] The fish has been a symbol of the Christian faith since the time of the catacombs. Fish symbols, however, are common to all ages and faiths. There is no sign that sport fishing had religious origins, though medieval monks, who usually lived near water and took fish for food, presumably enjoyed catching them.

and bait by professional fishermen, the kind of fish caught, how they were sold, and the like. His fisherman speaks for himself as to what he is about. A fragment goes as follows (P stands for Piscator; M for Magister):

M. What trade are you acquainted with?
P. I am a fisherman.
M. What do you get by your trade?
P. Food, clothing, and money.[7]

No sport here. And after Aelfric's *Colloquy* follow the remarkable centuries of near silence on fishing until at the beginning of the fifteenth century the *Treatise of Fishing* describes the ancient occupation for the first time in history as a sport.

Compare hunting. The sport goes far back in antiquity, falconry as far as 2000 B.C. in China. Among the ancient Greeks it was well regarded. Xenophon, historian, general, and sportsman, begins his treatise on hunting (c. 400 B.C.[?]) with the assertion that the art was invented by the gods and was the care of Apollo and Diana. "I therefore exhort the young," he says, "not to despise hunting, or any part of liberal education; for by such means men become excellent in military qualifications, and in other accomplishments by which they are necessarily led to think, act, and speak rightly."[8] After developing this theme at some length, he describes in the body of the treatise the qualifications of the hunter, his dogs, his equipment (nets, javelins, snares, and spears), and the technique of hunting hares, deer, boars, lions, leopards, and other animals; and then, in Chapter 12, restates the merits of the sport: "1. Concerning the modes of proceeding in the chase I have now spoken. Those who are fond of the pursuit will receive many benefits from it; for they will secure health for their bodies, greater keenness of sight and hearing, and a later old age. 2. It is also an excellent preparation for the toils of war. . . ." He shows in detail how the rigors of the chase train a young man in real action and keep him from viciousness or excessive pleasure of the senses. In a vein he may have learned from Socrates, of whom he was a disciple, Xenophon then makes a characteristically intricate Greek observation. Men love virtue, he says, but attain it only by labor. They will not neglect it if they see it bodily, "for everyone, when he is in sight of the object of his love, conducts him-

[7] Translation as given by Turrell, *op. cit.*, p. 2.
[8] *Xenophon's Minor Works*, translated by J. S. Watson (London: Bohn Library, 1857), p. 332 *et seq.*

self better than at other times, and neither does nor says anything unbecoming or wrong, lest it should be seen by that object." Thus hunting makes a good soldier and a good leader.

That Xenophon was read with interest for a long time is evident from a hunting treatise by the Greek writer Arrian, in the second century. He wrote a supplement to Xenophon, on coursing, beginning with a summary of "the advantages that accrue to mankind from hunting," as related by Xenophon.

When hunting literature reappeared in medieval Europe, it described what had become one of the most prominent features of the life of the nobility, and a protected privilege. "The noble of every age," said Balzac, "has done his best to invent a life which he and he only can live." Hunting, in addition to its inherent pleasures, performed that service. Men of noble rank not only hunted, but they also wrote about it, and it is from the tradition of their writing, rather than from fishing's own literary history, that the *Treatise of Fishing* emerged.

Because they were at the beginning of modern writing on sport and under the influence of the ancients, early writers of hunting treatises tended to be systematic and doctrinal; their observations on nature have been given a place in the history of science. On one level these writings went no further than such matters as the diseases of hawks; one work of this kind was written in England about 1200 by a mathematician and natural scientist, Adelard of Bath. On a higher level they dealt with all the elements of sport, including its place in the general scheme of things. Earlier in this chapter we advanced the thesis that the sporting treatise brought together the forces of chivalry and learning, chivalry in the high-minded argument for a sport, and learning in the manual of instruction. The aspect of chivalry needs explanation.

We often today think of chivalry as exaggerated courtly manners, as compared with our own manners, or with those of ancient Greece where they were incorporated less conspicuously in the way of life. The characters in the romantic literature of the Middle Ages often seem like children beside the Greeks. The writers of the Middle Ages—whose historic role is said to have been to tame the ferocity of medieval knights—celebrated courtesy, service, sacrifice, courage, honor, piety, heroism, compassion, fidelity, justice, love, and other qualities of mind and heart; and though this hardly gave a true picture of life outside the books, the chronicles indicate that it displayed the ideals of life as well as the state of mind of writers for several centuries. Chrétien de Troyes, the most celebrated poet of the twelfth century and the most influential upon later writers, whose manuscripts are the earliest extant in the Arthurian tradition, stated the case precisely in the little prologue to his story *Cligès:*

> Our books have informed us that the pre-eminence in chivalry and learning once belonged to Greece. Then chivalry passed to Rome, together with that highest learning which has now come to France. God grant that it may be cherished here, and that it may be made so welcome here that the honour which has taken refuge with us may never depart from France: God had awarded it as another's share, but of Greeks and Romans no more is heard, their fame is passed, and their glowing ash is dead.[9]

In this passage the medievalist R. W. Southern found the "secret revolution" of the eleventh and twelfth centuries: "all that we comprehend in the word 'civilization.'"[10]

It is not surprising that the same elements should crystallize at the same time in the literature of the ideal life of sport. Writers have rarely viewed sport as recreation without meaning. As the Greek Games were an expression of religion and love, modern sport is an expression of a secular code of chivalry and learning. The idealism of modern sport is identical with the ideals of chivalry, and chivalry is its apparent source. In sport, unlike life outside of sport, the rules are both understood without ambiguity and accepted without reservation; when one is broken, either there is an established penalty (another rule), or the game is over. Hence sports writers have always been moralists par excellence. Three hunting treatises in the two centuries preceding the writing of the *Treatise of Fishing* show the course of this tradition.

If modern writing on sport had only one originating point—unlikely as that assumption might be—a claim to it could be made on behalf of Frederick II's *Art of Falconry,* which he completed in Latin not long before he died in 1250. It is in any case the high point of treatise-writing in the early Middle Ages and the earliest complete model known in Europe. As the invention of the sonnet and the beginning of Italian poetry are at-

[9] *Chrétien de Troyes, Arthurian Romances,* translated by W. W. Comfort (Everyman edition, No. 698), p. 91.

[10] *The Making of the Middle Ages* (New Haven: Yale University Press, 1961), pp. 13–14.

tributed to Frederick II's court at Palermo, Sicily, it is appropriate that the beginning of the art of writing about sport in modern times should be found in that workshop. The Holy Roman Emperor, King of Sicily, King of Jerusalem, etc., who altered the history of Europe with the secularization of the state (and literature), was a great hunter, obsessed with the ancient royal sport of falconry: he says in his prologue that he prepared himself for thirty years to write the treatise. For his study of the art, he brought master falconers from "the four corners of the earth." The twelfth and thirteenth centuries were "the centuries of Aristotle," and Frederick gave himself to this influence. He caused Aristotle's zoology and two Arabic works on the diseases of hawks to be translated. From Aristotle also it is apparent that he learned the sense of logical order that the ancient philosopher gave to the medieval mind. Frederick II's treatise of falconry, however, rests upon direct observation and experience and is good enough to be considered the earliest modern scientific work on ornithology.

> As the ruler of a large kingdom and an extensive empire [Frederick writes] we were very often hampered by arduous and intricate governmental duties, but despite these handicaps we did not lay aside our self-imposed task and were successful in committing to writing at the proper time the elements of the art. *Inter alia,* we discovered by hard-won experience that the deductions of Aristotle, whom we followed when they appealed to our reason, were not entirely to be relied upon, more particularly in his description of the characters of certain birds.[11]

To this comment on the limitations of logic, he adds the observation—as if he had expected more—that "the Prince of Philosophers . . . was ignorant of the practice of falconry." What inspired Frederick to lay down this model for the organization of a sporting treatise is not known, but it appears to be in the tradition of Xenophon.

> Our main thesis, then [Frederick says], is *The Art of Falconry;* and this we have divided into two cardinal sections. The first contains the argument, by which we mean contemplative thought, or theory; the second illustrates practice, which portrays experimental action. In addition, a third subsection contains a part of the argument and includes certain data pertaining to both

[11] *The Art of Falconry,* translated and edited by Casey A. Wood and F. Marjorie Fyfe (Stanford University Press, 1943), p. 3. This magnificent work sums up present knowledge of Frederick's treatise and its background (for the Prologue of *The Art of Falconry,* see Appendix B). It was inspired by the earlier studies of Charles H. Haskins: see especially the *English Historical Review,* July 1921, pp. 334–55; and *Romanic Review,* Vol. XIII, 1922, pp. 18–27.

theory and practice. Our purpose is to present the facts as we find them. Up to the present time the subject of falconry has been devoid of both artistic and scientific treatment.

The medium we have chosen for this monograph is prose, with prologue and text.[12]

This design for writing a sporting treatise, providing a place for the meaning of sport before dealing with the art and science of it, has never been superseded. And each of these places Frederick filled with memorable content. He had a high degree of consciousness of the nature of sport: "Hunting itself," he says, "is nothing else but a form of bodily exercise and practices employed to capture animals." And (in the Mazarine Library version of his treatise) he takes one through a 589-page mental exercise in zoology, the breeding and care of falcons, lures, gerfalcons catching cranes, and a discourse on herons and river birds. He justifies this activity with the argument that falconry is the most noble of the several branches of hunting. From it one learns the secrets of nature. To practice it one needs to be skilled, for birds of prey are difficult to train; and the interesting problem is the training of the bird rather than the hunt itself. It is more noble to employ animals than artificial instruments in the hunt; and birds of prey are more noble than four-footed animals (presumably hounds employed in the chase). In conclusion he turns to the medieval doctrine that noble qualities are associated with a noble class:

> Here it may again be claimed that, since many nobles and but few of the lower rank learn and carefully pursue this art, one may properly conclude that it is intrinsically an aristocratic sport; and one may once more add that it is nobler, more worthy than, and superior to other kinds of venery.[13]

The early writers on sports, like Frederick, codifying their practices for the first time, thus were explicit about what they considered to be the sporting state of mind. Frederick's values—knowledge, skill, preference for the animate, belief in the myth and symbol of the hawk and in something intrinsically aristocratic (these things learned perhaps from his Greek models and Arab contemporaries)—are devoid, however, of romantic sentiments. He is disciplined about the nature of sport, raising it above mere exercise, but his emphasis falls chiefly on the values of skill and learning.

[12] *Ibid.*, p. 4.

[13] *Ibid.*, p. 6. Frederick also begged nobles everywhere to have his treatise read to them. Few of them would have been able to read Latin, if they read at all.

His chivalry was part classical, part oriental, and part medieval European. His learning was scientific in the modern empirical sense.

The Art of Falconry was the most important and most influential treatise on hunting in the early Middle Ages. It was circulated during the second half of the thirteenth century and translated into French. Several old books on falconry derived from it.[14] We are not concerned here, however, with the direct relationships between manuscripts, but with tradition.

In this sense Frederick's argument was "answered" in another treatise, a didactic poem, *La Chace dou Cerf,* written about mid-thirteenth century by an unknown author. This is the oldest treatise on hunting in French. Following the form of argument and instruction laid down by Frederick, it sets forth the case for a different branch of hunting (the chase *vs.* falconry) and raises equally high but quite different values. It brings medieval chivalry into sport with the words *honor, love,* and *faith.* And while the author upholds the royal rank of hunting, he makes a bow also to equality. His prologue is brief:

> There are some who attempt to rime and take much trouble about it; some do it to gain honour and others to gain money. Some concern themselves with love; many knights also go to tournaments to advance themselves; one draws (the sword), the other jousts with the lance. A loyal heart delights in many things; his faith guides him. There are such as love falcons, sparrow hawks, and merlin hawks, but some carry them on their wrist who in their hearts care little for them. He who meddles in a sport if he does not love it, whatever pains he takes can profit and avail little. If there is anyone who wishes to learn of a sport which surpasses others (whoever learns well is not easily wearied) I much wish to make you understand it. No man is the worse for learning well. The sport is so royal that there is neither king nor count nor [even] Gawain, if he were alive and loved it well, who would not be more honoured for that reason by all who understand it.
>
> "Good Sir, if all knew it, would it be less honoured than it is now?"
>
> "Nay, rather it would be more honoured, fair gentle friend, know it well."
>
> "Wherefore I pray you that you would say before all what it is."
>
> "Certainly, fair sweet friend, it is the amusement that one has from running hounds.[15]

Little about actual incidents in the hunt, or stories of hunting, can be

[14] *Romania,* ed. by Paul Meyer, Vol. XV, 1886, p. 278.

[15] Translated by H. E. L. Dryden, 1844, as corrected by Alice Dryden in her edition of 1908: a book of three hunting manuscripts entitled *The Art of Hunting* (Northampton, England: printed by William Mark), p. 119.

learned from treatises; but writing about hunting in the Middle Ages was not confined to a specialized literature. Hunting was a large and significant part of life—for many it was all of life that was not war—and a literary subject. An incident in the famous English romance *Sir Gawain and the Green Knight,* a narrative poem written by an unknown contemporary of Chaucer, gives some idea of what is meant by the lofty cliché "mighty hunter." There are three hunts in the story on three successive days, for the deer, the boar, and the fox, respectively, each vividly described in minute detail and with a symbolism in the story which is not of concern here. After a hard chase, on the second day, the boar is wounded and at bay (the climax of a boar hunt); the professional huntsmen are afraid and stand back and we see how the ideal medieval hunter goes in for the kill:

> But then came the lord himself, spurring his horse, and saw the boar standing at bay. He got down from his horse, and left it standing there, and drew his bright sword, and went forward with long strides, passing through the ford to where the grim beast was waiting for him. The boar watched him coming with his weapon in hand, and his bristles rose and he snorted so fiercely that many feared for the knight. The boar made straight at him and the man and beast fell locked together and the water swirled about them. But the beast had the worst of it, for the man watched his mark well at the first charge, and drove the sharp steel firmly into his throat, right up to the hilt, and pierced the heart. The boar snarled and gave up the fight and made away across the stream, but a hundred hounds fell on him, biting furiously, and the men drove him to open ground where the hounds finished him off.
>
> Then there was a loud hollaing, and the blowing of the kill on the loud horns, and the hounds bayed over the boar as their masters bade, they who had been the chief huntsmen in that long chase. Then one who was wise in woodcraft unlaced [i.e., cut up] the boar. He cut off the head, and fed the hounds with some of the flesh. Then they slung the carcase on a stout pole, and set off for home. The head was borne before the lord himself, who had slain the beast in the ford by the skill and the strength of his hands.[16]

About the time this was written—a little more than a hundred years after Frederick II died—there lived such a mighty hunter as this in France, who, as it happens, wrote the most famous of all hunting treatises, *Livre de Chasse.* This man was Gaston de Foix, a feudal lord who from his court at Orthez ruled over two principalities in the Pyrenees. His fame—and nickname, Gaston Phoebus (which also is given to his treatise)—was established

[16] *The Story of Sir Gawain and the Green Knight,* translated by M. R. Ridley (British Book Centre, 1951), pp. 65–66.

by the medieval chronicler Jean Froissart, of whom he was patron, the celebrity of the two men, as a result, to some extent brushing off on each other. Much lore has gathered around this point in history. Sir Kenneth Clark (*Landscape into Art*), for example, discovered that natural observation in landscape painting began in illustrated manuscripts on sport—*Livre de Chasse* one of them—a circumstance that led Clark to remark on the paradox that through the instinct to kill man achieved intimacy with nature. Gaston Phoebus has also been celebrated by his English biographer-editor W. A. and F. Baillie-Grohman, and by Theodore Roosevelt. Roosevelt, the greatest of American hunters, whom we thank for the vast forest and stream preserves in the West, wrote, under a White House dateline in 1904, a remarkable essay on Gaston Phoebus and related matters, lauding him as "a mighty lord and mighty hunter, as well as statesman and warrior."[17] Gaston Phoebus surely deserved superlatives, but an account of the chilling episodes of his life does not belong here. He died of apoplexy in 1391 after an all-day bear hunt.

Fourteen years later, Edward, Duke of York, grandson of Edward II, conspirator against two kings, and a famous hunter, was put in prison by Henry IV. There it is surmised he performed his work of translating Gaston's *Livre de Chasse* into English, with five new chapters, under the title *Master of Game*. Gaston's treatise thereby achieved the new distinction of being the first hunting treatise in the English language.[18] In 1406 Edward was free and appointed to the office of Master of Game under Henry IV. He died, a hero, in the English victory over the French at Agincourt in 1415; though, according to one account, he suffocated from the heat in his suit of armor. The author of the *Treatise of Fishing* acknowledged *Master of Game,* as follows:

> I will now describe the said four sports or games to find out, as well as I can, which is the best of them; albeit, the right noble Duke of York, late called the Master of Game, has described the joys of hunting, just as I think to describe (of it and all the others) the griefs.

[17] Edward, Duke of York, *Master of Game,* ed. by W. A. and F. Baillie-Grohman, with a Foreword by Theodore Roosevelt, 1904. London: Chatto & Windus. The edition used here is 1909. P. xix.

[18] Twici's *The Art of Hunting* was written in England in the early fourteenth century in Norman French. The author was huntsman to Edward II. His treatise, curiously, lacks a preliminary argument. It was translated into English about 1425 and was very influential in the hunting literature that followed. Text and translation are in Dryden, *op. cit.*

The treatise *Master of Game,* like its French original, follows the now familiar form of argument and instruction. Hunting (i.e., the chase), the author says, is better than hawking. It is so noble as to be called the "Master of Sports." And he writes: ". . . I will prove by various arguments in this little prologue that there is no man's life, of those that engage in noble games and sports, that is less displeasing to God than is the life of a fully trained and skillful hunter, nor any such life that more good comes from. The first argument is that the sport often causes a man to avoid the Seven Deadly Sins. Secondly, men are better horsemen, more just and intelligent, more accomplished, more gracious, more enterprising, and better acquainted with all districts and all routes, both short and long. All good habits and manners come from it, as well as the health of a man and of his soul." The hunter, he says, will avoid sins because in hunting he will not be idle; for idleness leads to lust and pleasure, dreams and evil imaginings. The author will prove how hunters live more joyfully than anyone else. "For when the hunter rises in the morning, he sees the sweet and fair morning and the weather clear and bright, and he hears the song of the small birds, which sing sweetly with great melody and full of love. . . ." He will prove, he says, that hunters live longer than others. ". . . For as Hippocrates says, full repletions of food kill more men than any sword or knife. But hunters eat and drink less than any other men of this world. . . . And since hunters eat little and [sweat] often, they should always live long and be healthy." He does not overlook war. "For if he [a man who is not a hunter] were in need or at war, he would not know what to do, for he would not be used nor accustomed to toil, and so another man would have to do what he ought to do."[19]

Now, in the early fifteenth century, we come to the *Treatise of Fishing,* which has no model in fishing history. The famous woodcut accompanying its first printed version (1496) showed the solitary, animated, and intent angler playing a fish with his rod held high in his left hand, his catch in a tub beside him on the bank of a stream. The town in the background suggests that he came out from there to the country for recreation. Today he might be a bank president on the Beaverkill, or a Butte, Montana, copper miner on the Big Hole. In those days he was likely to have been a merchant; very likely not a noble and not a landowner, since fishing had

[19] A modernized text of the complete prologue to *Master of Game* is in Appendix A; the matter in quotation marks above is from that text.

none of the dignity, ceremony, and hierarchal associations of medieval hunting. If he read the *Treatise of Fishing* it would have been for practical instruction and not to learn the language and manners of an aristocrat. Fishing was an inexpensive sport, and, though sophisticated in technique, it was not yet divided into specializations. A man could do it all with his hands: a good part of the *Treatise of Fishing* is occupied with instruction on making your own tackle. But that is not all he would have learned from his reading.

The *Treatise of Fishing* is formed in three parts: (1) the argument, (2) the instruction, and, in the complete 1496 version, (3) further argument establishing the concept of the angler through his moral qualities. The treatise begins, as we have seen, by defining the sport with the rule of rod, line, and hook, and lauds it above other good and honorable hunting sports in which there is pleasure without repentance and which lead to a fair and long age. The good life derives from merry thought, moderate work, and moderate diet, as opposed to contentious company, an uncongenial occupation, and places of debauchery. Rise early, as the angler does, and according to the adage you will be holy, healthy, and happy. Therefore, learn your fishing tackle, how to fish (at each level from the bottom to the top of the water), the kinds of fish, the weather, and baits, hooks, artificial flies, and rods and how to make them, as the treatise shows. In conclusion, the author gives the order to anglers, possibly a take-off on official proclamations: "I charge and require you in the name of all noble men that you do not fish in any poor man's private water . . . without his permission and good will." Don't break a man's fish traps. Don't break a hedge. Shut the gate. Fish not for material gain but for solace and health of body and soul. This way you will avoid the vice of idleness. Don't take too many fish, which you can easily do if you fish according to the instructions. Conserve the fish in the water. So enjoined you will have the blessing of God and St. Peter. From this beginning the angler with his rod and pursuit of pleasure was in time to be identified in a vast number of writings as philosopher, scholar, and teacher, and his sport as gentle, solitary, contemplative, passionate, cheerful, and innocent.

Did the author learn the design of the treatise and some of these sentiments from *Master of Game?* The great scholar of the second edition of the *Book of St. Albans,* Joseph Haslewood, in his book in 1810, commented that the commendation of hunting in *Master of Game* "awakened the jealousy of the author of the Treatise upon Angling." The historian of fly fishing J. W. Hills, upon seeing the relation of the two treatises in 1920, had the brilliant insight "that all sport is one." Both the first hunting writer and the first fishing writer, in English, apply the measure of what is noble. Both speak of skill and the avoidance of idleness, of living longer with good diet and exercise, of joy in the presence of nature, and other benefits to body and soul. The hunter is more just, intelligent, accomplished, gracious, enterprising, learned, and well mannered; and the fisherman more specifically respects his neighbor. In a word, both are chivalrous and learned. But they also differ. Hunting is worldly; it is good training for the warrior. Fishing is solitary and reflective. Even the rod is designed to be used also as a walking stick that will keep secret where you are going. And though if you fish according to the instructions, you should catch fish, it does not matter if you do not. Thus though the two treatises are similar in sporting sentiment, they part widely in the experiences peculiar to each sport. Whether the *Treatise of Fishing* drew upon *Master of Game,* as it seems, or upon another source, does not matter. The simple facts are that the modern history of writing about hunting has its first classic in Frederick's treatise on falconry, and the modern history of writing about sport fishing has its first classic and its first known writing in the *Treatise of Fishing,* and the two treatises have in common their aesthetics and the state of mind called sport.

The *Treatise of Fishing* presumably appealed to an audience wider than that of privileged hunters. Language alone suggests different readers for *Master of Game* and the fishing treatise. *Master of Game,* and other early hunting treatises in England, employed a hunting terminology that was largely Norman French, the language of the court and the official language of England after 1066. The English of the *Treatise of Fishing* is the language of ordinary people. It is simple native prose with few long words: most are of one syllable, and most of the remainder are of two syllables, not a language for discussing Aristotle but good enough for love and war and hunting and fishing. The *Treatise of Fishing* is one of the best and most durable pieces of prose writing of its time. It is a rare thing to be able to go that far back in sport and find words so fresh and up to date (only a few of its words are archaic; only some of its "technology" is obsolete).

Courtly literature of sport was written for a knightly class which had extraordinary leisure and aspired to make a way of life of it. Later on, unchanged in essence, the literature of sport was written for an ever widening audience until we come to the millions of sportsmen with their new leisure today. The *Treatise of Fishing,* while first in fishing, also marked a turning point in the general history of sports-writing both in style and in its probable readers. The treatise was available in manuscript during the fifteenth century, transcribed no one knows how many times, and when it made its first appearance in print in the second *Book of St. Albans* in 1496, it was in a hunting context. As hunting, hawking, and heraldry were interests of the nobility which could be acquired, the *Book of St. Albans* served as a handbook for gentlemen. The author of the *Treatise of Fishing,* however, writing, as we have seen, near the beginning of the century for all who were "virtuous, gently, and freeborn," cannot be held responsible for the less felicitous advertisements introduced into the book by its first printer near the end of the century. Wynkyn de Worde made no bones about selling the social merits of sport. At the conclusion of the treatise of coat armor, he, or his shop editor, entered the following notice:

> Here we shall make an ende of the moost specyall thynges of the boke of the lygnage of cote armurys: and how gentylmen shall be knownen from ungentylmen. And consequently shall folowe a compendyous treatyse of fysshynge wyth an angle whiche is right necessary to be had in this present volume: by cause it shewyth afore the manere of hawkynge & huntynge wyth other dyvers maters right necessary to be knowen of noble men and also for it is one of the dysportes that gentylmen use. And also it is not soo labororyous ne soo dishonest to fysshe in this wyse as it is w^t nettes & other engynes whyche crafty men done use for theyr dayly encrease of goods.[20]

In an epilogue to the fishing treatise, de Worde explained why he included it with the other treatises in the book:

> And for by cause that this present treatyse sholde not come to the hondys of eche ydle persone whyche wolde desire it yf it were empryntyd allone by itself & put in a lytyll plaunflet therfore I haue compylyd it in a greter volume of dyuerse bokys concernynge to gentyll & noble men. to the entent that the forsayd ydle persones whyche sholde have but lytyll mesure in the sayd dysporte of fysshying sholde not by this meane vtterly dystroye it.

It has been inferred from these expressions of the printer that literacy in the fifteenth century extended to classes regarded by de Worde as lower

[20] By "labororyous," the printer meant professional, that is, not sporting; and by "dishonest" he meant, in this context, ungentlemanly.

than that embraced by the term "gentlemen" (though he did later, in 1532, yield on exclusiveness by publishing a separate edition of the fishing treatise). More to the point here, however, is the implication that at the end of the fifteenth century hunting and fishing were an acceptable combination within the same covers, needing only a mild apology for their connection. In the following century the hunting and fishing treatises of the *Book of St. Albans* were often published together, from which one may conclude that fishing had become a fashionable sport. Yet the *Treatise of Fishing*, though a best-seller, attracted no known literary competition for most of the two centuries.

During the 157 years between the first printing of the *Treatise of Fishing* and the first edition of *The Compleat Angler,* the few angling writers who appeared went on to develop the concept of the angler. Only five angling books worthy of note—exclusive of the sixteen or more reprints of the *Treatise of Fishing*—are known to have been published in this period in the English language. The second book on angling, *The Arte of Angling,* first published in 1577 by an anonymous author, and certainly known to early fishing writers, including Walton, who borrowed from it but never mentioned it, was lost to angling history until a single surviving copy was recently discovered in an attic in England and brought to the United States by the collector Carl Otto von Kienbusch, and printed at Princeton in 1956. The *Arte,* the first writing on the sport in prose dialogue, has two characters, Piscator and Viator (Wayfarer).[21] Piscator (the pupil in Aelfric) is the teacher, Viator the student. The *Arte* is a fine little book, the best use of dialogue on the subject of angling outside of Walton's. Piscator is testy but hospitable. He treats of angling as an art and a science, and "as of that pleasure that I have always most recreated myself withal, and had most delight in, and is most meetest for a solitary man, and is also of light cost." He speaks of the fellowship, ruling out, however, "the sluggard sleepy sloven," the poor man, the angry man, the fearful man, and the busybody, who can stay at home or, if they like, hunt or hawk. The character of the angler is described in thirteen "gifts":

> Vi[ator]. Why then, I pray you, what gifts must he have that shall be of your company?
>
> Pi[scator]. 1. He must have faith, believing that there is fish where he cometh to angle. 2. He must have hope that they will bite. 3. Love to the

[21] Adopted by Walton, who after his first edition changed "Viator" to "Venator."

> owner of the game. 4. Also patience, if they will not bite, or any mishap come by losing of the fish, hook, or otherwise. 5. Humility to stoop, if need be to kneel or lie down on his belly, as you did today. 6. Fortitude, with manly courage, to deal with the biggest that cometh. 7. Knowledge adjoined to wisdom, to devise all manner of ways how to make them bite and to find the fault. 8. Liberality in feeding of them. 9. A content mind with a sufficient mess, yea, and though you go home without. 10. Also he must use prayer, knowing that it is God that doth bring both fowl to the net and fish to the bait. 11. Fasting he may not be offended withal, but acquaint himself with it, if it be from morning until night, to abide and seek for the bite. 12. Also he must do alms deeds; that is to say, if he meet a sickly poor body or doth know any such in the parish that would be glad of a few fishes to make a little broth withal (as often times is desired of sick persons), then he may not stick to send them some or altogether. And if he have none, yet with all diligence that may be [he] try with his angle to get some for the diseased person. 13. The last point of all the inward gifts that doth belong to an angler, is memory, that is, that he forget nothing at home when he setteth out, nor anything behind him at his return.[22]

The third book on angling is Leonard Mascall's *A Booke of Fishing with Hooke and Line* (1590), which has some distinction in the field of fish conservation but is otherwise little more than an edited version of the *Treatise of Fishing.*

The fourth[23] is John Dennys' treatise in verse, *Secrets of Angling* (1613), the first angling poem. He begins with a play on the elevated opening line of Vergil's *Aeneid* (*Arma virumque cano:* Of arms and the man I sing):

> Of Angling, and the Art thereof I sing,
> What kind of tooles it doth behove to have;
> And with what pleasing bait a man may bring
> The fish to bite within the water wave. . . .

Dennys confesses:

> Not that I take upon me to impart
> More than by others hath before been told;
> Or that the hidden secrets of this art,
> I would unto the vulgar sort unfold. . . .

[22] *The Arte of Angling*, 1577, ed. by Gerald Eades Bentley, with an Introduction by Carl Otto von Kienbusch, and Explanatory Notes by Henry L. Savage (Princeton University Library, 1956), p. 32.

[23] We omit John Taverner's *Certaine Experiments concerning Fish and Fruite* (London, 1600), which fishermen read for its remarkable observations on water life.

It is not known who all the others are by whom this knowledge has been told, but the author of the *Arte* is one of them. From him Dennys appears to have taken the thirteen gifts of the angler, calling them "The Qualities of an Angler." He gives twelve instead of thirteen; the odd one, alms, he combines with love. Dennys appears to be the first in didactic angling-writing to draw upon the ancient pastoral and piscatory, which he acknowledges by paying farewell respects to Neptune and all his monsters on entering Arcadia and the gentle haunts of perch and trout. To the second edition of *Secrets of Angling*, the editor, William Lawson, added this now established gift of the trout to the angler: "The trout," he said, "makes the angler most gentlemanly, and readiest sport of all other fishes."

The year after the poem was first published, Gervase Markham set it back to prose (with a few additions from the *Treatise of Fishing*), in a work entitled *The Pleasures of Princes,* the fifth known book in the history of angling. He had also some new and original ideas on the angler. The twelve "inward qualities of the mind" were not enough, he said. The angler must also be a general scholar, knowing of the liberal sciences, a grammarian, a writer "without affectation or rudeness," of sweet speech, "to persuade, and intice other[s] to delight in an exercise so much laudable"; he must have strong arguments "to defend, and maintain his profession against envy or slander"; he should know the sun, moon, and stars, from which to guess the weather; countries, highways, and paths to lakes and streams; he should know geometrical angles so as to describe the channels and windings of rivers, and the "art of numbering" so as to be able to take soundings; and music to dispose of melancholy.

Thus the angler emerging from the Elizabethan Age could be told from an "ungentleman." It is not far from here to the personification of this image in *The Compleat Angler* in 1653. One writer, however, intervened with the sixth book on the sport. He was Thomas Barker, a cook by profession, who wrote a rare little treatise which he called *The Art of Angling* (1651). So well established had the literary image of the angler become in his time that Barker felt constrained to apologize: "I do crave pardon," he said, "for not writing scholar like." But Barker was an able fishing writer, the first to proceed directly to the kill, to speak of a reel, and to invent new trout flies. By Turrell's conferment he is the "father of poachers." Walton acknowledged Barker alone among the angling writers before himself.

Walton merged the basic outline of the *Treatise of Fishing* with the dialogue technique, the characters, and some of the content of *The Arte of Angling* (1577), and with elements of the pastoral. Along with everything he could find in classical, Biblical, and medieval traditions he brought along his contemporary "band of musicians," the great poets who were his friends and neighbors, and, in his fifth edition, got Charles Cotton to make the angler actually complete with a treatise on fly-fishing, the first specialized treatment of that subject, and still one of the best. Into the pleasant ensemble Walton breathed his personality and idyllic mood. The effect of this most popular of English idyls upon writing on the sport of fishing was inspiring and disastrous.

For seventy-four years after his fifth edition, Walton was in eclipse; then, with the benediction of Sam Johnson, he was revived and, even before the nineteenth-century renaissance of angling, was canonized and made the model of the angler. Although he had warned of the limits of making "an angler by a book" alone, Walton, the least imitable of angling writers, for a long time thereafter was closely imitated with idyls upon an idyl. One of the first to see the danger was Sir Walter Scott, who said: "The palm of originality, and of an exquisite simplicity which cannot, perhaps, be imitated with entire success, must remain with our worthy patriarch, Izaak." (Scott also defended Walton against Byron, who condemned Walton for his posture of innocence in a blood sport.)

Up to this time there were fewer than a hundred titles in angling literature; they were soon to begin multiplying into the thousands of titles today, by far the largest library in sport. Most of the classics were from the seventeenth century; the eighteenth produced little. On the eve of the great developments of the nineteenth century, two courses presented themselves to the angling writer, one the Waltonian tradition, the other a direct, empiric approach to the sport. Each course was taken by large numbers of writers. In England, Walton ruled, at least formally—ninety editions of his book were reported by Westwood and Satchell in their angling bibliography in 1883—though the best writers went their own way.

The difficulty of imitating Walton in America was described by Washington Irving in his sentimental travesty "The Angler," one of the sketches published in 1819. He and a group of friends read Walton one winter and determined to become anglers like him. As soon as the weather was good they went up to the highlands of the Hudson, "as stark mad as was ever Don Quixote from reading books of chivalry." One of the party, fully harnessed for the field with all the angler's equipments, "was as great a matter of stare and wonderment among the country folk, who had never seen a regular angler, as was the steel-clad hero of La Mancha among the goat-herds of the Sierra Monera." Irving hooked himself instead of the fish, tangled his line in the trees, lost his bait, broke his rod, and in a short while gave up fishing, lay down under a tree, and spent the rest of the day reading Izaak Walton, "satisfied that it was his fascinating vein of honest simplicity and rural feeling that had bewitched me, and not the passion for angling." With a bow to Walton for his idyl and another to the *Treatise of Fishing* for its maxims, Irving concluded that angling was suited neither to him nor to America, but only to England, where there is "rule and system" and where "every roughness has been softened away from the landscape." Walton had misled him.

The American continent, as it happened, was explored in detail in the century that was dominated both here and abroad by a romantic view of nature. Most writing on fishing in England in the nineteenth century was immersed in that romanticism. In the United States sport fishing did not become prominent until the middle of the century. George Washington Bethune, a reformed Dutch clergyman and scholar, in 1847 introduced Walton (keeping himself anonymous for fear of censure) with one of the most notable editions of *The Compleat Angler,* and the influence of Walton grew until the turn of the new century when it declined. Bethune also discussed and quoted from the *Treatise of Fishing;* an edition of it was not published in the United States until George W. Van Siclen's in 1875.[24] A new spirit, however, came early into American fishing. On the frontier men had hunted and fished not as a recreation but to live. The act of going to the wilderness was itself a sought-out adventure with its own romanticism, and as sport began to flourish, hunting and fishing absorbed this new sense of frontier excitement, which in the United States has never left them, especially in the West. So we have two literatures of fishing, one of retirement to old meadows, the other of going out to new waters. The *Treatise of Fishing* produced no cult, as Walton did, and by its nature could not. What the treatise did was to establish the elements of sport in rule, courtesy, and learning, and find in fishing a tolerable state of mind.

[24] The notable editions of *The Treatise of Fishing with an Angle,* after the numerous reprints of the sixteenth century, were Haslewood's in 1810, William Pickering's (Baskerville) edition in 1827, and M. G. Watkins' edition in 1880. Van Siclen reprinted the edition of 1827. Thomas Satchell printed a transcript of the manuscript in 1883.

CHAPTER 2

Modernized Text of the Earliest Surviving Version of the Treatise (from the Manuscript: 1450)

The *Treatise of Fishing* survives in two basic versions, each of which, it appears, was transcribed independently from a now lost original. The older version survives in a single manuscript copied in about 1450. The first printed text is in the second *Book of St. Albans* (1496). A modernization of the text of the manuscript appears in this chapter; a similar modernization of the first printed version is contained in Chapter 3. The manuscript is incomplete, several pages having been lost long ago, but it is of special interest because it is close in time to the original. A description of the manuscript, together with a facsimile and line-for-line transcript, is in Chapters 6 and 7.

THE TREATISE OF FISHING WITH AN ANGLE (1450)

Solomon in his Proverbs says that a glad spirit makes a flowering age—that is to say, a fair age and a long one.[1] And since it is so, I ask this question, "What are the means and cause to bring a man into a merry spirit?" Truly, in my simple judgment, it seems to me, they are good and honest sports and games in which a man's heart takes pleasure without any repentance. Then this follows—that good and honorable recreations are the cause of man's fair old age and long life. Therefore, I will now choose

[1] Proverbs 17:22 (Vulgate): Animus gaudens aetatem floridam facit.

among four good sports and honorable pastimes, that is to say, among hunting, hawking, fowling, and fishing, particularly angling with a rod or a pole, a line, and a hook. And thereof I will treat as far as my simplicity will permit, both for the above-mentioned saying of Solomon and also for the statement of medical science made in this manner:

Si tibi deficiant medici, medici tibi fiant
Haec tria—mens laeta, labor et moderata diaeta.[2]

That is to say: If a man lacks physicians or doctors, he shall make three things his doctors or physicians, and he will never have need of more. The first of them is merry thought. The second is work in moderation. The third is a good diet of pure foods and suitable drinks. First, then, if a man wishes to be merry and have a glad spirit, he must avoid all contentious company and all places of disputes and quarrels, where he might have a cause of melancholy.[3] And if he will have a labor which is not excessive, he must then arrange for himself, for his heart's pleasure—without care, anxiety, or trouble—a merry occupation which may rejoice his heart and his spirit in a respectable manner. And if he wishes to be moderate in diet, he must avoid all places of debauchery, which is the cause of overindulgence and sickness, and he must withdraw himself to a place of sweet and hungry[4] air, and eat nourishing and digestible foods.

I will now describe the said four sports or games to find out, as well as I can, which is the best of them; albeit, the right noble Duke of York, lately called the Master of Game,[5] has described the joys of hunting, just as I think to describe (of it and all the others) the griefs. For hunting, to my mind, is too much work. The hunter must run all day and follow his hounds, laboring and sweating very painfully. He blows on his horn till his lips blister; and when he thinks it is a hare, very often it is a hedgehog.

[2] This seems to be a variant of a maxim in the eleventh-century *Regimen Sanitatis Salernitanum:* Si tibi deficiant medici, medici tibi fiant Haec tria, mens laeta, requies, moderata diaeta. For one of the best-known versions of the proverb, see Robert Burton, *The Anatomy of Melancholy* (1621), Part 2, Sec. 2, Mem. 6, Subs. 4.

[3] An excess of black bile in the body, a pathological condition which could produce all manner of dangerous ailments—as well as a gloomy frame of mind.

[4] Hunger-producing, conducive to a hearty appetite.

[5] Edward of Norwich, second Duke of York, 1373–1415, translator of the book called *The Master of Game.* See Appendix A.

Thus he hunts, and when he comes home in the evening, rain-beaten, sorely pricked by thorns and with his clothes torn, wet-shod, befouled, some of his hounds lost, some crippled[6]—such griefs happen to the hunter and many others which, for fear of the displeasure of those that love it, I dare not report in full. Truly, it seems to me that this is not the best recreation or sport of the four mentioned.

Hawking

This sport and pastime of hawking is laborious and right troublesome also, as it seems to me, and that is the honest truth. The falconer often loses his hawks, the hunter his hounds; then all his sport is gone and finished. Very often he shouts and whistles till he is painfully thirsty. His hawk goes above[7] and does not choose to pay him any attention when he would have her fly at the game. At last she will consent. Then, with improper feeding, she will get the frounce, the ray, the cray,[8] and many another sickness that brings her to the souce.[9] These sports seem to me to be beneficial, but they are not the best of the four mentioned.

[6] *Surbatted,* bruised in the feet, footsore from too much running on rough ground.

[7] Or, she takes to a bough of a tree; the Middle English can be read either way.

[8] *Frounce,* a disease of hawks, characterized by sores in the mouth and throat. *Ray* (or *rye* or *ree*), a disease which produces a swelling of the hawk's head and legs; cf. also the modern dialectal *ray* "diarrhoea in cattle and sheep." *Cray,* a sort of constipation, in which the excrements are hard, chalk-like, and difficult to pass. The choice of two diseases which rhyme and can have opposite meanings may suggest that the writer had a flippant attitude toward hawking. All three diseases will be found together, however, and in the same order as above, in two fifteenth-century books on hawking; see the *Book of St. Albans* (1486), sig. a4, and British Museum manuscript Harley 2340 in Thomas Wright and J. O. Halliwell, *Reliquiae Antiquiae* (London, 1845), I, 294–95. These books are later than the treatise.

[9] Or *source,* rising or mounting up of a bird, in this case, probably the mounting up of a hawk getting into position to swoop on the prey. According to some writers, the word (cf. French *sous,* "under, beneath") refers to the hawk's downward flight upon its prey; see John Hodgkin, *Proper Terms* (Supplement to the Transactions of the Philological Society, 1907–1910), p. 100. Either way, the writer of the treatise seems to have misused the word here, for the diseases mentioned would not assist the hawk to fly in any direction—quite the contrary. Possibly the writer was not an expert in hawking terminology.

Fowling[10]

The sport and game of fowling seems to me poorest of all, for in the summer season the fowler has no luck. And in the hardest and coldest weather he is sorely vexed, for he would go to his traps, but he cannot because of the cold. Many a trap and many a snare he makes, and many he loses. In the morning he walks in the dew; he also goes wet-shod and very cold to dinner the next day and sometimes to bed, before he has eaten well on anything that he gets by fowling. Much more of the same I could tell, but my displeasure[11] or anger makes me leave off. It seems to me that hunting, hawking, and fowling are so toilsome and unpleasant that none of them can succeed in bringing a man into a merry frame of mind, which is the cause of a long life according to the said proverb of Solomon.

Fishing

Undoubtedly then, it follows that it must needs be the sport or game of fishing with an angle-rod—for every other kind of fishing is also right toilsome and unpleasant, often causing men to be very wet and cold, which many times has been seen to be the main cause of sickness and sometimes of death. But the angler can have no cold nor discomfort nor anger, unless he be the cause himself, for he cannot lose more than a line or a hook, of which he can have plenty of his own making, or of other men's making, as this simple treatise will teach him; so then his loss is no grievance. And he can have no other grievances, unless some fish breaks away from him when he[12] is on his hook, in the landing of that same fish, or in any case, he does not catch him. This is no great hardship, for if he fails with one, he cannot fail with another, if he does as this treatise which follows will instruct him —unless there are no fish in the water where he is angling. And yet, at the very least, he will have his wholesome and merry walk at his own ease, and also many a sweet breath of various plants and flowers that will make

[10] Trapping or snaring birds.

[11] *Magyf*, a variant of *mawgre*, displeasure, ill will. Perhaps the displeasure and anger are due to the author's own experience with bird-catching; or perhaps the author has left out something and means to say "for fear of provoking displeasure and anger."

[12] The fish. Fish are masculine in this treatise.

him right hungry and put his body in good condition. He will hear the melodies of the harmony of birds. He will also see the young swans or cygnets following their brood swans, the ducks, the coots, the herons, and many other birds with their broods, which seems to me better than all the noise of hounds and blasts of horns and other amusements that falconers and hunters can provide, or the sports that fowlers can make. And if the angler catches the fish with difficulty, then there is no man merrier than he is in his spirits. Also, whoever wishes to practice the game or sport of angling, he must pay heed to the sense of the old proverb, that is, these verses:

> Surge, miser, mane sed noli surgere vane,
> Sanctificat, sanat, ditat quoque surgere mane.[13]

This is to say, he must rise early, which thing is right profitable to a man in these ways. One is for health of the soul, for it shall cause a man to be holy, if anything can make him pleasing to God.[14] The second cause is that it will produce bodily health and will cause him to live long. The third, it will cause him to be rich, temporally and spiritually, in goods and in goodness. Thus I have proved, according to my purpose, that the sport of angling is the true means that causes a man to be merry-spirited, which (according to the said proverb of Solomon and the teaching of medicine) makes a flowering age and a long life. And therefore, to all those that are virtuous, gentle,[15] and freeborn, I write this simple treatise, by following which you can have the whole art of angling to amuse yourselves as you please, in order that your age may be the more flourishing and last the longer.

Then if you want to be crafty in angling, you must first learn to make your tackle, that is to say, your rod, your lines of different colors, and your hooks. After that, you must know how you should angle and in what places of the water; how deep and what time of the day for what manner of fish in what weather; how many impediments there are to angling; and especially with what baits for each different fish in every month of the year;

[13] An old schoolbook aphorism; cf. Anthony Fitzherbert, *The Book of Husbandry* (1534), edited by W. W. Skeat for the English Dialect Society, Vol. 37, p. 101. For other variants of it, see *Twelfth Night,* II, iii, 3, and *Poor Richard's Almanac.*

[14] If he is ever to be on good terms with God.

[15] Having noble qualities, or being of gentle birth.

how you must make your baits-bread,[16] where you will find the baits, and how you will find them, and how you will keep them; and the most difficult thing, how you are to make your hooks of steel and of iron,[17] some for you to dub[18] and some for the float, as you will afterward hear. All these things you will find openly depicted to your eye.

How You Must Make Your Rod

And how you should make your rod skillfully, I will tell you. You must cut, between Michaelmas and Candlemas,[19] a fair, smooth staff six feet long, or longer if you wish, of hazel, willow, or aspen; and heat it in an oven when you bake, and set it as exactly straight as you can make it; then let it cool and dry for four weeks or more. Then take and bind it tight with a good cord to a bench or to an exactly squared timber. Then take a plumber's[20] wire that is straight and strong and sharp at one end. Heat the sharp end in a charcoal fire till it is hot, and pierce the staff with it through the pith of the staff—first at the one end and afterward at the other until it is all the way through. Then take a bird spit[21] and burn the hole as you think fit, until it is big enough for your purpose and like a taper of wax;[22] and then wax it. Then let it lie still for two days afterward, until it is thoroughly cold; then unbind it and let it dry in a smokehouse or up under the house-roof till it is thoroughly dry. In the same season, take a rod of white hazel and beath it[23] even and straight, and let it dry in the

16 That is, bait-food, food used as bait. Cf. also the baits made of various ingredients and baked like bread (1496 version). But *brede* in this passage could also be *breed* (propagate) or a variant of *braid* (how you must make the trick, or stratagem, of your bait). The interpretation given above seems slightly more plausible than the others.

17 *Osmund,* iron of high quality imported from the Baltic area.

18 To clothe, dress up. This seems to be the earliest instance of dubbing, or dressing up, a hook; it evidently means to put an artificial fly on the hook. This promise of flies was fulfilled in the 1496 printed version (see Chapter 3 and Chapter 8). The text above suggests that the flies were in the lost pages of the manuscript.

19 That is, between September 29 and February 2.

20 A plumber, a worker in lead.

21 A spit or skewer for roasting birds.

22 That is, make the hole decreasing in size, tapering.

23 That is, soak it in hot water to make it pliable, so that it can be straightened.

same way as the staff; and when they are dry, make the rod fit the hole in the said staff, so that it will go halfway into the staff in a continuous line. And to make the other half of the crop,[24] take a fair shoot of blackthorn, crabtree, medlar, or juniper, cut in the same season and well beathed and straightened; and bind them together neatly so that all the crop may exactly enter into the above-mentioned hole. Then shave the staff down and make it taper-wise waxing.[25] Then ferrule the staff well at both ends with hoops of iron or latten,[26] with a spike in the lower end fastened with a removing device for pulling the crop in and out. Then set your crop a handbreadth inside the upper end of your staff in such a way that it will be as big there as at any other place above. Then, with a cord of six hairs, strengthen your crop at the upper end as far down as the place where it is tied together; and double the cord and tie it firmly in the top with a noose to fasten your fishing line on. And thus you will make yourself a rod so perfect and suitable that you can walk with it, and no one will know what you are going to do; and it will be light and nimble to fish with at your pleasure and desire.

To Color Your Lines

After you have made your rod, you must learn to color your lines of hair in this manner. First you must take, from the tail of a white horse, the longest hair that is to be had, and the rounder it is the better. And when you have separated it into six bunches, then color every part by itself in a different color, such as, yellow, green, brown, tawny, russet, and dusky color. First, to make your yellow hair: Take a half-gallon of small ale and crush in it three handfuls of walnut leaves and a quarter of alum, and put them all together in a brass pan and boil them well together.[27] And when it is cold, put in your hair that you wish to have yellow, until it is as dark as you want to have it, and then take it out.

[24] The top part of anything; the upper section of the fishing rod, to be made of the two kinds of wood.

[25] Increasing in size like a taper.

[26] An alloy resembling brass.

[27] Small ale is probably weak or inferior ale (like the expression "small beer"). The word *quarter* probably stands for a quarter of a pound.

To Make Green Color

You must take small ale, the quantity of a quart, and put it in a little pan, and add to it half a pound of alum. Put your hair in it, and let it boil half an hour. Then take your hair and let it dry. Then take a half-gallon of water and put it in a pan, and add two handfuls of weld[28] or waxen,[29] and press it down with a heavy weight, and let it boil softly half an hour. And when it turns yellow in the scum, put in your hair and with it half a pound of copperas well beaten to powder. And let it boil half-a-mile-way.[30] Then set it down and let it cool five or six hours, take out your hair and let it dry, and there you will have the best green that ever was for the water. And the more copperas you put in, the greener it will be.[31]

* * * * * *

With How Many Hairs You Shall Angle for Every Fish

First, for the minnow,[32] with a line of one hair. For the growing roach,[33] the bleak,[34] the gudgeon,[35] and the ruff[36] with a line of two hairs. For the dace[37] and the great roach, with a line of three hairs. For the perch,[38] the flounder,[39] the bream,[40] with a line of four hairs. For the chevin-

[28] Or *olds;* a yellow dye made from the plant *Reseda luteola.*
[29] Or *wyxen;* apparently another name for weld.
[30] The time it would take to walk half a mile.
[31] There is no apparent lacuna in the manuscript, but there is a gap in the text equal to about six pages of the manuscript.
[32] The European species *Phoxinus phoxinus;* perhaps also, the stickleback (*Gasterosteus aculeatus*).
[33] The European *Rutilus rutilus.* The great roach farther on in the list is probably the full-grown roach.
[34] The fresh-water bleak (*Alburnus lucidus*).
[35] *Gobio gobio,* or *G. fluviatilis.*
[36] The fresh-water ruff (*Acerina cernua*).
[37] The European *Leuciscus leuciscus.*
[38] The European *Perca fluviatilis.*
[39] One of the European flounders; probably *Flesus flesus.*
[40] The European fresh-water *Abramis brama.*

chub,[41] the tench,[42] the eel,[43] with a line of six hairs. For the trout,[44] the grayling,[45] the barbel,[46] and the great chevin,[47] with a line of nine hairs. For the great trout, grayling, and perch, with a line of twelve hairs. For a salmon,[48] with fifteen. For the pike,[49] you must take a good fine line of packthread, made in the manner of a chalkline made brown with your coloring as described above, strengthened with wire to prevent biting asunder. Your lines must be plumbed[50] with lead, and the plumb[51] nearest the hook must be a full foot and more away from it, and every plumb of a size in keeping with the thickness of the line. There are three ways of weighting. First, for a running ground-line[52] and for the float set upon the lying ground-line,[53] ten plumbs all running together. On the lying ground-line, ten or twenty[54] small plumbs. For the float, weight it so heavily that the least pluck of any fish can pull it down into the water. And make the plumbs round and smooth so that they will not get caught on stones or weeds, which would hinder you greatly in your sport of angling.

How You Shall Make Your Floats

You are to make your floats in this manner. Take a good cork that is clean, without many holes; bore it through with a small hot iron; and put a quill in at the larger hole. Then shape them in the manner of a dove egg,

[41] Same as chevin or chub (*Leuciscus cephalus*). Perhaps *chub* is an explanatory synonym, i.e., "For the chevin (chub)," etc.
[42] *Tinca tinca,* or *T. vulgaris.*
[43] The European *Anguilla anguilla.*
[44] Brown trout (*Salmo trutta*), the only trout in England at the time.
[45] The European *Thymallus thymallus.*
[46] *Barbus fluviatilis.*
[47] Probably the full-grown chub.
[48] The Atlantic salmon (*Salmo salar*).
[49] *Esox lucius.*
[50] Weighted with lead weights.
[51] A weight, usually of lead; generally used like a sinker.
[52] A ground-line free at one end, so that it could move upon the bottom.
[53] A fixed, stationary line for bottom fishing.
[54] Perhaps an error for "nine or ten."

smaller and larger as you like, and make them smooth on a grindstone.[55] And your float, for one hair, should be no bigger than a pea; for two hairs, like a bean; for twelve hairs, like a walnut; and so forth, for every line according to its size. Every sort of line must have a float for angling, except only the ground-line—and even the running ground-line must have a float. The lying ground-line without float.[56]

How Many Kinds of Angling There Are

Now that I have taught you to make your tackle, I will tell you how you must understand that there are six ways of angling. One is at the bottom for the trout. Another, at the bottom at an arch of a bridge or at a standing[57] (where it ebbs and flows) for bleak, roach, and dace. The third is without a float for all kinds of fish. The fourth, with a minnow for the trout, without any plumb or float; the same way for roach and dace with a line of one or two hairs baited with a fly.[58] The fifth is with a dubbed hook for the trout and the grayling.[59] And for the principal point of angling, always keep yourself away from the water and from the sight of the fish—far back on the land or else behind a bush or a tree—so that the fish may not see you. For if he does, he will not bite. And take care that you do not shadow the water any more than you can help, for that is a thing which will frighten the fish, and if he is frightened, he will not bite for a good while afterward. For every kind of fish that feeds at the bottom, you must angle for him in the middle of the water,[60] and somewhat more beneath than above; for always the greater the fish, the nearer he will lie to the bottom of the water, while the smaller fish commonly swims above. The

[55] *Gynston,* literally "machine stone," which sounds like some kind of grindstone. Or this could be an error for *grynston,* a spelling variant of *grindstone.*

[56] Was there supposed to be an illustration here, or was the verb dropped?

[57] Standing water by the seashore. Or perhaps a standing-place, such as a pier, a dock, or a sea wall.

[58] Probably a natural fly.

[59] The sixth method seems to be missing because the fourth listed is really two combined.

[60] Parts of this passage have apparently been left out; cf. the corresponding passage in the 1496 version.

sixth good point is: when the fish bites, that you be not too hasty to smite[61] him, nor too late. You must wait till you suppose that the bait and the hook are well into the mouth of the fish, and then strike him. And this is for the ground-line. And for the float: when it seems to you to be pulled softly under the water or else carried softly upon the water, then smite him. And see that you never oversmite[62] the strength of your line, lest you break it. And if you happen to hook a great fish with a small line, you must lead him in the water and labor there, until he is overcome and wearied. Then take him as well as you can, and beware that you do not hold beyond the strength of your line. And if you can avoid it at all, do not let him go out on the end of the line straight from you, but keep him always under the rod, and always hold him strait.[63] Thus you can sustain his leaps and his dives with the help of your hand.

In What Place Is the Best Angling

Here I will declare in what places of the water you must angle to have the best luck. You should angle in a pool or in standing water, in every place where it is at all deep. There is no great choice in a pool,[64] for it is but a prison for fish, and they live for the most part in captivity and hungry like a prisoner. Therefore, it takes the less art to catch them. But, in any case, you should angle in every spot where it is deep, and clear at the bottom, as in gravel or clay without mud or weeds, and especially if there is a whirly-pit[65] of water, or a covert—such as a hollow bank or great roots of trees or long weeds floating on top of the water—where the fish can hide themselves at various times. Also in deep, swift streams and in waterfalls and weirs, floodgates and mill pits,[66] and wherever the water rests by the bank and the current runs close by and it is deep and clear at the bottom.

[61] To hook the fish by a quick pull on the line, to strike him.
[62] Overtax, strike too hard.
[63] The instruction seems to mean, "keep the line taut, allow no slack."
[64] A pond in which fish are penned up to be used as they are needed.
[65] A whirlpool or a very strong eddy.
[66] Probably millraces.

And in other places where you can see any fish rising and feeding at the top.

What Time of the Day Is Best for Angling

You must know that the best time to angle is from the beginning of May to September. The biting time is early in the morning from four o'clock until eight; in the afternoon, from four until eight, but this is not so good as in the morning. And if there is a cold, whistling wind and it be a dark, lowering day, then the fish will usually bite all day. For a dark day is much better than any other clear weather. From the beginning of September until the end of April, angle at any time of the day. Also, many pool fish will bite best at noontime. And if you see the trout or the grayling leap at any time of the day, angle for him with a dub[67] appropriate to that same month. And where the water ebbs and flows, the fish will bite in some place at the flood tide, although after that they will rest behind pilings or arches of bridges and in other such places.

In What Weather Is the Best Angling

You should angle, as I said before, in dark lowering weather when the wind blows softly, and in the summer season when it is burning hot.[68] From September to April and in a fair sunny day, it is good to angle. And if the wind in that season comes from any part of the north,[69] the water then is good. And when there is a great wind, when it snows, rains, or hails, or there is thunder or lightning, and also in consuming[70] heat, that is not the time to angle.

The Twelve Impediments

Which cause men to catch no fish, apart from other common causes which may happen by chance, are these. The first, if your tackle is not

[67] An artificial fly, a hook disguised with an artificial fly.

[68] Something may have been omitted here. The 1496 version says that burning hot weather is not good for angling.

[69] The manuscript has *oriente,* i.e., "east," with *northe* written over it. On the whole, "northeast" seems more improbable here than "north."

[70] *Niming,* seizing; i.e., consuming, devouring, or stupefying.

good and well made. The second is if you do not angle in biting time. The third, if the fish are frightened by the sight of any man. The fourth, if the water is very thick, white, or red as lees,[71] from any flood recently fallen. The fifth, if the fish will not stir either for cold or fair weather. The sixth is if the water is very hot. The seventh, if it rains. The eighth, if it hails or snows. The ninth, if there is any tempest of any storm. The tenth, if there is a great wind from any direction. The twelfth,[72] if the wind is from the north[73] or northeast or southeast; for generally, both in winter and in summer, if the wind blows from any part of these points, the fish will not usually bite nor stir. The west and the south winds are right good, yet of the two the south is better.

Baits to Angle with

And now that I have told you how to make your tackle and how you are to fish with it, it is reasonable that you should know with what baits you must angle for every kind of fresh-water fish in each month of the year —which is the most important thing in this sport of angling. Unless these baits are known, all your skills hitherto written about will avail little or nothing to your purpose, for you cannot bring a hook into a fish's mouth unless there is food on it that pleases him.

Bait for the Salmon

And because the salmon is the goodliest fish that a man can angle for in fresh water, therefore I intend to begin with him. The salmon is a noble fish, but he is cumbersome to catch, for generally he is only in very deep waters and great rivers, and for the most part he keeps to the middle of the stream so that a man cannot come at him easily. And he is in season from the month of March until Michaelmas, in which season you should angle for him with these baits, when they are to be had. First, with a bleak, just as you do for the trout with a minnow; and with a red worm[74] in the beginning and the end of the said season; and also with a worm that grows

[71] Dregs, sediment of wine.

[72] Number eleven was omitted. This probably should be poor choice of bait, which was placed second in the 1496 version and does not appear here.

[73] An error for *east* (?).

[74] A kind of earthworm.

in a dunghill; and especially with an excellent bait that grows in the water-suckle.[75] But the salmon does not stay at the bottom, but at the float. Also you may happen to catch him (but this is seldom seen) with an artificial fly at his leaping, just as you do a trout or a grayling.

For the Trout

The trout is a dainty fish and free biting. He is in the season as the season is.[76] He will not be found anywhere except in clean gravel-bottom water and in a stream. And you can angle for him at all times with a lying or running ground-line, except in leaping time, and then with an artificial fly; and early with an early ground-line, and later in the day with a float-line. You must angle for him in March with a minnow hung on your hook by the lower lip, without float or sinker, drawing it up and down in the stream till you feel him hooked. In the same season, angle for him with a ground-line with a red worm as the surest bait. In April, take the same baits; also, in the same season, take a lamprey, also the cankerworm that grows in a dock root, and the red snail. In May, take a stone fly,[77] and the grubworm under the cow turd,[78] and the dor-worm,[79] and a bait that grows on a pine-tree leaf. In June, take the red worm and nip off the head, and put a codworm[80] on the hook in front of it. In July, take the little red

[75] A water plant; probably a local name for the English water dock (*Rumex hydrolapathum*).

[76] His biting habits depend upon the time of year(?). However, "season" here may refer to availability or edibility, in which case the interpretation should be that the trout is in season at any time of the year. In the case of salmon there is stronger reason to speak of seasons, since as a migratory fish it would not be available at all times, nor would it be particularly palatable in autumn, when it spawns. In the passage on salmon, March is given as the beginning of the season, and this corresponds roughly to the early runs into the rivers; and the season is properly ended in September, at the onset of spawning. The printed (1496) version gives "March to Michaelmas" as the season also for trout. For either fish, this season would correspond to the period when the flesh was in best condition for eating.

[77] Probably a species of *Perla*.

[78] This habitat is not so well known to modern anglers as a source of bait. The reference here could have been to a species of earthworm, but the next bait specified is the "dor-worm," clearly the larvae of some insect. According to a recent British study ("The Larval Inhabitants of Cow Pats," by B. R. Lawrence, *Journal of Animal Ecology*, 23 (2): 234, 1954), the larvae of two true or two-winged flies (Diptera) are common inhabitants, and likely the grubworms referred to in the treatise.

[79] Several insects have borne this name. The *dor-worm* is the larva of some fly, beetle, or bee.

[80] The larva of a European caddis fly.

worm and the codworm together. In August, take the fly,[81] the little red worm, the herlesoke,[82] and bind the hook. In September, take the red worm and the minnow. In October, take the same, for they are special baits for the trout at all times.[83]

[81] Probably the *flesh fly*, "blowfly"; cf. 1496 version.
[82] Some insect or worm (?). But a *herl* is the fiber from the shaft of a feather; it was used for making artificial flies.
[83] The rest of the manuscript is lost.

CHAPTER 3

Modernized Text of the First Printed Version of the Treatise (from the Second Book of St. Albans: *1496)*

This second version of the *Treatise of Fishing,* in order of appearance, is the more complete one as well as the first to be printed. Its publication in the second *Book of St. Albans* in 1496, along with other treatises on hunting, hawking, and heraldry, placed it in the context of a gentleman's handbook. This printed version of the treatise on fishing varies in many details from the manuscript version, fills in missing pages, and has two important sections presumably lost from the end of the earlier version, namely, one on the twelve trout-fly dressings, the second on the concluding charge to anglers to follow a code of good behavior: shut the gate, etc. The modernization here is made for the benefit of the reader unfamiliar with Middle English type style; a facsimile of the original print with a line-for-line transcript is in Chapter 8.

Solomon in his Proverbs says that a good spirit makes a flowering age, that is, a fair age and a long one. And since it is so, I ask this question, "What are the means and the causes that lead a man into a merry spirit?" Truly, in my best judgment, it seems that they are good sports and honest games in which a man takes pleasure without any repentance afterward. Thence it follows that good recreations and honorable pastimes are the cause of a man's fair old age and long life. And therefore, I will now choose among four good sports and honorable pastimes—to wit, among hunting, hawking, fishing, and fowling. The best, in my simple judgment, is fishing, called angling, with a rod and a line and a hook. And thereof I will treat as my simple mind will permit, both for the above-mentioned saying of Solomon and also for the statement that medical science makes in this manner:

> Si tibi deficiant medici, medici tibi fiant
> Haec tria—mens laeta, labor, et moderatadiaeta.[1]

You shall understand, that is to say, that if a man lacks physician or doctor, he shall make three things his physician and doctor, and he will never need any more. The first of them is a merry thought. The second is

[1] For explanatory notes to this portion of the treatise, see the manuscript version, Chapter 2.

work which is not excessive. The third is a moderate diet. First, if a man wishes to be always in merry thoughts and have a glad spirit, he must avoid all quarrelsome company and all places of dispute, where he might have any causes of melancholy. And if he wishes to have a labor which is not excessive, he must then arrange for himself, for his heart's ease and pleasure—without care, anxiety, or trouble—a merry occupation which may rejoice his heart and in which his spirits may have a merry delight. And if he wishes to have a moderate diet, he must avoid all places of debauchery, which is the cause of overindulgence and sickness. And he must withdraw himself to places of sweet and hunger-producing air, and eat nourishing foods and also digestible ones.

Now then I will describe the said sports or games to find out, as truly as I can, which is the best of them; albeit the right noble and very worthy prince, the Duke of York, lately called the Master of Game, has described the joys of hunting, just as I think to describe it and all the others. For hunting, to my mind, is too laborious. For the hunter must always run and follow his hounds, laboring and sweating very painfully. He blows on his horn till his lips blister; and when he thinks he is chasing a hare, very often it is a hedgehog. Thus he hunts and knows not what. He comes home in the evening rain-beaten, scratched, his clothes torn, wet-shod, all muddy, this hound lost and that one crippled. Such griefs happen to the hunter—and many others which, for fear of the displeasure of them that love it, I dare not report. Thus, truly, it seems to me that this is not the best recreation or game of the four mentioned.

The sport and pastime of hawking is laborious and troublesome also, as it seems to me. For often the falconer loses his hawks, as the hunter his hounds. Then his pastime and sport is gone. Very often he shouts and whistles till he is terribly thirsty. His hawk takes to a bough and does not choose to pay him any attention. When he would have her fly at the game, then she wants to bathe.[2] With improper feeding she will get the frounce, the ray, the cray, and many other sicknesses that bring them to the upward flight. Thus, by proof, this is not the best sport and game of the four mentioned.

The sport and game of fowling seems to me poorest of all. For in the

[2] This odd statement is an error due to someone's mistaking the rare word *baythe*, "to consent, agree," for *bathe*, "to take a bath." For the correct reading, see the manuscript version.

winter season the fowler has no luck except in the hardest and coldest weather, which is vexatious. For when he would go to his traps, he cannot because of the cold. Many a trap and many a snare he makes, yet he fares badly. In the morning time, in the dew, he is wet-shod up to his tail. Much more of the same I could tell, but dread of displeasure makes me leave off. Thus, it seems to me that hunting and hawking and also fowling are so toilsome and unpleasant that none of them can succeed nor be the true means of bringing a man into a merry frame of mind, which is the cause of his long life according to the said proverb of Solomon.

Undoubtedly then, it follows that it must needs be the sport of fishing with a hook. (For every other kind of fishing is also toilsome and unpleasant, often making folks very wet and cold, which many times has been seen to be the cause of great sicknesses.) But the angler can have no cold nor discomfort nor anger, unless he be the cause himself. For he can lose at the most only a line or a hook, of which he can have a plentiful supply of his own making, as this simple treatise will teach him. So then his loss is not grievous, and other griefs he cannot have, except that some fish may break away after he has been caught on the hook, or else that he may catch nothing. These are not grievous, for if the angler fails with one, he may not fail with another, if he does as this treatise teaches—unless there are no fish in the water. And yet, at the very least, he has his wholesome and merry walk at his ease, and a sweet breath of the sweet smell of the meadow flowers, that makes him hungry. He hears the melodious harmony of birds. He sees the young swans, herons, ducks, coots, and many other birds with their broods, which seems to me better than all the noise of hounds, the blasts of horns, and the clamor of birds that hunters, falconers, and fowlers can produce. And if the angler catches fish, surely then there is no man merrier than he is in his spirit. Also whoever wishes to practice the sport of angling, he must rise early, which thing is profitable to a man in this way. That is, to wit: most for the welfare of his soul, for it will cause him to be holy; and for the health of his body, for it will cause him to be well; also for the increase of his goods, for it will make him rich. As the old English proverb says in this manner: "Whoever will rise early shall be holy, healthy, and happy."

Thus have I proved, according to my purpose, that the sport and game of angling is the true means and cause that brings a man into a merry spirit, which (according to the said proverb of Solomon and the said teaching of medicine) makes a flowering age and a long one. And therefore, to all you that are virtuous, gentle, and freeborn, I write and make this simple treatise which follows, by which you can have the whole art of angling to amuse you as you please, in order that your age may flourish the more and last the longer.

If you want to be crafty in angling, you must first learn to make your tackle, that is, your rod, your lines of different colors. After that, you must know how you should angle, in what place of the water, how deep, and what time of day; for what manner of fish, in what weather; how many impediments there are in the fishing that is called angling; and especially with what baits for each different fish in every month of the year; how you must make your baits-bread, where you will find the baits, and how you will keep them; and for the most difficult thing, how you are to make your hooks of steel and iron, some for the artificial fly and some for the float and the ground-line, as you will afterward hear all these things expressed openly for your knowledge.

And how you should make your rod skillfully, here I will teach you. You must cut, between Michaelmas and Candlemas, a fair staff, a fathom and a half long and as thick as your arm, of hazel, willow, or aspen; and soak[3] it in a hot oven, and set it straight. Then let it cool and dry for a month. Then take and tie it tight with a cockshoot cord,[4] and bind it to a bench or a perfectly square, large timber. Then take a plumber's wire that is smooth and straight and sharp at one end. And heat the sharp end in a charcoal fire till it is white-hot, and then burn the staff through with it, always straight in the pith at both ends, till the holes meet. And after that, burn it in the lower end with a spit for roasting birds, and with other spits, each larger than the last, and always the largest last; so that you make your hole always taper-wax.[5] Then let it lie still and cool for two days. Untie it then and let it dry in a house-roof in the smoke until it is thoroughly dry. In the same season, take a fair rod of green hazel, and soak it even and straight,

[3] That is, soak it in hot water to make it pliable, so that it can be straightened. *Bethe,* the word used here, is probably an error; the manuscript has *beke,* which makes better sense.

[4] A cord used for fastening a net across an open space (or "cockshoot") in the woods to catch birds.

[5] Waxed with wax from a taper(?); increasing in diameter like a taper(?). The manuscript is clearer on this point.

and let it dry with the staff. And when they are dry, make the rod fit the hole in the staff, into half the length of the staff. And to make the other half of the upper section, take a fair shoot of blackthorn, crabtree, medlar, or juniper, cut in the same season and well soaked and straightened; and bind them together neatly so that the upper section may go exactly all the way into the above-mentioned hole. Then shave your staff down and make it taper-wax. Then ferrule the staff at both ends with long hoops of iron or latten in the neatest manner, with a spike in the lower end fastened with a running device for pulling your upper section in and out. Then set your upper section a handbreadth inside the upper end of your staff in such a way that it may be as big there as in any other place above. Then, with a cord of six hairs, strengthen your upper section at the upper end as far down as the place where it is tied together; and arrange the cord neatly and tie it firmly in the top, with a loop to fasten your fishing line on. And thus you will make yourself a rod so secret that you can walk with it, and no one will know what you are going to do. It will be light and very nimble to fish with at your pleasure. And for your greater convenience, behold here a picture of it as an example:

After you have made your rod thus, you must learn to color your lines of hair in this manner. First, you must take, from the tail of a white horse, the longest and best hair that you can find; and the rounder it is, the better it is. Divide it into six bunches, and you must color every part by itself in a different color, such as, yellow, green, brown, tawny, russet, and dusky colors.

And to make a good green color on your hair, you must do thus. Take a quart of small ale and put it in a little pan, and add to it half a pound of alum, and put your hair in it, and let it boil softly half an hour. Then take out your hair and let it dry. Then take a half-gallon of water and put it in a pan. And put in it two handfuls of a yellow dye, and press it with a tile-stone, and let it boil softly half an hour. And when it is yellow on the scum, put in your hair with half a pound of green vitriol, called copperas, beaten to powder, and let it boil half-a-mile-way. And then set it down and let it cool five or six hours. Then take out the hair and dry it. And it is then the finest green there is for the water. And ever the more you add to it of copperas, the better it is. Or else instead of copperas, use verdigris.

Another way, you can make a brighter green, thus. Dye your hair with blue dye[6] until it is a light blue-gray color. And then seethe it in yellow vegetable dye as I have described, except that you must not add to it either copperas or verdigris.

To make your hair yellow, prepare it with alum as I have explained before, and after that with yellow vegetable dye without copperas or verdigris.[7]

Another yellow you shall make thus. Take a half-gallon of small ale, and crush three handfuls of walnut leaves, and put them together. And put in your hair till it is as deep a yellow as you want to have it.

To make russet hair, take a pint and a half of strong lye and half a pound of soot and a little juice of walnut leaves and a quart[8] of alum; and put them all together in a pan and boil them well. And when it is cold, put in your hair till it is as dark as you want it.

To make a brown color, take a pound of soot and a quart of ale, and seethe it with as many walnut leaves as you can. And when they turn black, set it off the fire. And put your hair in it, and let it lie still until it is as brown as you wish to have it.

To make another brown, take strong ale and soot and blend them together, and put therein your hair for two days and two nights, and it will be a right good color.

To make a tawny color, take lime and water, and put them together; and also put your hair therein four or five hours. Then take it out and put it in tanner's ooze[9] for a day, and it will be as fine a tawny color as is required for our purpose.

The sixth part of your hair, you must keep still white for lines for the dubbed[10] hook, to fish for the trout and grayling, and to prepare[11] small lines for the roach and the dace.

[6] Literally: Let woad your hair in a woad-vat.

[7] The first break in the manuscript occurs at about this point. For several pages, the 1496 print is sole authority for the text of the treatise.

[8] Error for *quarter*, i.e., a quarter of a pound.

[9] The liquid from a tanner's vat, a mixture of tanbark juices, etc.

[10] Covered with an artificial fly.

[11] *Rye*, i.e., *ray*, "to array, dress up, prepare."

When your hair is thus colored, you must know for which waters and for which seasons they will serve. The green color in all clear water from April till September. The yellow color in every clear water from September till November, for it is like the weeds and other kinds of grass which grow in the waters and rivers, when they are broken. The russet color serves for all the winter until the end of April, as well in rivers as in pools or lakes. The brown color serves for that water that is black, sluggish, in rivers or in other waters. The tawny color for those waters that are heathy or marshy.

Now you must make your lines in this way. First, see that you have an instrument like this picture drawn hereafter. Then take your hair and cut off from the small end a large handful or more, for it is neither strong nor yet dependable. Then turn the top to the tail,[12] each in equal amount, and divide it into three strands. Then plait each part at the one end by itself, and at the other end plait all three together. And put this last end in the farther side of your instrument, the end that has but one cleft. And fix the other end tight with the wedge the width of four fingers from the end of your hair. Then twist each strand the same way and pull it hard; and fasten them in the three clefts equally tight. Then take out that other end and twist it sufficiently in whichever direction it is inclined. Then stretch it a little and plait it so that it will not come undone. And that is good. And to know how to make your instrument, behold, here it is in a picture. And it is to be made of wood, except the bolt underneath, which must be of iron.

When you have as many of the lengths as you suppose will suffice for the length of a line, then you must tie them together with a water knot[13] or else a duchess knot. And when your knot is tied, cut off the unused short ends a straw's breadth from the knot. Thus you will make your lines fair

[12] That is, the top to the bottom; reverse half the hair so as to make each strand of uniform strength from end to end.

[13] Probably the knot later known as the fisherman's knot.

and fine, and also very secure for any kind of fish. And because you should know both the water knot and also the duchess knot, behold them here in picture. Contrive them in the likeness of the drawing.

[Illustration missing[14]]

You must understand that the subtlest and hardest art in making your tackle is to make your hooks, for the making of which you must have suitable files, thin and sharp and beaten small; a semi-clamp of iron; a bender;[15] a pair of long and small tongs; a hard knife, somewhat thick; an anvil; and a little hammer. And for small fish, you must make your hooks in this manner, of the smallest square needles of steel that you can find. You must put the square needle in a red charcoal fire till it is of the same color as the fire is. Then take it out and let it cool, and you will find it well tempered for filing. Then raise the barb with your knife and make the point sharp. Then temper it again, for otherwise it will break in the bending. Then bend it like the bend pictured hereafter as an example. And you must make greater hooks in the same way out of larger needles, such as embroiderers' or tailors' or shoemakers' needles, or spear points; and of shoemakers' awls, especially, the best hooks are made for great fish. And the hooks should bend at the point when they are tested; otherwise they are not good. When the hook is bent, beat the hinder end out broad, and file it smooth to prevent fraying of your line. Then put it in the fire again, and give it an easy red heat. Then suddenly quench it in water, and it will be hard and strong. And that you may have knowledge of your instruments, behold them here in picture portrayed.

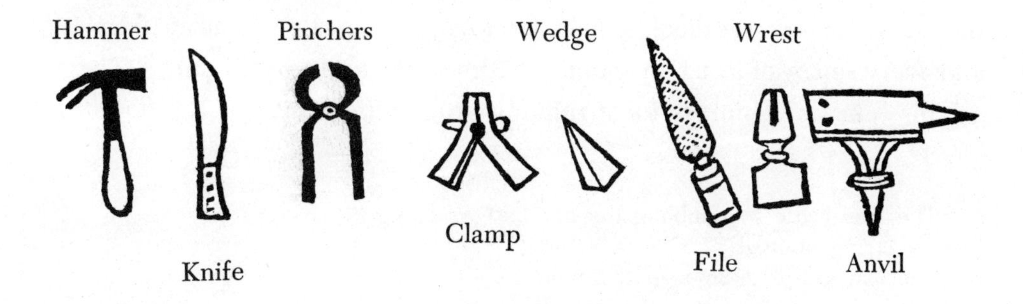

[14] Probably missing because the printer was unable to reproduce the knots.
[15] An instrument for bending, called a *wrest* below.

When you have made your hooks in this way, then you must set them on your lines, according to size and strength in this manner. You must take fine red silk thread, and if it is for a large hook, then double it, but not twisted. And otherwise, for small hooks, let it be single. And with it, bind the line thick for a straw's breadth from the point where the one end of your hook is to be placed. Then set your hook there, and wrap it with the same thread for two-thirds of the length that is to be wrapped. And when you come to the third part, then turn the end of your line back upon the wrapping, double, and wrap it thus double for the third part. Then put your thread in at the hole[16] twice or thrice, and let it go each time round about the shank of your hook. Then wet the hole and pull it until it is tight. And see that your line always lies inside your hooks and not outside. Then cut off the end of the line and the thread as close as you can, without cutting the knot.

Now that you know with what size hooks you must angle for every fish,[17] I will tell you[18] with how many hairs you must angle for each kind of fish. For the minnow, with a line of one hair. For the growing roach, the bleak, the gudgeon, and the ruff, with a line of two hairs. For the dace and the great roach, with a line of three hairs. For the perch, the flounder, and small bream, with four hairs. For the chevin-chub, the bream, the tench, and the eel, with six hairs. For the trout, grayling, barbel, and the great chevin, with nine hairs. For the great trout, with twelve hairs. For the salmon, with fifteen hairs. And for the pike, with a chalkline made brown with your brown coloring as described above, strengthened with a wire, as you will hear hereafter when I speak of the pike.[19]

Your lines must be weighted with lead sinkers, and you must know that the sinker nearest the hook should be a full foot and more away from it, and every sinker of a size in keeping with the thickness of the line.[20] There are three kinds of sinkers for a running ground-line. And for the float set

[16] The loop made by doubling the line and wrapping it.
[17] Something omitted(?).
[18] The manuscript resumes at this point.
[19] The carp is omitted here, but mentioned later.
[20] The sentences which follow are not clear and may have been misread by the printer; cf. the manuscript version.

upon the stationary ground-line, ten weights all joining together. On the running ground-line, nine or ten small ones. The float sinker must be so heavy that the least pluck of any fish can pull it down into the water. And make your sinkers round and smooth so that they do not stick in stones or in weeds. And for the better understanding, behold them here in picture.

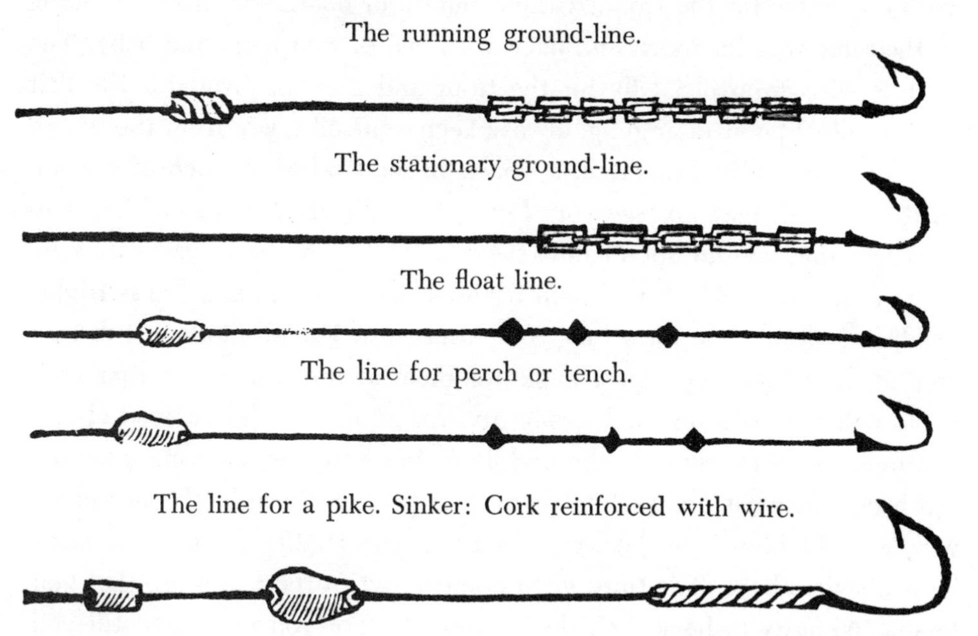

Then you are to make your floats in this manner. Take a good cork that is clean, without many holes; and bore it through with a small hot iron; and put a quill in it, even and straight. Ever the larger the float, the larger the quill and the larger the hole. Then shape it large in the middle and small at both ends, and especially sharp in the lower end, and similar to the pictures following. And make them smooth on a grinding stone,[21] or on a tilestone. And see that the float for one hair is no larger than a pea; for two hairs, like a bean; for twelve hairs, like a walnut; and so every line according to proportion. All kinds of lines that are not for the bottom must have floats, and the running ground-line must have a float. The stationary ground-line without float.

[21] Perhaps a whetstone, more likely a grindstone revolving on an axle.

Now I have taught you to make all your tackle. Here I will tell you how you must angle. You shall angle:[22] understand that there are six ways of angling. The one is at the bottom for the trout and other fish. Another is at the bottom at an arch or at a pool,[23] where it ebbs and flows, for bleak, roach, and dace. The third is with a float for all kinds of fish. The fourth, with a minnow for the trout, without plumb or float. The fifth is running in the same way for roach and dace with one or two hairs and a fly. The sixth is with an artificial fly for the trout and grayling. And for the first and principal point in angling, always keep yourself away from the water, from the sight of the fish, either far back on the land or else behind a bush, so that the fish may not see you. For if they do, they will not bite. Also take care that you do not shadow the water any more than you can help, for that is a thing which will soon frighten the fish. And if a fish is frightened, he will not bite for a long time afterward. For all kinds of fish that feed at the bottom, you must angle for them at the bottom, so that your hooks will run or lie on the bottom. And for all other fish that feed above, you must angle for them in the middle of the water, either somewhat beneath or somewhat above. For always the greater the fish, the nearer he will lie to the bottom of the water; and ever the smaller the fish, the more he will swim above. The third good point is: when the fish bites, that you be not too hasty to hook the fish, nor too late. For you must wait till you suppose that the bait is fairly in the mouth of the fish, and then wait no longer. And this is for the ground-line. And for the float, when you see it pulled softly under the water or else carried softly upon the water, then strike. And see that you never strike too hard for the strength of your line, lest you break it. And if you have the fortune to hook a great fish with a small tackle, then you must lead him in the water and labor with him there until he is drowned and overcome. Then take him as well as you can or may, and always beware that you do not hold beyond the strength of your line. And as much as you can, do not let him come out of the end of your line straight from you, but keep him always under the rod and always hold him strait, so that your line can sustain and bear his leaps and his plunges with the help of your crop and of your hand.

Here I will declare to you in what place of the water you must angle.

[22] Redundant.

[23] *Stang*, a variant spelling of *stank*, "a pond"; but cf. the manuscript version.

You should angle in a pool or in standing water, in every place where it is at all deep. There is not much choice of such places in a pool. For it is but a prison for fish, and they live for the most part in hunger like prisoners; and therefore it takes the less art to catch them. But in a river, you must angle in every place where it is deep and clear at the bottom, as in gravel or clay without mud or weeds, and especially if there is a kind of whirling of water or a covert—such as a hollow bank or great roots of trees or long weeds floating above in the water—where the fish can cover and hide themselves at certain times when they like. Also it is good to angle in deep, swift streams, and also in waterfalls and weirs, and in floodgates and mill-races. And it is good to angle where the water rests by the bank and where the current runs close by and it is deep and clear at the bottom; and in any other places where you can see any fish rise or do any feeding.

Now you must know what time of the day you should angle. From the beginning of May until it is September, the biting time is early in the morning from four o'clock until eight o'clock; and in the afternoon, from four o'clock until eight o'clock, but this is not so good as in the morning. And if there is a cold, whistling wind and it be a dark, lowering day,[24] for a dark day is much better to angle in than a clear day. From the beginning of September until the end of April, angle at any time of the day. Also, many pool fishes will bite best at noontime. And if you see the trout or grayling leap at any time of the day, angle for him with an artificial fly appropriate to that same month. And where the water ebbs and flows, the fish will bite in some place at the ebb, and in some place at the flood. After that, they will rest behind the stakes or pilings and arches of bridges and in other places of that sort.

Here you should know in what weather you must angle: as I said before, in a dark, lowering day when the wind blows softly. And in the summer season when it is burning hot, then it is useless. From September until April in a fair, sunny day, it is right good to angle. And if the wind in that season comes from any part of the east, the weather then is no good. And when there is a great wind, and when it snows, rains, or hails, or there is a great tempest, as with thunder or lightning, or sweltering[25] hot weather, then it is not good for angling.

[24] Something omitted (?); see manuscript version.
[25] *Swoly,* "sultry, oppressively hot."

Now you must know that there are twelve kinds of impediments which cause a man to catch no fish, apart from other common causes that may happen by chance. The first is if your tackle is not adequate or suitably made. The second is if your baits are not good or fine. The third is if you do not angle in biting time. The fourth is if the fish are frightened by the sight of a man. The fifth, if the water is very thick, white or red from any flood recently fallen. The sixth, if the fish do not stir because of the cold. The seventh, if the weather is hot. The eighth, if it rains. The ninth, if it hails or snow falls. The tenth is if there is a tempest. The eleventh is if there is a great wind. The twelfth, if the wind is in the east, and that is worst, for generally, both winter and summer, the fish will not bite then. The west and north winds are good, but the south is best.

And now that I have told you, in all points, how to make your tackle and how you must fish with it, it is reasonable that you should know with what baits you must angle for every kind of fish in each month of the year, which is the gist of the art. And unless these baits are well known by you, all your other skill hitherto avails little to your purpose. For you cannot bring a hook into a fish's mouth without a bait. These baits for every kind of fish and for every month follow here in this manner.

Because the salmon is the most stately fish that any man can angle for in fresh water, therefore I intend to begin with him. The salmon is a noble fish, but he is cumbersome to catch. For generally he is only in deep places of great rivers, and for the most part he keeps to the middle of the water, so that a man cannot come at him. And he is in season from March until Michaelmas, in which season you should angle for him with these baits, when you can get them. First, with an earthworm in the beginning and end of the season. And also with a grubworm that grows in a dunghill. And especially with an excellent bait that grows on a water-dock plant. And he does not bite at the bottom but at the float. Also you may catch him (but this is seldom seen) with an artificial fly at such times as he leaps, in like manner and way as you catch a trout or a grayling. And these baits are well proven baits for the salmon.[26]

[26] This is reminiscent of the formula *probatum est* (i.e., the remedy has been proved, or tested) which so often follows a medical recipe in the medieval collections. The formula takes different shapes in the medical books and is often translated into English in various ways: *probatum est pro certo, quod probatur, quod probatum est secundum R. de O.* (according to the Rector of Oswaldkirk, a forgotten authority on medicine), *yt ys preuyd, þis ys a medycyne prouyd, þis ys prouyd, it is trew & prouede, þis medycyne is prouede on warantyse,* etc. For examples, see W. R. Dawson, *A Leechbook or*

The trout, because he is a right dainty fish and also a right fervent biter, we shall speak next of him. He is in season from March until Michaelmas. He is in clean gravel bottom and in a stream. You can angle for him at all times with a lying or running ground-line, except in leaping time and then with an artificial fly; and early with a running ground-line, and later in the day with a float-line. You must angle for him in March with a minnow hung on your hook by the lower nose, without float or sinker, drawing it up and down in the stream till you feel him hooked. In the same time, angle for him with a ground-line with an earthworm as the surest bait. In April, take the same baits, and also the lamprey, otherwise called "seven eyes,"[27] also the cankerworm that grows in a great tree, and the red snail. In May, take the stone fly and the grubworm under the cow turd, and the silkworm, and the bait that grows on a fern leaf. In June, take an earthworm and nip off the head, and put a codworm on your hook in front of it. In July, take the big red worm and the codworm together. In August, take a flesh fly[28] and the big red worm and the fat of bacon, and bind them about your hook. In September, take the earthworm and the minnow. In October, take the same, for they are special for the trout at all times[29] of the year. From April to September the trout leaps; then angle for him with an artificial fly appropriate to the month. These flies you will find at the end of this treatise, and the months with them.

The grayling, also known as the umber,[30] is a delicious fish to man's mouth. You can catch him just as you do the trout, and these are his baits.

Collection of Medical Recipes of the Fifteenth Century (London: Macmillan, 1934), pp. 20, 24, 30, 34, 36, etc.; Fritz Heinrich, *Ein mittelenglisches Medizinbuch* (Halle: Max Niemeyer, 1896), pp. 75, 92, 114, 125, 144, 157, etc.; Gottfried Müller, *Aus mittelenglischen Medizintexten* (Leipzig: Bernhard Tauchnitz, 1929), pp. 65, 66, 79, etc.; Margaret S. Ogden, *Liber de Diversis Medicinis* (Early English Text Society, CCVII; London, 1938), pp. 24, 28, 29, 30, etc.; Herbert Schöffler, *Beiträge zur mittelenglischen Medizinliteratur* (Halle: Max Niemeyer, 1919), pp. 238, 243, 256, etc. All of these medical books are roughly contemporary with the manuscript of the *Treatise of Fishing*.

[27] Called "seven eyes" because of its seven pairs of gill slits which look like eyes.

[28] Some kind of blowfly.

[29] The manuscript ends at this point, and from here on the 1496 print is sole authority.

[30] A recently borrowed French term. Most of the fish names are native formations, like *grayling*, or older borrowings from Latin, French, or Scandinavian.

In March and in April, the earthworm. In May, the green worm,[31] a little ringed worm, the dock canker, and the hawthorn worm. In June, the bait that grows between the tree and the bark of an oak. In July, a bait that grows on a fern leaf; and the big red worm, and nip off the head and put a codworm on your hook in front of it. In August, the earthworm, and a dock worm. And all the year afterward, an earthworm.

The barbel is a sweet fish, but it is a queasy food and a perilous one for man's body. For commonly, he introduces the fevers; and if he is eaten raw, he may be the cause of a man's death, as has often been seen. These are his baits. In March and in April, take fair, fresh cheese, lay it on a board, and cut it in small square pieces the length of your hook. Then take a candle and burn it on the end at the point of your hook until it is yellow. And then bind it on your hook with arrowmaker's silk, and make it rough like a welbede.[32] This bait is good for all the summer season. In May and June, take the hawthorn worm and the big red worm; nip off the head and put a codworm on your hook in front; and that is a good bait. In July, take the earthworm chiefly and the hawthorn worm together. Also the water-dock leaf worm and the hornet worm[33] together. In August and for all the year, take mutton fat and soft cheese, of each the same amount, and a little honey; and grind or beat them together a long time, and work it until it is tough. Add to it a little flour, and make it into small pellets. And that is a good bait to angle with at the bottom. And see to it that it sinks in the water, or else it is not good for this purpose.

The carp is a dainty fish, but there are only a few in England, and therefore I will write the less about him. He is a bad fish to catch, for he is so strongly reinforced in the mouth that no weak tackle can hold him. And as regards his baits, I have but little knowledge of them, and I would hate to write more than I know and have tested. But I know well that the earthworm and the minnow are good baits for him at all times, as I have heard

[31] Many of these baits cannot be identified with any certainty, although we believe that anyone living in the fifteenth century in the place where the treatise was written would recognize them instantly.

[32] Possibly a woodlouse or a millepede, both crustaceans. J. O. Halliwell's *A Dictionary of Archaic and Provincial Words* (London: John Russell Smith, 1852) has "*Welbode.* The insect [*sic*] millepes," and "*Wolbode.* A millepes."

[33] The larva of a hornet(?); more likely a "horned worm" of some kind, cf. the horned beetle, horned snail, etc.

reliable persons say and also found written in trustworthy books.[34]

The chub is a stately fish, and his head is a dainty morsel. There is no fish so greatly fortified with scales on the body. And because he is a strong biter, he has the more baits, which are these. In March, the earthworm at the bottom, for usually he will bite there then, and at all times of the year if he is at all hungry. In April, the ditch canker that grows in the tree; a worm that grows between the bark and the wood of an oak; the earthworm; and the young frogs when the feet are cut off. Also, the stone fly, the grubworm under the cow turd, the red snail. In May, the bait that grows on the osier leaf and the dock canker, together upon your hook. Also a bait that grows on a fern leaf, the codworm, and a bait that grows on a hawthorn. And a bait that grows on an oak leaf and a silkworm and a codworm together. In June, take the cricket and the dor;[35] and also an earthworm with the head cut off and a codworm in front, and put them on the hook. Also a bait on the osier leaf, young frogs with three feet cut off at the body and the fourth at the knee. The bait on the hawthorn and the codworm together; and a grub that breeds in a dunghill; and a big grasshopper. In July, the grasshopper and the bumblebee of the meadow. Also young bees and young hornets. Also a great, brindled fly that grows in paths of meadows, and the fly that is among anthills.[36] In August, take wortworms[37] and maggots until Michaelmas. In September, the earthworm; and also take these baits when you can get them; that is to say: cherries, young mice without hair, and the honeycomb.

The bream is a noble fish and a dainty one. And you must angle for him with an earthworm from March until August, and then with a butterfly and a green fly,[38] and with a bait that grows among green reeds, and a bait that grows in the bark of a dead tree. And for young bream, take maggots. And from that time forth for all the year afterward, take the

[34] This is the only bit of angling lore allegedly drawn from books. In view of the medieval fondness for citing authorities wherever possible, it seems likely that most of the treatise was written from personal experience and oral tradition.

[35] The *dor-worm,* a larva of some sort.

[36] A winged ant, either queen or drone.

[37] Probably a caterpillar that feeds on cabbages.

[38] Probably a green-colored natural fly.

earthworm and, in the river, brown bread. There are more baits, but they are not easy, and therefore I pass over them.

A tench is a good fish, and heals all sorts of other fish that are hurt, if they can come to him.[39] During most of the year he is in the mud; he stirs most in June and July, and in other seasons but little. He is a poor biter. His baits are these. For all the year, brown bread toasted with honey in the shape of a buttered loaf, and the big red worm. And for the chief bait, take the black blood in the heart of a sheep and flour and honey. Work them all together somewhat softer than paste, and anoint the earthworm therewith—both for this fish and for others. And they will bite much better thereat at all times.

The perch is a dainty fish and surpassingly wholesome, and a free-biting fish. These are his baits. In March, the earthworm. In April, the grubworm under the cow turd. In May, the sloe-thorn worm and the codworm. In June, the bait that grows in an old fallen oak, and the green canker. In July, the bait that grows on the osier leaf, and the grub that grows on the dunghill, and the hawthorn worm, and the codworm. In August, the earthworm and maggots. All the year thereafter, the earthworm is best.

The roach is an easy fish to catch. And if he is fat and penned up, then he is good food, and these are his baits. In March, the readiest bait is the earthworm. In April, the grub under the cow turd. In May, the bait that grows on the oak leaf and the grub in the dunghill. In June, the bait that grows on the osier and the codworm. In July, houseflies and the bait that grows on an oak; and the nutworm[40] and mathewes[41] and maggots till Michaelmas; and after that, the fat of bacon.

The dace is a noble fish to catch, and if it[42] be well fattened, then it is good food. In March, his bait is an earthworm. In April, the grub under the cow turd. In May, the dock canker and the bait on the sloe thorn and on the oak leaf. In June, the codworm and the bait on the osier and the white grubworm in the dunghill. In July, take houseflies, and flies that grow in anthills; the codworm and maggots until Michaelmas. And if the water is

[39] We regret not knowing more about this remarkable observation.

[40] Perhaps the larva of the nut weevil (*Balaninus nucum*), which lays eggs in green hazelnuts or filberts.

[41] Worms or maggots of some kind; cf. *mathe*, "maggot," etc.

[42] Neuter pronoun(!). Fish are generally masculine in this treatise.

clear, you will catch fish when others take none. And from that time forth, do as you do for the roach, for usually in their biting and their baits they are alike.

The bleak is but a feeble fish, yet he is wholesome. His baits from March to Michaelmas are the same as I have written before for the roach and dace, except that, all the summer season, as far as possible, you should angle for him with a housefly; and, in the winter season, with bacon and other bait made as you will know hereafter.

The ruff is a right wholesome fish, and you must angle for him with the same baits in all seasons of the year and in the same way as I have told you for the perch; for they are alike in fishing and feeding except that the ruff is smaller. And therefore he must have the smaller bait.

The flounder is a wholesome fish and a noble one, and a subtle biter in his own way. For usually, when he sucks his food, he feeds at the bottom; and therefore you must angle for him with a lying ground-line. And he has but one kind of bait, and that is an earthworm, which is the best bait for all kinds of fish.

The gudgeon is a good fish for his size, and he bites well at the bottom. And his baits for all the year are these: the earthworm, the codworm, and maggots. And you must angle for him with a float, and let your bait be near the bottom or else on the bottom.

The minnow, when he shines in the water, then he is better.[43] And though his body is little, yet he is a ravenous biter and an eager one. And you must angle for him with the same baits as you do for gudgeon, except that they must be small.

The eel is an indigestible fish, a glutton, and a devourer of the young fry of fish. And because the pike also is a devourer of fish, I put them both behind all others for angling. For this eel, you must find a hole in the bottom of the water, and it is blue-blackish. There put in your hook till it be a foot within the hole, and your bait should be a big angle-twitch[44] or a minnow.

The pike is a good fish, but because he devours so many of his own kind

[43] *Byttyre,* "bitter," makes poor sense here, and the author often confused *e* with *i* (or *y*); cf. manuscript version. The "better" minnows may be those with bright streaks or spots on the bellies or sides.

[44] An earthworm, angleworm.

as well as of others, I love him the less.[45] And to catch him, you must do thus. Take a small cod hook, and take a roach or a fresh herring, and a wire with a hole in the end. And put the wire in at the mouth and out at the tail, down along the back of the fresh herring. Then put the line of your hook in after it, and draw the hook into the cheek of the fresh herring. Then put a sinker on your line a yard away from your hook, and a float midway between; and cast it in a hole which the pike frequents. And this is the best and surest device for catching the pike. There is another way of catching him. Take a frog and put it on your hook at the back side of the neck between the skin and the body, and put on a float a yard distant, and cast it where the pike haunts, and you will have him. Another way: take the same bait and put it in asafetida and cast it in the water with a cord and a cork, and you will not fail to get him. And if you care to have good sport, then tie the cord to the foot of a goose, and you will see a good tug-of-war[46] to decide whether the goose or the pike will have the better of it.

Now you know with what baits and how you must angle for every kind of fish. Now I will tell you how you must keep and feed your live baits. You must feed and keep them all together, but each kind by itself and with such things as those in and on which they live. And as long as they are alive and fresh, they are excellent. But when they are sloughing their skin or else dead, they are no good. Out of these are excepted three kinds, that is, to wit: hornets, bumblebees, and wasps. These you must bake in bread, and afterward dip their heads in blood and let them dry. Also except maggots, which, when they are grown large with their natural feeding, you must feed further with mutton fat and with a cake made of flour and honey; then they will become larger. And when you have cleansed them with sand in a bag of blanket,[47] kept hot under your gown or other warm thing for two or three hours, then they are best and ready to angle with. And cut off the leg of the frog at the knee, the legs and wings of the grasshopper at the body.

The following are baits made to last all the year. The first are flour and

[45] The sentiment against cannibal fish has been a lasting but not always consistent one among anglers.

[46] *Haling*, "hauling, pulling."

[47] A kind of heavy woolen cloth.

lean meat from the hips of a rabbit or a cat, virgin wax, and sheep's fat. Bray them in a mortar, and then mix it at the fire with a little purified honey; and so make it up into little balls, and bait your hooks with it according to their size. And this is a good bait for all kinds of fresh-water fish.

Another: take the suet of a sheep and cheese in equal amounts, and bray them together a long time in a mortar. And then take flour and mix it therewith, and after that mingle it with honey and make balls of it. And that is especially for the barbel.

Another, for dace and roach and bleak: take wheat and seethe it well and then put it in blood a whole day and a night, and it will be a good bait.

For baits for great fish, keep this rule especially: When you have taken a great fish, open up the belly, and whatever you find in it, make that your bait, for it is best.

These are the twelve flies with which you must angle for the trout and grayling; and dub them just as you will now hear me tell.[48]

March

The Dun Fly: The body of dun wool and the wings of the partridge. Another Dun Fly: the body of black wool; the wings of the blackest drake;[49] and the jay under the wing and under the tail.[50]

April

The Stone Fly: the body of black wool, and yellow under the wing and under the tail; and the wings, of the drake. In the beginning of May, a good fly: the body of reddened[51] wool and lapped about with black silk; the wings, of the drake and of the red capon's hackle.

[48] Owing to the fact that we discuss the interpretation of these fly dressings in detail in Chapter 5, our text here is calculated to avoid as much as possible the resolution of issues discussed there. Identification of the natural prototypes of these artificial flies is also attempted in that chapter.

[49] Feather material, probably from a mallard.

[50] The European jay (*Garrulus glandarius*).

[51] *Roddyd;* cf. *rud,* "to make red."

May

The Yellow Fly: the body of yellow wool; the wings of the red cock's hackle and of the drake dyed yellow. The Black Leaper: the body of black wool and lapped about with the herl[52] of the peacock's tail; and the wings of the red capon with a blue head.

June

The Dun Cut: the body of black wool, and a yellow stripe along either side; the wings, of the buzzard,[53] bound on with hemp that has been treated with tanbark. The Maure Fly: the body of dusky[54] wool; the wings of the blackest breast feathers of the wild drake. The Tandy Fly at St. William's[55] Day: the body of tandy[56] wool; and the wings the opposite, either against the other,[57] of the whitest breast feathers of the wild drake.

July

The Wasp Fly: the body of black wool and lapped about with yellow thread; the wings, of the buzzard. The Shell Fly at St. Thomas' Day:[58] the body of green wool and lapped about with the herl of the peacock's tail; wings, of the buzzard.

August

The Drake Fly: the body of black wool and lapped about with black silk; wings of the breast feathers of the black drake with a black head.

[52] Fibers from the shaft of a tail feather.
[53] The European buzzard, of the hawk family.
[54] Printed *dolke;* error for *doske,* "dusky." The tall variety of fifteenth-century S often resembles an *l.*
[55] The festival of St. William of York (William Fitzherbert, Archbishop of York, twelfth century) was celebrated June 8.
[56] Possibly "tawny."
[57] With the sections of drake breast feathers set back to back.
[58] Thomas à Becket. This is not the day of his martyrdom (December 29), but the day of his translation, i.e., when his bones were enshrined, July 7.

These pictures are put here as examples of your hooks:[59]

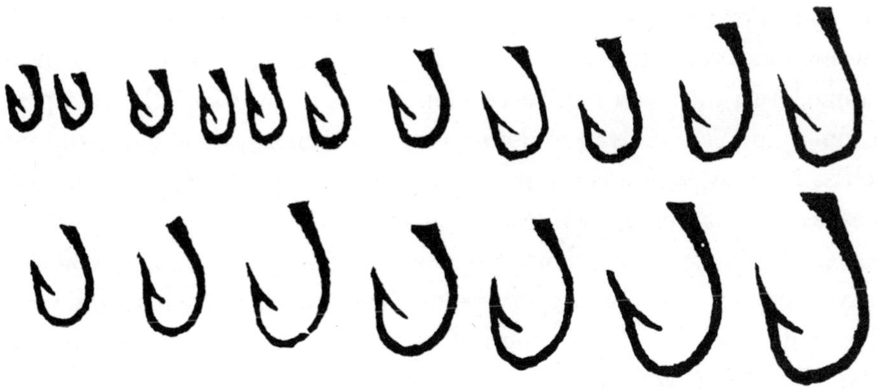

Modernized Text of the First Printed Version of the Treatise

Here follows the order[60] made to all those who shall have the understanding of this aforesaid treatise and use it for their pleasures.

You that can angle and catch fish for your pleasure, as the above treatise teaches and shows you: I charge and require you in the name of all noble men that you do not fish in any poor man's private water (such as his pond, or tank, or other things necessary for keeping fish in) without his permission and good will. And that you be not in the habit of breaking any men's fish traps lying in their weirs and in other places belonging to them, nor of taking the fish away that is caught in them. For after a fish is caught in a man's trap, if the trap is laid in the public waters, or else in such waters as he rents, it is his own personal property. And if you take it away, you are robbing him, which is a right shameful deed for any noble man to do, a thing that thieves and robbers do, who are punished for their evil deeds by the neck and otherwise when they can be discovered and captured. And also if you do in the same manner as this treatise shows you, you will have no need to take other men's fish, while you will have enough of your own catching, if you care to work for them. It will be a true pleasure to see the fair, bright, shining-scaled fishes outwitted by your crafty means and drawn out on the land. Also, I charge you, that you break no man's hedges in going about your sports, nor open any man's gates without shutting them again. Also, you must not use this aforesaid artful sport for covetousness, merely for the increasing or saving of your money, but mainly for your

[59] Not, as we should expect, of the flies. The latter may have been too difficult for the printer to reproduce. We illustrate our conception of the flies in Chapter 5.

[60] Possibly by a different author; or perhaps an editor worked this section over. There is a slight change of style.

enjoyment and to procure the health of your body and, more especially, of your soul. For when you intend to go to your amusements in fishing, you will not want very many persons with you, who might hinder you in your pastime. And then you can serve God devoutly by earnestly saying your customary prayers. And in so doing, you will eschew and avoid many vices, such as idleness, which is the principal cause inciting a man to many other vices, as is right well known. Also, you must not be too greedy in catching your said game,[61] as in taking too much at one time, a thing which can easily happen if you do in every point as this present treatise shows you. That could easily be the occasion of destroying your own sport and other men's also. When you have a sufficient mess, you should covet no more at that time. Also you should busy yourself to nourish the game in everything that you can, and to destroy all such things as are devourers of it. And all those that do according to this rule will have the blessing of God and St. Peter. That blessing, may He grant who bought us with his precious blood!

* * * * * *

And in order that this present treatise should not come into the hands of every idle person who would desire it if it were printed alone by itself and put in a little pamphlet, I[62] have therefore compiled it in a larger volume of various books pertaining to gentle and noble men, to the end that the aforesaid idle persons, who would have but little moderation in the sport of fishing, should not by this means utterly destroy it.

[61] The quarry, i.e., the fish. The writer of the treatise proper does not use *game* in this sense.
[62] Wynkyn de Worde, who added this paragraph.

CHAPTER 4

The Legend of Dame Juliana

The Treatise of Fishing with an Angle, though strictly speaking anonymous, is usually attributed to Dame Juliana Berners, who, according to legend, was a nun and a sportswoman in the fifteenth century. She was, as the legend goes, noble in birth and spirit, sociable, solitary, dashing, beautiful, learned, and intellectual. In some accounts she fled to field sports to avoid love; in another she might have retired to a convent "from disappointment." The seeming conflict between nun and sportswoman together with the scarcity of evidence for assertions made about her, have been the cause of spirited argument among generations of antiquaries.

If Juliana is a myth, she is a myth not of anglers but of these antiquaries. She was neither discovered nor invented by anglers, nor have they added anything to her story. Anglers are almost alone responsible, however, for adopting her as the author of the *Treatise of Fishing.* She is still the only candidate, and is entrenched now both in libraries and legend. The history of the Juliana legend, and the association of her legend with fishing—two separate matters—are the subject of this chapter.

There is no doubt, if by-lines mean anything, that Dame Juliana was a hunting writer or compiler. The solid fact about her is that her name, in the spelling "Barnes," is attached to the first hunting treatise printed in English, in 1486; and it is repeated, in the spelling "Bernes," in another printing in 1496. On that evidence she is the first woman writer to publish in print in the language. In the first printing the hunting treatise was part of a larger compilation dealing with hunting, hawking, and heraldry, and known as the *Book of St. Albans.* In the second it was again part of this book, and to the book had been added *The Treatise of Fishing with an Angle*. Hence the connection, whatever its merits, between Juliana and the first writing on sport fishing. Two and a half centuries passed without notice of this connection by anglers, while antiquaries developed the legend. That legend, completed in its essentials, appears to have been brought into fishing literature in 1760 by John Hawkins in his introduction to the eighth edition of *The Compleat Angler*.

This was at the time of the first Walton revival. Hawkins was a London lawyer and a friend and biographer of Samuel Johnson. Johnson, it is said, encouraged him to edit Walton, and for a long time his was the standard reissue of the famous idyl, reprinted many times down into the nineteenth century. Dame Juliana came into the book only incidentally. Reviewing early writing on fishing, Hawkins made the following observations on the second *Book of St. Albans* (1496). "This book," he said, "was written by Dame *Julyans Bernes*, prioress of the nunnery of *Sopwell*, near St. *Albans;* a lady of noble family, and celebrated for her learning and accomplishments, by *Leland, Bale, Pits,* and others. . . ."[1] Since that time Juliana has been an angling personality. Sir Henry Ellis, who made the first bibliography of angling books, in 1811, repeated more or less the same information, and the ascription was followed thereafter by other angling bibliographers, though often with some sign of skepticism.[2]

The sources given by Hawkins are eminent early English antiquaries. The legend had only recently been rounded out by other antiquaries in their chambers, as far from field and stream as one can get. They left behind a historical riddle and a suspicion among some people in favor of a colorful Juliana.[3]

The *Book of St. Albans,* in which Dame Juliana first appeared, is the most celebrated book on field sports in English, the first English sporting book to be printed, and one of the earliest English printed books, issued nine years after Caxton's first in England. Its subjects—hunting, hawking,

[1] *The Compleat Angler,* by Izaak Walton, ed. by John Hawkins, 1760, Introduction, p. xxii.

[2] Pickering contradicted Hawkins in his notable little separate edition of the *Treatise of Fishing,* in 1827, but Hawkins' assertions prevailed in the angling world.

[3] The most recent is Alfred Duggan's whimsical essay in *Sports Illustrated,* May 13, 1957, p. 76. Duggan's piece was part of a series, in the other part of which this book originated.

and heraldry—were among the fundamentals of a polite education and necessary for the competent discussion of literature as well as correct behavior. The book appears to have been meant to assist newly risen persons of means in learning these arts, especially their terminologies, as aristocratic graces. It begins simply, "In so moch that gentill men and honest persones haue grete delite in hawkyng and desire to haue the maner to take hawkys. . . ." Only the hunting treatise, which is placed between the others, has an indication of an author or compiler. It concludes: "Explicit [i.e., finished] Dam Julyans Barnes in her boke of huntyng." No more information about her is given in the book.

The Legend of Dame Juliana

The code of hunting in Juliana's treatise was thought by some to have come down from Tristram, the legendary knight who was long believed to have invented the terminology of hunting. Listen to your dame, she says, in one place, and in another, pay heed to Tristram. There is no conflict between these injunctions. Learning hunting terms was part of the upbringing of a page, so that "dame" in the hunting treatise would be a natural expression for the mistress-tutor he would attend in training for knighthood. By calling his attention to Tristram she would remind him of the chivalric tradition of hunting.

The fifteenth-century attitude toward Tristram as hunter and provider of a glossary of gentlemanly terms was stated clearly by Sir Thomas Malory in his story *Isode the Fair,* written probably in the 1460s:

> And so Trystrams lerned to be an harper passyng all other, that there was none suche called in no contrey. And so in harpynge and on instrumentys of musyke in his youthe he applyed hym for to lerne. And aftir, as he growed in myght and strength, he laboured in huntynge and in hawkynge—never jantylman more that ever we herde rede of. And as the booke seyth,[4] he began good mesures of blowynge of beestes of venery and beestes of chaace and all maner of vermaynes, and all the tearmys we have yet of hawkynge and huntynge. And therefore the booke of [venery, of hawkynge and huntynge is called the booke of][5] sir Trystrams.
>
> Wherefore, as me semyth, all jantyllmen that beryth olde armys ought of ryght to honoure sir Tristrams for the goodly tearmys that jantylmen have

[4] The modern editor, Eugène Vinaver, says: "Malory's description of a gentleman's education is to a large extent original; and the phrase 'as the booke seyth' is used merely to conceal a departure from the source" (Vol. 3, p. 1445).

[5] Vinaver notes that the words in brackets were added by Caxton in his edition of Malory in 1485.

and use and shall do unto the Day of Dome, that thereby in a maner all men of worshyp may discever a jantylman frome yoman and a yoman frome a vylayne. For he that jantyll is woll drawe hym to jantyll tacchis[6] and to folow the noble customys of jantylmen.[7]

Juliana's hunting treatise, in fact, was not for the most part an original work. A. L. Binns has shown that it is difficult to single out one stage of its development and call it "authorship";[8] the term "compiler" is more appropriate than "author." The manuscript used by the printer has not survived, but Binns has compared the printed version with two extant independent manuscripts which have similar texts,[9] and concluded that all three are copies, with variations, of a lost parent original. He traces the tradition of Juliana's hunting treatise in the *Book of St. Albans,* as follows: Some of it was taken from an Anglo-Norman treatise, Twici's *L'Art de Venerie* (c. 1328). This treatise with some other materials became Twici in English (c. 1425). From there much went into the unknown but postulated treatise that would be the parent of the *Book of St. Albans.* Into this parent went also matter from *Livre de Chasse* (c. 1387) via its English translation, *Master of Game* (c. 1406). *Master of Game* had in it also some new material. So did the parent of the *Book of St. Albans* hunting treatise. From this parent then came the three similar extant treatises. The question of "authorship" of Juliana's treatise thus extends over two centuries of development. Whether she compiled the version in the *Book of St. Albans,* or an earlier one, is not known.

The manuscript possibly was in a monastic library, though more likely on a merchant's sparse bookshelf; copies of it were surely in circulation in manuscript at the end of the century. Early printers turned to such old surviving manuscripts, having before them the prospect of converting into the new medium of communication all the writing in existence that was within reach and profitable to publish, together with new writing for which there was demand. The demand for treatises had been proven: they were a

[6] Qualities.

[7] *The Works of Sir Thomas Malory,* edited by Eugène Vinaver in Three Volumes (Oxford: Clarendon Press, 1947), Vol. 1, p. 375.

[8] A. L. Binns, *A Manuscript Source of the Book of St. Albans,* John Rylands Library, 1950. See also E. F. Jacob in *Bulletin of the John Rylands Library,* Vol. 28, 1944.

[9] MS. Lambeth 49 (unprinted) in Lambeth Palace Library, and MS. Rawlinson Poet. 143 (unprinted) in the Bodleian Library.

prominent form of manuscript writing and publishing in the vernacular, and were widely circulated in the fifteenth century.

The Legend of Dame Juliana

The printer of the first *Book of St. Albans* disdained to identify himself, merely setting down the information that it was "translatyt and complytyt togedyr at Seynt Albons" in 1486. He was the second printer in England, the first to print color, and he printed eight books. His identity has been determined, in part, by indirect means. One of his books was reprinted in 1497 by Caxton's apprentice and successor, Wynkyn de Worde, who referred to its first printer as the "one sometime schoolmaster of St. Albans," and by that appellation he has since been known. It is assumed that his shop was in the Hertfordshire town of St. Albans, twenty miles northwest of London, that he had access to the library of the famous Abbey of St. Albans, if he was not himself a monk, and that he may have found his manuscripts there, monasteries being then the principal repositories of learning. Nearby was the nunnery of Sopwell and the river Ver, which were to figure in the legend to come. The book of hunting, hawking, and heraldry having, according to a custom of the time, no title or title page, came to be called the *Book of St. Albans.*

The second printing, in 1496, was made by Wynkyn de Worde in small folio in his shop at the sign of the Red Pale at Westminster, London. Wynkyn de Worde is generally regarded as the first English commercial printer. Caxton, though a merchant and bookseller, was also a scholar and an editor. A modern student of Wynkyn de Worde, Henry Plomer (*Wynkyn de Worde and His Contemporaries*), says that de Worde would not have been capable of writing the prologues and epilogues to his books and that these were probably written by his assistant, Robert Copland, who later became a notable printer on his own. If that was indeed the case, Copland has the distinction of being the first employed professional editor of printed works. Wynkyn de Worde in 1496 had just begun an extraordinarily successful business which would publish some eight hundred books before his death in 1534, most of them printed "At the Sign of the Sun" in Fleet Street, where he operated after 1500. The *Book of St. Albans,* which he reprinted several times in whole and in separate parts, led the entire list in popularity.

The most important departure de Worde made from the 1486 St. Albans edition was to add to his edition the illustrated treatise, never before printed, to which he gave the title *Here Begins the Treatise of Fishing with an Angle.* Below this title he placed the woodcut of the angler. There was no sign of an author.

In announcing the fishing treatise at the end of the preceding treatise on coat armor, Wynkyn de Worde explained that it belonged in the volume because like hawking and hunting, fishing is a gentleman's sport. In a similar vein, in another note at the end of the fishing treatise, the printer added the further information that he had put the fishing treatise into the larger volume of treatises, instead of publishing it separately, to keep it out of the hands of idle persons, that is, persons who were not gentlemen. Perhaps Copland actually drafted these notes (and edited the fishing treatise). They have been accepted by scholars for the past two centuries as suggesting that the printer regarded the *Treatise of Fishing* as a separate and independent work by an author unknown to him, and so constitute formidable evidence against Juliana's authorship. Sometime later, about 1532–34, Wynkyn de Worde made a separate quarto, or pocket-size, edition of the fishing treatise, probably for streamside use, again giving no author.[10]

The first printer of the fishing treatise, however, is late on the scene. The treatise was written closer to the beginning of the century in which it was printed. The sole surviving manuscript copy of this earlier version of the treatise (now in the Yale Library) is incomplete, without illustration, and varies in detail from the 1496 version; the consensus of specialists who have studied the characteristics of the writing places it as a copy transcribed around 1450. (See Chapter 6, for a facsimile of its text.) Both the printed and manuscript versions have long been believed to have derived from a lost parent manuscript written early in the fifteenth century.[11] The manuscript copy has no sign of its author; the end part, where the author's name might have been placed, is missing. Thus both the

[10] Eloise Pafort, *Notes on the Wynkyn de Worde Editions of the* Boke of St. Albans *and Its Separates,* Vol. 5 in "Studies in Bibliography" (University of Virginia Bibliographical Society, 1952–53), pp. 43–52. The only surviving copy of the 1532–34 quarto edition of the *Treatise of Fishing* is in the Morgan Library in New York.

[11] The reason for dating the lost parent manuscript early in the fifteenth century is as follows: The treatise reference to Edward, Duke of York, speaks of him as "late called Master of Game." Edward–grandson of King Edward III–succeeded to his title in 1402, became Master of Game to Henry IV in 1406. Henry IV died in 1413. Edward died in 1415. His biographer-editor, Baillie-Grohman, surmises that he probably wrote *Master of Game* while at leisure in prison in 1405. The fishing treatise thus could not have acknowledged *Master of Game* earlier than 1406, and so could not have existed in the form we know it before that year. The word *late* is ambiguous. If, as it seems, it means "lately," the date of the fishing treatise could be any time after 1406. If it means

manuscript and the first printing of the fishing treatise appear anonymous.

Juliana, however, as noted earlier, reappeared in Wynkyn de Worde's *Book of St. Albans* as the only author mentioned. He confirmed her authorship of the hunting treatise as follows: "Explicit dame Julyans Bernes doctryne in her boke on huntynge." The spellings Barnes, Bernes, and later, Berners, have been believed by some authorities to be variations of the same name; this belief has been questioned by others. Spelling aside, hers being the only author's name in the *Book of St. Albans,* it is not surprising that the whole book should have eventually been ascribed to her, if only for convenience.

The Legend of Dame Juliana

The *Book of St. Albans* was reprinted many times by different printers in the sixteenth century. The first reprint of the first edition which ascribed the whole work to Juliana was in 1595; the editor, Gervase Markham, called it, *The Gentleman's Academie; Or, The Books of St. Albans: . . . All compiled by Juliana Barnes, in . . . 1486.*

Here the simple facts end.

The first pieces of the legend of Juliana appeared in 1559, sixty-three years after the fishing treatise was first printed. In the interim a number of events intervened and were to have their effect: Henry VIII, the Reformation, the expropriation and abolition of monasteries, the beginning of what is called the Renaissance, and the rise of antiquaries and chroniclers seeking to preserve and celebrate the record of medieval England as it dissolved into the modern era.

One of these antiquaries was John Bale (1495–1563). One of his books, published in 1559(?), was *Lives of the Most Eminent Writers of Great Britain* (*Scriptorum Illustria Majoris Britanniae . . .*), a series of short biographies. About Juliana he was flowery:

Juliana Barnes. XXXIII

> She was an illustrious female, eminently endowed with superior qualities both mental and personal. Amongst the many solaces of human life she held the sports of the field in the highest estimation. This heroic woman saw that they were the exercises of noble men after wars, after the administration of

that Edward is deceased, the date is after 1415. Since the surviving copy of the manuscript is placed at about 1450, the author must have written the original copy between the extreme dates of 1406 and 1450. The word *late* in reference to the Duke of York suggests a date close by, say between 1406 and 1420.

justice, or the concerns of the state. She had learned, perhaps, that Ulysses instituted such diversions after the conquest of Troy, and that they received commendation from Plato, as the sources of renewed enjoyment to those who suffered, either from domestic calamities, or the injuries of war. These arts therefore this ingenious woman was desirous to convey in her writings as the first elements of nobility; with the persuasion, that those youths, in whose hearts resided either virtue or honour, would cultivate them to guard against vain sloth. Since, as Seneca says, "love is generated in youth by luxury; and nourished by idleness basking in the lap of fortune." And Ovid says, "Take away idleness, and the arts of Cupid perish." To these treatises she added the Art of Heraldry. Hence she wrote in her native tongue, I. The Art of Hawking. II. The Art of Hunting. III. On the Laws of Arms; and is said to have edited a small work on Fishing. She flourished in the year of our Lord 1460, in the reign of Henry the VIth.[12]

This vignette started a story which has run through four centuries. Here were Juliana's fine personal qualities, the subjects and elevated themes of

[12] Translation as given by Joseph Haslewood. From the notes to his facsimile edition of the second *Book of St. Albans*, London, 1810, p. 5. The translation is slightly biased. For example, it says Juliana was "eminently endowed with superior qualities both mental and personal." The Latin, *corporis & animi dotibus abundaus, ac formae elegantia spectabilis,* would be more exactly translated as "abounding in gifts of body and spirit, and remarkable for her physical beauty." Haslewood's translation is more compatible with the theory of the nun. One could bias it the other way by emphasizing the grace of her figure. Facsimile of Bale's Latin text follows:

IVLIANA BARNES. XXXIII.

IVliana Barnes, illuſtris fœmina, corporis & animi dotibus abundans, ac formæ elegantia ſpectabilis, inter alia humanę uitæ ſolatia, uenationes et aucupia in magnis habebat delicijs. Has uidit heroica mulier, nobilium uirorum exercitationes eſſe poſt bella, poſt actiones forenſes, uel poſt adminiſtrationes in republica. Nouitq; fortaſsis Vlyſſem has artes inſtituiſſe poſt captum Ilion, & eſſe à Platone laudatas, ut eſſent nouæ uoluptatis ſolatia, his qui parentes amiſerant, aut ex bellis incommoda ſenſerant. Eas igitur artes ingenioſa uirago, per ſcripta dare ſtuduit, tanquam nobilitatis elementa præcipua: perſuadens, ut contra deſidiam inanem his uterentur iuuenes illi, quibus eſt cordi uel uirtus uel honeſtas. Quoniam (ut inquit Seneca) amor iuuentæ gignitur luxu, ocio nutritur inter læta fortunæ bona. Et Ouidius:

Ocia ſi tollas, periere Cupidinis artes.

His addidit tertiam, Heraldorum ſcilicet artem. Vnde ſcripſit in Anglico ſermone,

Artem aucupariam,	*Lib. 1. Quoniam generoſi atq; honeſti.*
Artem uenatoriam,	*Lib. 1. Sicut in libro de arte aucup.*
De legibus armorum,	*Lib. 1. In ſequenti opere tractatur.*

Dicitur & de piſcatione edidiſſe opuſculum. Heraldorum uerò heroicam philoſophiam à ueteranis militibus didiciſſe fertur. Claruit anno à diuini uerbi incarnatione 1460, regnante adhuc Henrico eius nominis ſexto.

her writing, a specific date when she was living, and, weak as it is, a connection between her and the fishing treatise. To what extent is Bale reliable?

He offers no means of verifying what he says. Yet within the conventions of panegyric, he exerts some accuracy of expression. His praise is transparently interpretative; it could be based on inferences from the *Book of St. Albans*. He makes a nice distinction between weak and strong statements. She "perhaps" learned about Ulysses and Plato, but she definitely wrote three treatises. She "is said" to have edited a small work on fishing. It is possible that Bale wrote this after a perusal of the 1486 edition of the *Book of St. Albans*—he spells her name "Barnes," as it is in that edition—and with indirect knowledge of the 1496 edition and its fishing treatise. If, as some later scholars have believed, his mention of the fishing treatise means that he saw only the 1496 edition, why did he change the spelling of her name from "Bernes" to "Barnes"? Aside from which book he read, he may be reporting literally that he heard it said that she wrote the fishing treatise. The connection is as weak as he makes it. But the date when she "flourished," 1460, he asserts as a fact without qualification. Without this, one might dismiss Bale as simply the troubadour of an old English writer. Certainly he leaves an impression that he knew something—not much, but something persuasive enough to inspire him to these distinctions in expression.

Bale has always been a controversial personality. Some modern authorities hold his antiquarian works in high esteem. C. S. Lewis says of them, "Here Bale is sincerely concerned with fact, and is free both from literary adornment and scurrility, which elsewhere, for Bale, are much the same thing."[13] The scurrility Lewis speaks of was in religious conflict: Bale, a Carmelite monk turned against the Church, was a bitter campaigner for the Reformation. He is also credited with visiting monasteries and saving important records from them when they were banned by Henry VIII, but several early scholars say that much of what Bale reported on the contents of monasteries, he took from a contemporary, John Leland (1506–52), who is the ghost in the Juliana story.

Leland, who called himself "Antiquarius," was Henry VIII's librarian and chaplain; he has been called court antiquary to Henry VIII, though

[13] *English Literature in the Sixteenth Century* (Oxford: Clarendon Press, 1954), p. 296.

he may not have had such a title. He was the first English antiquary and is usually acknowledged as the "father" of the art. Modern antiquaries regard him—and most early antiquaries—as credulous, but thank him for precious records of the past. Though his manuscript notes were not printed until the early eighteenth century, the importance of his work was immediately recognized, and demonstrated by the use made of his notes by several other antiquaries, among them Bale. Leland's collection of the lives and works of about six hundred English writers and scholars before 1500 lay behind Bale's work in that field.

Leland, it appears, saw the great disaster to learning in the disorderly closing of the monasteries, and planned a great work on the glories of England's past. He persuaded the king to give him a commission—in his own words, "to peruse and diligently to serche al the libraries of monasteries and collegies of this yowre noble Reaulme, to the intente that the monumentes of auncient Writers as welle of other Nations, as of this 'yowr owne Province mighte be brought owte of deadely darkenes to lyvely lighte. . ."[14] From about 1534 to 1542—a period during which hundreds of religious houses were closed, or, as in the case of great abbeys like Westminster and St. Albans, surrendered—Leland traveled through England and Wales, searching through the fast disappearing records of the past. He examined and made notes on books, manuscripts, catalogues, and other records, and reported not only on religious houses, churches, and libraries, but also on towns, houses, castles, bridges, and streams. The kind of detail he noticed (to give a fisherman's example) was this: "Dour in Ewys Land a great House of Whyt Monkes suppressed, and thereby runneth a Broke cawlled Worme."[15] He had a fisherman's eye too for the "trouts" and other fish to be found in the many waters. Reporting on his visit to the Abbey of St. Albans, he recorded a controversy between town and Abbey over the Abbey's great fishpond, as a consequence of which the pond was drained.

Leland's work is arranged mainly in three parts: the *Itinerary,* which is the field work, the *Collectanea,* which is the library work, and "*De Viris Illustribus, Sive de Scriptoribus Britannicis,* his biographies of writers. No one has presented any direct evidence that Leland found anything at St. Albans concerning Dame Juliana or that he wrote anything about her from

[14] Leland's *The Itinerary,* ed. by Thomas Hearne, 1710–12, Vol. 1, p. 1.
[15] *Ibid.,* Vol. 5, p. 10.

any source. Yet his presence in the legend was to become pervasive. Leland went insane in 1550, or perhaps a little earlier, after which his notes fell into other hands. He died in 1552, in the house, it is said, of a London printer-historian, Reginald Wolfe, a strange coincidence as we shall see.

Not long after Bale wrote about Dame Juliana, aspects of her character were described in similar terms by Raphael Holinshed (d. 1580), Shakespeare's principal source for the historical plays. In his chronicle of Edward IV, Holinshed wrote: "Julian Bemes, a gentlewoman endued with excellent giftes bothe of body and minde, wrote of certaine treatises of hauking and hunting, delighting greatly hirselfe in those exercises and pastimes: She wrote also a book of the law[s] of arms, and knowledge apperteynning to harolds. . . ."[16] Bemes is easily recognized as a likely misprint for Bernes. Fifteen lines above this item, Holinshed makes a statement, in another connection, with the double acknowledgment, "as Bale noteth out of Lelande." The question is, did Holinshed note Juliana out of Bale or Leland or some other source? The spelling "Bemes," corrected to "Bernes," might suggest that it was not out of Bale, who called her "Barnes." Holinshed worked as translator for Reginald Wolfe, who had come into possession of some of Leland's notes. After Wolfe died in 1573, Holinshed, working in part from Leland's notes, carried on Wolfe's work, which in 1577 became the famous chronicles.

The next words on Juliana came from the Catholic priest and antiquary John Pits (1560–1616). Pits, on leaving Oxford in 1578, went into voluntary exile on the continent, and lived chiefly in Germany and France, where he spent most of his life teaching and writing. Curiosity about lives of writers, which existed in antiquity and has not since abated, occupied Pits as it had Leland and Bale. Pits's lives of English writers (*De Illustribus Angliae Scriptoribus,* published in Paris in 1619) made him in a way Bale's opposite number in a Protestant-Catholic contest to establish biographies of writers of worth. Pits claimed that Bale was not original and merely misrepresented Leland. Critics in turn say Pits himself very likely never saw Leland's work. He drew on Bale but left out of his list some of Bale's Protestant writers, and added some Catholic writers whom Bale had ignored. Both, however, were agreed in their appreciation of Juliana. The following is a translation of Pits on Juliana from the Latin:

[16] Holinshed's *Chronicles,* 1577, Vol. II, p. 1355.

Concerning Juliana Barnes

Juliana Barnes, born of a noble rank, was a manlike woman endowed with brilliant gifts of nature. She was a Minerva in her studies and a Diana in hunting, lest by pursuing leisure she might be involved in the charms of Venus. For they say that at home she was almost always studying the chase and fowling, and often followed those exercises in the forests and fields. Entertaining her mind with these honorable delights and training her body, she so arranged the whole course of her life that she either prudently might avoid illicit desires or vigorously overcome them. She also is said not to have overlooked fishing. Moreover, she engaged in military matters and read and wrote much concerning the art of heraldry; surpassing her sex in talent, constancy, and fortitude, *you may even say that she surpassed the male sex.* Accordingly she wrote certain works in the English language that afterward were rendered into Latin.

Concerning the Art of Fowling, one book. That it is for one who is noble and respectable.

Concerning the Art of Hunting, one book. As in the case of the Art of Fowling.

Concerning the Art of Fishing, one book.

Concerning the Laws of Armor, etc., one book. It is treated in the work following [i.e., after the fishing treatise].

I find nothing concerning other arts or subjects. She flourished in the year 1460 after the Incarnation, when Henry VI was in danger with regard to the throne of England.[17]

[17] John Pits, *Relationum Historicarum,* 1619, p. 649. Facsimile of Pits' text:

De Iuliana Barne.

1460.
849.

IVLIANA Barnes illuſtri loco in Anglia nata, virago præclaris naturæ dotibus imbuta. Mineruam ſtudijs, Dianam imitata venationibus, nè otium ſectata, Veneris implicaretur illecebris. Ferunt enim illam domi ferè ſemper venationes & aucupia ſpeculatam, eademque exercitia non rarò in ſyluis & agris ſecutam. His honeſtis delicijs animum oblectans, corpus exercens, omnem vitæ curſum ita inſtituit, vt illicitas voluptates vel cautè ſemper declinauerit, vel conſtanter certauerit, & fortiter ſuperauerit. Piſcationem etiam non omiſiſſe perhibetur. Imò rei militari ſe immiſcuit, & de arte Haraldorum multa legit atque etiam ſcripſit; ingenio, conſtantia, fortitudine ſexum ſuperans, *Quin imò dicas ſexum ſuperaſſe virilem.* Scripſit igitur idiomate Anglico quædam poſteà facta Latina

De arte aucupij, *Librum vnum.* Quoniam generoſi atque honeſti.
De arte venatoria, *Librum vnum.* Sicut in libro de arte aucupij.
De piſcatione, *Librum vnum.*
De legibus armorum, *Librum vnum.* In ſequente opere tractatur.

De alijs nihil inuenio. Claruit anno poſtquàm Verbum caro factum eſt 1460, Henrico ſexto de regno Angliæ periclitante.

In being long on rhetoric and short on fact, Pits is very like Bale: but did Pits get his information from Bale or Leland or from some other source? He does not say.

The Leland mystery continued on toward its climax through William Burton (1575–1645), Robert Burton's elder brother, a topographer and antiquary best known for his *Description of Leicestershire.* Burton had means and retired to the country to devote his life to his researches. In his book he takes his crack at Bale, saying that Bale "collected almost his whole worke [on writers] out of Leland" and that Bale suppressed this fact.[18] Among Burton's credentials for making an observation on this subject is the circumstance that he owned several volumes of Leland's original manuscripts and had access to others, and worked on them all. He was, it appears, an incessant Leland scholar, preserving some of the old antiquary's decaying pages by making transcripts of them. Burton acknowledges his debt to Leland in his book on Leicestershire in these words: "This John Leland . . . had a Commission granted him by King *Henry* the eight, in the 25. yeare of his raigne; to view, peruse, and take to his owne use any Record or Manuscript, in any Abbey or religious house within the Realme: Out of which Records he collected many things together into diuers Bookes, foure volumes of which I haue in my custody, and most truely acknowledge them to haue afforded mee many worthy notes of antiquity."[19]

The Leland documents, it appears, came to Burton by a circuitous route. When Leland was declared a lunatic, his elder brother, who oddly had the same name and is called John Leland Senior, was given possession of Leland's properties. The story is that the boy-king Edward VI, whose brief reign coincided with the time of Leland's unhappy end, heard of them, presumably from his scholarly tutor, Sir John Cheke, whom he commanded to seize the documents. (It is not clear how Reginald Wolfe managed to keep some of them.) Sir John afterward gave four of Leland's Latin volumes to Humphrey Purefoy, a cousin of William Burton, and at one time a member of Queen Elizabeth's Privy Council. From him they passed to his son, Thomas Purefoy of Barwell in Leicestershire, who in 1612 bequeathed them to Burton. These were three volumes of the *Collectanea,* and one on writers, *De Viris Illustribus.* After working over them and other Leland

[18] *Description of Leicestershire,* 1622, p. 17.
[19] Pp. 39–40.

manuscripts for a number of years, Burton, in 1632, presented his Leland manuscripts to the Bodleian Library at Oxford, where they were eventually edited and published, and where the originals still remain.

These men went to the grave with their secrets, as even antiquaries do, and most of the seventeenth century passed without event in this sphere. Another generation of antiquaries arose and began to examine the signs of the past.

In the year 1700 the county historian Sir Henry Chauncy (1632–1719) had a few words to say about Dame Juliana in his account of St. Albans in his book *The Historical Antiquities of Hertfordshire.* He reviewed the history of printing in England as follows:

"William Caxton, Mercer of London, brought this noble Art of Printing into England, which was first practiced in the Abby of St. Peter at Westminster; then John Insomuch, a Monk and Schoolmaster in this Town [St. Albans], erected a Printing Press in this Monastery, where several Books were printed; one entitled the *Fruit of Time,* another *The Gentlemans Recreation,* or the *Book of St. Albans,* so term'd because printed here in a thin Folio, *anno* 1481. and compiled by Julian Barnes the Abbess of Sopwell . . ." (p. 449). In another place (p. 160) unrelated to this, Chauncy gives the pedigree of the ancient family of Berners, without Juliana.

Chauncy's information about the *Book of St. Albans* is shaky, his title for the book and date of publication both being incorrect. And the name he gives to the printer, John Insomuch, has never been verified; scholars have observed that he may have obtained it by mistake from the opening words of the *Book of St. Albans:* "In so much that gentill men. . . ." Yet Chauncy's remarks have attracted attention from scholars. The most interesting thing he does is to identify Juliana as "Abbess of Sopwell." He seems to have had his own independent source for this information—Hertfordshire was his home county. But Chauncy was not the first to make Juliana a nun and head of Sopwell.

This truly novel addition to the story of Juliana was first printed in 1697. A scholar, Edward Bernard, published at Oxford a catalogue[20] listing early printed books and manuscripts in the library of Dr. John Moore, Bishop of Ely (1646–1714). Owing to his possession of this great library, which is said to have contained about 29,000 books and 1800 manuscripts,

[20] *Catalogi Librorum Manuscriptorum Angliae et Hiberniae,* Bodleian Library, Oxford, 1697.

Moore has been known as the "father of black-letter collectors." One of Moore's books, listed in Bernard's catalogue,[21] was a copy of the *Book of St. Albans* (1486). The catalogue entry has the following printed annotation: "It is said to have been made by the Lady *Julian Berners,* Lady Prioress of Sopwell Nunnery, near St. Albans; in which Abby of St. Albans it was first printed in the year abovesaid [i.e., 1486]."

Three important events occurred in this passage: for the first time, so far as one knows, Juliana's name appeared in print in the variation "Berners"; for the first time she was identified in print as a nun, specifically "Prioress of Sopwell"; and for the first time it is said in print that the *Book of St. Albans* was first printed in the Abbey.

The origin of this note can be determined by a reasonable surmise which would seem difficult to fault. Bishop Moore's library was bought in 1714 by George I and given to Cambridge. The copy of the *Book of St. Albans* which was listed in the 1697 catalogue is still, in 1962, in the University Library at Cambridge.[22] On a blank leaf at the beginning of the book, but not part of the collation, the following observations are written in longhand:

> This Booke was made by the Lady Julian Berners, daughter of Sr James Berners, of Berners Roding, in Essex, Knight, & Sister to Richard Lord Berners. She was Lady Prioresse of Sopwell, a Nunnery neere St. Albons, in wch Abby of St. Albons this was first printed 1486, 2 H. 7. She was living 1460, 39 H. 6. according to John Bale, Centur.[8] Fol. 611.

This note must be the source of the annotation in the 1697 catalogue of Moore's library, and whatever its merits, it provides the earliest source of the information that Juliana was Lady Juliana Berners and Prioress of Sopwell, and that the book was first printed in the St. Albans Abbey. It also identifies the Berners family and places her in it; and repeats the information from Bale that she was living in 1460.

On other pages in this copy of the *Book of St. Albans* are further notes in the same hand: one set quotes the opening lines of Bale's description of Juliana and attributes them more or less equally to both Bale and Leland; another note says that this copy of the *Book of St. Albans* belonged to William Burton, who received it from "my cousin" Thomas Purefoy in

[21] No. 9419.233.4, on page 367.

[22] No. 4214 in the published *Catalogue of the Fifteenth-Century Printed Books in the University Library, Cambridge.*

1612. It was from Thomas Purefoy, as we have seen, that Burton inherited the Leland manuscripts; presumably the copy of the *Book of St. Albans* came along with them. These notes were written by William Burton in his own hand and so carry his high authority for their content. There can be no doubt that the Juliana legend rests on Burton's assertions written into his copy of the *Book of St. Albans*.[23]

Here we are at dead center of the Juliana mystery. All of the essential elements of the legend have been laid down. They hint that Leland found records concerning Dame Juliana at the St. Albans Abbey, which he is known to have visited, and wrote about her in his notes, after which these notes were in part used by Bale and later seen by Burton, who drew further upon them. Whether or not the Burton notes are believed, we are clearly dealing here with legend, since they remain unverified in Leland's records or elsewhere. Yet it is a peculiar origin for a legend, for Burton can hardly be supposed to have written the notes with such conviction without his having seen some evidence that convinced him. Perhaps someday this evidence will turn up.[24]

The contents of the Burton notes reached the antiquarian public almost simultaneously by two routes. One was by way of Thomas Hearne (1678–1735), Oxford antiquary and editor of the first published editions of Leland's works. The other was by way of Conyers Middleton (1683–1750), Cambridge antiquary and historian.

First, Thomas Hearne.

Hearne is known chiefly for publishing for the first time Leland's *Itinerary* (1710–12) and *Collectanea* (1715). He worked for years with Leland's manuscripts, many of them the transcripts made by Burton. In 1731 Hearne edited another work, in the preface to which he discussed, largely in Latin, which scholars still used in the early eighteenth century, the question of Juliana Berners and the *Book of St. Albans*.[25] He wished to praise the good life of the monks of the Middle Ages, which, he says, included playing games. But into later editions of their written works, he charges,

[23] See Appendix C for facsimiles of Burton's notes and evidence that they are in fact in his hand.

[24] We have had Leland's printed works searched without avail. However, many of Leland's manuscripts were lost, and we have not searched his unprinted manuscripts.

[25] *Walteri Hemingford, Historia de Rebus Gestis Edwardi I. Edwardi II. & Edwardi III.*, ed. by Thomas Hearne, Oxford, 1731.

their enemies sometimes introduced alien words to bring the religious into disrepute. So with the *Book of St. Albans* by Juliana Barnes, "or rather Berners," prioress of Sopwell. To account for the earthy language of parts of the hunting treatise, he supposes that some Wyclifist editor inserted into its inventions of collective nouns such phrases as: a pontificality of prelates, a dignity of canons, a discretion of priests, a superfluity of nuns, and an abominable sight of monks, the last of which in one version he reports was written, "An hominable (sic) shyt (sic) of mocks." Purged of this mischief, the treatise, he has no doubt, is the text of Juliana Barnes, "than which prioress," he says, as if he were her personal troubadour, "there was no other either more beautiful or even more learned."

The source of his knowledge of Juliana's title and connections, Hearne tells us, is William Burton in the notes in Bishop Moore's copy of the *Book of St. Albans.* He has also some new information, from memoranda by a contemporary, John Bagford, "that illustrious man, by far the greatest expert on the origin of the art of printing." Bagford (1650–1716), a shoemaker and well-known professional collector of books, had written, according to Hearne, this interesting note about the *Book of St. Albans:* "The first that I ever saw had been the book of John Leland, after it came into the hands of Burton of Leicestershire, and is now in the collection of the bishop of Ely (Dr. Moore). . . ." Thus if one wishes to believe this unsupported but plausible word of Bagford, Burton's copy of the *Book of St. Albans,* in which he wrote the founding words of the legend of the nun, had appropriately come down to Burton from Leland. If this were a proven fact, it would prove nothing, and yet it seems to add another connecting link to the past. The important matter is what Burton wrote in the book when it was his.

A few years later Hearne recorded the Burton notes in his own copy of the *Book of St. Albans,* and these were to reach another antiquary in the next century and form the cornerstone of a study of Juliana in a great work on the second *Book of St. Albans.* Before we come to that, the eighteenth century has more to offer.

The second route by which the legend of Juliana was spread, and the one that appears to have brought it into fishing literature, was through Conyers Middleton, Cambridge University librarian, who had charge of Bishop Moore's library there. Middleton studied the "Burton" copy of the *Book of St. Albans.* In 1735 he published *A Dissertation Concerning the Origin of Printing in England,* later reprinted as *The Origin of Printing.*

In it, Middleton identifies the copy of the *Book of St. Albans* and says: "After the first Treatise of Hawking and Hunting *&c.*, is added, *Explicit Dam Julyans Barnes in her boke of huntyng*. Tho' her Name be subjoin'd to the first Part only, yet the whole is constantly ascribed to her, and passes for her Work. She was of a noble Family, Sister to *Richard* Lord *Berners* of *Essex*, and Prioress of *Sopwell* Nunnery near *St. Albans:* She lived about the year 1460, and is celebrated by *Leland* and other Writers for her uncommon Learning and Accomplishments, under the Name of *Juliana Berners*" (p. 14).

Middleton did not provide his sources—even so late as this, antiquaries seemed to think it sufficient to make unsupported assertions—but it appears from the similarity of the information and even language that his statements derive from the Burton notes. Of the early authorities he specifies only Leland, and fails to give the tie. As this was the first publication of the information about Juliana for a moderately wide audience, it is a landmark in the legend. Indeed, it appears that the legend went directly from Middleton into angling literature. It was just twenty-five years later that John Hawkins, as we have seen, described Dame Juliana in almost identical words in the introduction to his edition of *The Compleat Angler*. Hawkins, however, made one important departure from Middleton. Whereas Middleton (out of the Burton) dealt only with the first edition of the *Book of St. Albans,* Hawkins attributed the whole of the second edition to Dame Juliana, thereby attaching the legend of the nun and noblewoman to the fishing treatise. Hawkins gives no source, but his assertions about Dame Juliana clearly derive from Middleton (or Middleton's source); and presumably he made the connection with the fishing treatise via Bale and Pits.

Thus, in sum, although Bale is factually weak, and Pits is weaker, and Holinshed is cryptic, and Chauncy is full of error, and the Burton notes provide no verification, and Leland, to whom better knowledge of Juliana is ascribed, remains silent in the background, the legend crystallized publicly in Hearne, Middleton, and Hawkins.

From Middleton, it appears, the legend spread to numerous works of biography and reference, and provoked opposition. William Oldys (1696–1761), a free-lance London antiquary of distinction—to whom anglers owe a debt for his life of Izaak Walton's fly-fishing companion Charles Cotton, in Hawkins' edition of Walton—became the first influential critic of the legend. In a note appended to his life of Caxton in *Biographia Britannica* in 1748, Oldys made an analysis of the prevailing beliefs about Dame Juliana and the *Book of St. Albans*. Here at mid-eighteenth century a new and more demanding sense of proof had entered the antiquarian mind—as represented by Oldys—together with disbelief in the old authorities. Oldys scoffs: "This book [*Book of St. Albans*] . . . is ascrib'd to an illustrious and heroic Lady of great gifts in body and mind; a second Minerva in her studies, and another Diana in her diversions; in short, an ingenious *Virago*, as Bale and Pits call her, who lived about 1460, and yet she was no less than an Abess, as Sir Henry Chauncy, or Prioress, as Dr. Middleton calls her, of the strict and mortified Nunnery at Sopwell in Hertfordshire; who says also, that she was sister to Richard Lord Berners of Essex. But that the said Juliana Barnes was such a religious Lady, and so nobly descended, no author, as yet, has attempted to prove. . . ."

Oldys offers, as he himself notes, the first detailed description and critique of the individual treatises in the *Book of St. Albans*. He allows Juliana only the hunting treatise; but, oddly, he thought she versified it from a tract on hunting by Sir Tristram; his source, John Manwood's *Laws of the Forest* (1665 edition), enabled a later scholar (Haslewood) to trace the error to a sixteenth-century reprint of the *Book of St. Albans*. Although Oldys knew the original editions of the book, and the writings on the subject from Bale to the catalogue of Bishop Moore's library to Chauncy to Middleton, he apparently was not aware of the Burton notes. He regards Chauncy as important enough to attack him directly. Oldys takes no stock in the St. Albans printer as either monk or schoolmaster. He doubts Chauncy saw the original editions, since the title and date are wrongly given. Moreover, he says, Chauncy contradicts himself, calling Juliana the Abbess of Sopwell in one place, "when he has a distinct chapter upon the religious foundation there and only calls it a Priory; but mentions nothing of Juliana Barnes, in that place." Nor can Oldys find a sister to Richard Lord Berners in a pedigree anywhere.

For Oldys, Dame Juliana is "Mrs. Barnes," a term that did not necessarily mean married. Unlike Hearne and his predecessors, he cannot tolerate the notion that Juliana could be both nun and sportswoman. "And indeed," he says, "such a contrast of characters in one person, is apt to raise very contesting ideas. One cannot reconcile the notions those subjects inspire, of their authors being so expert and familiarly practiced in those robust and masculine exercises, with the character of such a sedate, grave, pious, matronlike Lady, as the Prioress of a Nunnery is imagined to be;

a conjunction of such extreams, seeming quite unnatural. Indeed, we have, and so we may have had, your romping, roaring hoydens, that will be for horsing and hunting after the wildest game, in the most giddy company; but to join so much of these rough and impetuous diversions, as is required to obtain the proficiency aforesaid, with the most serene and solemn profession of a mortified and spiritual life in herself, and the charge or care of training it in others, must make an unaccountable mixture. In that light, there appears such a motley masquerade, such an indistinction of petticoat and breeches, such a problem and concorporation of sexes, according to the image that arises out of several representations of this religious Sportswoman or Virago, that one can scarcely consider it, without thinking Sir Tristram, the old Monkish Forester, and Juliana, the Matron of the Nuns, had united to confirm John Cleveland's *Canonical Hermophradite. . . .*"

Oldys is the first scholar categorically to contradict the statements of Bale and Pits linking Juliana to the fishing treatise. He says: ". . . it [the *Treatise of Fishing*] is neither ascribed to her, nor anybody else; but only printed in this larger volume of those subjects relating to the Gentry and Nobility; that every idle and ordinary person might not be able to purchase it, as they would if it had been published in a little pamphlet by itself."

This did not, as we have seen, deter Hawkins twelve years later from declaring her the author of the fishing treatise. Nor did Oldys stop the legend of Juliana, even among antiquaries. On the contrary, his arguments against the reasonableness of supposing that a nun could be a sportswoman were to provoke a new train of thought in support of the legend.

In 1810 a genial London antiquary, Joseph Haslewood (1769–1833), reprinted Wynkyn de Worde's edition of the *Book of St. Albans,* in facsimile, and wrote the master collection of notes on the book and Juliana. Although Haslewood advances a point of view with which one might not agree, and makes a few errors in detail, his work is in a class by itself; no student of the *Treatise of Fishing* or the second *Book of St. Albans* could well do without consulting it. Although only 150 copies were printed, the book became the basis of all scholarship on Juliana until the latter part of the nineteenth century, when it was put into eclipse by an unfair attack, which will be discussed later. Haslewood paid the price for the extent of his belief in Juliana.

Haslewood built on the foundation of scholarship laid by Oldys, and made further researches that brought into public view the Burton notes, the contents of which Middleton had relayed without giving the authority. Haslewood put them into print, explained them, and wove his thesis about Juliana around them. He did not, however, print the notes directly from the Burton copy of the *Book of St. Albans* (the one in Moore's library), but indirectly from the accurate record of them left by Thomas Hearne in 1733.

Though his diary makes no mention of it, Hearne, it appears, had obtained for himself a copy of the first edition of the *Book of St. Albans;* this copy is now in the Bodleian Library. He inscribed his name on a blank leaf with the date, September 28, 1732. Below his name he made some notes about the Burton copy of the *Book of St. Albans,* based on a letter he had received in 1732 from an antiquary friend, Thomas Baker, at Cambridge.

Like Hearne before him, Haslewood found the Burton notes persuasive, and saw no difficulties in Juliana's supposed dual role of nun and sportswoman; indeed it was his counterargument to Oldys on this point that got him posthumously into trouble.

Haslewood is cautious and precise. He begins his review of the legend in the passive voice: "Julyans, or Juliana, Barnes, otherwise Berners, who has been generally designated as the authoress of the present volume, is supposed to have been born, towards the latter end of the fourteenth century, at Roding-Berners, in the hundred of Dunmow and county of Essex. The received report is, that she was daughter of Sir James Berners, of Roding-Berners, Knight, whose son Sir Richard was created Baron Berners, temp. Hen. IV. and that she once held the situation of Prioress of Sopwell Nunnery, in Hertfordshire" (Haslewood, p. 5).

He then cites the texts of Bale, Holinshed, and the Burton notes (as reported by Hearne) that make her a prioress and member of the Berners family, as "the only biographical incidents which can now be traced in the life of this lady." And, he says, "Wherever the canvas has been enlarged, or the colours given with higher tints, by later writers, the attempt has uniformly proceeded from the desire of producing novelty. Even these scanty materials have been doubted in several particulars, so far as to render necessary some further observations on her family, title, station, and authorship" (p. 7).

The Berners family, he says, is old and honorable; its pedigree comes from Chauncy and others. Barnes, Bernes, and Berners, he finds, are variations of the same name, with Barnes most frequent. Sir James married

Anna, daughter of John Berew. With a nice euphemism for the politics of that era, Haslewood says of Sir James: "He fell a victim to the turbulence of party, and was beheaded in 1388, as one of the evil counsellors of his imbecile master, Richard II. He left issue three sons; Richard, Thomas, and William; and, as now supposed, a daughter named Julyans. Of his estates in Essex, which became confiscated under the attainder, there was a partial restoration to the widow, the year after execution . . . the family still appear to have retained their rank among the wealthy, and shared in the courtly favours of the Monarch. The widow took for her second husband an illegitimate branch of royalty, in Sir Roger Clarendon, knight, natural son of Edward Prince of Wales" (pp. 7–8). Haslewood neglected to add that in another turbulence of party Sir Roger in 1402 was hanged by Henry IV.

Observing that doubt about Juliana as a Berners had arisen owing to the absence of a female offspring in the Berners' pedigree, Haslewood launches a conjecture: the silence of the pedigree "might well arise from the final circumstance of her entering a convent, and taking the requisite vows of celibacy. From that period it was usual for the relatives to consider such monastic devotees as no longer branches of the family stock; and if they became strangers to their own kindred, much more so were they likely to become to the world at large: Hence, perhaps, her name would scarcely be preserved beyond the archives of her own society" (pp. 8–9).

Here Haslewood calls upon Leland to extend his chain of conjecture. Leland, he recounts, visited religious houses and made notes of manuscripts; perhaps such notes—upon the Sopwell Nunnery, where the superior survived Leland—came into the hands of Burton, who possessed four volumes of Leland, which Burton acknowledges "to have afforded mee many worthy notes of antiquity." The fact that Burton troubled to make this note on Juliana's authorship in his copy of the *Book of St. Albans,* impressed Haslewood. He thought Burton would not "retain such an entry in his own copy, unless assured of its correctness" (p. 10). "Her being 'Lady Prioress of Sopwell,'" Haslewood observed, "is corroborated by Chauncy in part, in his account of St. Albans, which adds such presumptive evidence in support of the note, as to leave the whole statement indubitable. To this may be added the confirmation derived from the unquestioned repetition of all our best antiquaries" (p. 10).

With this position established, Haslewood makes further conjectures entirely of his own. He sets forth the Berners family tree, and enters into it

Juliana's name "as a new bough." He describes his handiwork as "a pedigree that swells the extinct peerage; and in which the name of another descendant, John Lord Berners, *the translator of Froissart,* has long appeared, like the solitary arm of a decayed tree still bearing fruit, all that remains to awaken interest or enquiry of the parent stem. Together then let them be placed, equally honourable to the respective periods they adorned; and stand, like remaining columns which once graced the portal of a desolated mansion, still, amidst ruins, mocking the violence and destructive ravages of time" (p. 10). The pleasure of mocking time is a clue to the passion—and perhaps the folly—of the antiquary.

Haslewood goes on, with qualifications. Juliana's title "Dame," from the colophon to the hunting treatise, is sometimes confused with "Lady." But in her time it meant "neither rank, age, nor character," and could be applied equally to a concubine, a virgin sister of a king, a gentlewoman, or a wife. However, in the Benedictine order of nuns, a distinction was made between a nun's origin in wealth or in poverty; and in that class system, the wealthy were called "Dame," and a humble lay-sister upon being elected to higher office would also be called "Dame." "The title of 'Dame Julyans Barnes,'" he says, "was therefore of no real importance; it was neither hereditary, nor derived from nobility or power; it was a local term, serving as a proper and respectful address to 'a gentlewoman,' and might be plainly modernized to 'Mrs. Julyans Barnes'" (p. 13). The title "Dame," he says, neither confirms nor conflicts with the story, but is consistent with it.

Haslewood is prepared now for what gagged Oldys: the inconsistency of character in the roles of nun and sportswoman. He quotes Pits's description of Juliana—as repeated ironically by Oldys—as a "second Minerva in her studies, and another Diana in her diversions." The conceptual difficulty of reconciling nun and sportswoman, Haslewood thinks, arose from the use of the first person in the hunting treatise. Presumably he had in mind such lines as, "Lystyn to yowre dame, and she shall yow lere." Haslewood agrees with Oldys that no nun of Sopwell would likely have been out in the field hunting and hawking in the manner taught by the "dame." He cites the history of this nunnery:

"The monastery of Sopwell was founded about the year 1140. Two women, religiously inclined, having made themselves an habitation by wradling boughs of trees with wattles, and stakes, close to Einwood, and within the precincts of the Abbey of St. Albans, where they passed their time in continual acts of devotion, severe abstinence, and strict chastity, Jeoffry, then Abbot, was induced to erect them into a cell, subordinate to the mother abbey, appropriating convenient buildings to their use, and directing the women to adopt the vest of nuns, according to the Order of St. Benedict. 'Moreover the Abbot, tender for the credit and safety of his Nuns, ordained that they should be inclosed in their house under locks and bolts, and the seal of the Abbot for the time being; and that none should be taken into their college but a select and limited number of virgins':[26] which were not to exceed the number of thirteen. How long they continued to live under lock and seal is not recorded. The laws certainly fell into some disregard, as in 1338, Michael, then Abbot, revived certain of the rules, eleven in number, enjoining a more rigid observance of them in future. By these rules it was, amongst other things, ordained, 'That a little bell do ring in the morning, as notice to rise and appear; and that none leave the dormitory before the bell rings. That the garden door be not opened (for walking) before the hour of prime, or first hour of devotion; and in summer, that the garden and the parlour doors be not opened until the hour of none [nine] in the morning: and to be always shut when the curfew rings. That no sister hold conversation in the parlour without her cowl on, and her face covered with a veil. No nun to lodge out of the house, and no guest within it.'[27]

"Notwithstanding the variation, suspension, or trifling relaxation of such restrictions, usually arising from the progress of time, in all institutions; yet was it the duty of the Superior of Sopwell Priory, to enforce some remnant of its laws;—*her* manners formed a model to the monastic votaries; and her presence was uniformly necessary to regulate the daily acts of devotion.[28] Under such restrictions it is impossible to believe that the staid

[26] Quoted from Chauncy, p. 466.

[27] [Footnote from Haslewood.] *History of the Ancient and Royal Foundation, Called the Abbey of St. Alban, &c. by the Rev. Peter Newcome,* 1795, p. 468.

[28] [Footnote from Haslewood.] It seems certain that the Abbot for the time being (or his deputy, the prior), in whom alone, according to the History of the Abbey, (p. 220) "was the power to make the prioress, without any consent or leave of the sisters," always selected those not too far advanced in life to perform the duties of the office in person, and when they became disqualified by age, they were removed. The following are all the names of the ladies holding the office, that I have met with; but the list must be incomplete.

Domina Johanna prioresse de Soppewelle.

1330. Domina Philippa died, and was succeeded by Alice de Pekesdene.

prioress could, while in the exercise of such an important station, devote her time, without impeachment, to the diversions of the field. That resignation and strict piety might indulge in partial and innocent amusements, may be credited; but to hold familiarity with hawks; to study their singular propensities; to collect recipes for the destruction of their vermin; exceed the attention of a menial ostreger in their care; or, by following the pleasures of the chace, surpass a huntsman in knowledge of the art and technicalities of venery; and withal, to suppose a holy prioress wandering over champaign and through woodland, as the prey either on wing, or of fleet foot, might deviously guide, is forming a character of such inconsistent shreds, that, when blended together, it appears rather fitted for some partial creation of fiction, than the faithful delineation of real life" (pp. 14–16).

Oldys was not more eloquent in denouncing the idea of a nun in the field.[29] But Haslewood did not need the argument. He had another line of thought which would explain the prowess of a nun.

Haslewood, like Oldys, declined to attribute all the treatises in the *Book of St. Albans* to Juliana. In addition to the hunting treatise in Wynkyn de Worde's edition, he gives her, on a "probable" basis, a small part of the hawking treatise, a short list of beasts of chase, and another short one of persons, beasts, fowls, etc.

"Even these compilations," he says, "upon examination, will be found to display a varied and extensive knowledge of the passing world. The terms of familiarity applicable to the ordinary classes of society, prove them to have been collected by one mixing unreservedly with mankind; and not the local or casual gatherings, of a simple recluse in a nunnery.

1416. Domina Matilda de Flamstede, is mentioned as formerly prioress. She probably resigned the situation from age, as she died in 1430, and had "lived in the rules of religion 60 years and 18 weeks; and in the whole, 81 years and 8 weeks" —Ib. p. 311.

1426. Domina Leticia Wyttenham.

1480. Joan Chapell, from the infirmity of age set aside, and Elizabeth Webb appointed in her stead.

1553. Joan Pigott, prioress at the time of abolishing of the convents, and living at this period.

No date has anywhere been assigned for the period that Dame Julyans is supposed to have held the office; she might be an intermediate prioress between Leticia Wyttenham and Joan Chapell.

[29] Both were mistaken, according to A. L. Binns, who says that nuns did hunt and bishops tried to stop it.

But why should it be believed that our authoress passed her whole life immured in a cloister? If conjecture may supply the absence of facts, how easily can a more consistent outline be furnished?" (P. 16.)

Here for the first time in the long history of increments provided by the eminent antiquaries of Britain, Haslewood brings Juliana to life:

"Let us suppose her educated in a convent [and a footnote from an old manuscript says that before the Reformation young women were educated at nunneries in needlework, confectionary, surgery, physic, writing, drawing, and the like]; the teens passed with relations in the vicinity of the court; at times partaking of the amusements of the field, then a favourite pursuit with ladies of family; forming a common-place book, according to the literary plan of that period, on various subjects; from disappointment retiring to a cloister, where an advancement to the office of superiour commonly attended courtly connections; amidst the hours of listless solitude, either seeking amusement by the translation of a treatise upon hunting, from the French language; or versifying the general rules of the sport from her own collections; whereby it became set forth with the affixture of 'Dame Julians Barnes';—and the sketch is at least plausible. It unites all the supposed characteristics of our authoress, without violating probability, or distorting consistency.

"To conclude," says Haslewood, "the facts resolve themselves into very few particulars. Her name to the Book of Hunting stands most prominent. Next, the date given by Bale, whose delineation of her appears to have been drawn from the second edition of the work, as he attributed to her pen the Treatise on Angling then first printed: her being prioress of Sopwell, which rests on the united authorities of Burton and Chauncy, though the date remains to be discovered by some more fortunate investigator: and lastly the probability of her being related to the Berners family.—Such is the extent of information of the life of our authoress, who, if the above separation of the pieces which were really written by her prove just, will have the literary claim materially narrowed; yet this is a circumstance rather to her advantage than otherwise . . . by freeing her character from the weight of censure, by which it has long been shadowed, and giving it a fairer claim to be considered as feminine" (pp. 16–17).

The peculiarity of Haslewood's reasoning is that he makes precise statements about the historical record, varied in strength and weakness according to circumstances; and in arriving at conclusions, he appears to believe, on the principle of corroboration, that a number of weak observations add up to a strong, "indubitable" one. His long conjecture about Juliana's possible life at court makes more legend, and yet it is also a logical reply to the reasoning of Oldys that a nun could not reasonably be supposed to have a knowledge of sports. Haslewood shows that if you believe Bale and Chauncy and believe in the Burton notes, there is no inconsistency between sportswoman and nun, the first role being at court, the second in the cloister.

But Haslewood is categorical in denying Juliana authorship of the fishing treatise. He says:

"While the unbusied and volatile spirits of the age unite in exhilarating the passions by the chase; the philosopher, student, and sedentary man, need a less boisterous recreation; and therefore become anglers. Hence the works extant upon that art display the erudition of its pursuers. Knowledge and philanthropy, acting under the genial influence of the solitude attached to the diversion, combine to enforce the best moral principles, while the novice is in eager pursuit of technical instruction. No works that treat upon subjects of art surpass, in this particular, the interesting essays upon angling: and to precede near seventy different English writers, who have more or less thus judiciously enlarged upon the science, stands the anonymous author of the present treatise: a treatise supposed to be the earliest didactic attempt upon the subject, printed in any language.

"Neither for Juliana Barnes, the monkish schoolmaster, nor anyone who assisted in compiling the original Book of St. Albans, can there be consistently advanced a claim of authorship in this 'little pamphlet.' The treatise of hawking is formed, without adornment, by recipes promiscuously gathered; that of hunting is a string of technical phrases attached to venery; and neither of them is interspersed with judicious and sentimental precepts, like the introduction and end of the present tract. It commences with a parable from Solomon, not in the dull and grave monotony that might appear the dubious and fanatical progeny of a gloomy cloister, but with an interesting and candid familiarity discussing what is "good disport," and "honest game"; and enforcing the mild principles of virtue and rational piety, for the obtainment of a cheerful, or, as it is quaintly termed, 'a merry spirit.' Whatever ravage or spoliage birds, dogs, and horses, might create, is not antecedently considered: neither check, limitation, nor regret, is given to the destructive pursuits of hawking and hunting: but here, at the conclusion, the peaceable angler, whose instrument of pleasure and mischief is converted into a walking staff, is solemnly charged not to seek amusement by fishing in the poor man's several water, without license; nor to break any gins, or wears; nor take any fish there found; neither break any man's hedge; nor open gates without shutting again; and, finally, not to pursue this disport ravenously, by taking too much at one time. Such simple and inartificial observations form a strong and illustrative fact, of a pen superior to any concerned in the other more laboured compilements.

"The period of writing this [fishing] treatise may be fixed, with some confidence, to have been early in the fifteenth century" (pp. 60–61).

After Haslewood almost everything widely known about Juliana had its source directly or indirectly in his book. Then toward the end of the nineteenth century Haslewood was accused by William Blades (1824–90), printer-antiquary and Caxton specialist, of having written a "sham biography" of Dame Juliana. This occurred in a chapter on authorship in Blades's 1881 facsimile edition of the first *Book of St. Albans,* which is still the standard modern edition of that work, as Haslewood's is of the second *Book of St. Albans.* Blades wrote almost nothing on the authorship that could not have been drawn from Haslewood, made no acknowledgment of his borrowings, and misrepresented Haslewood's opinions. One would never know from Blades, for example, that both Haslewood and Oldys had declared the *Treatise of Fishing* anonymous; or that both of them had observed that "Dame Juliana Barnes" could mean "Mrs. Barnes."

At the center of his attack, Blades says that Haslewood "supplied a full-blown biography of the authoress, giving particulars of her birth and education, the occupations of her youthful days, and a most imposing pedigree." Haslewood, he says, "attributes to her the authorship of all four works in the Book of St. Albans. The difficulty of accounting for a lady so placed writing upon such subjects, is cleverly, if not satisfactorily settled by assuming that she passed her teens at court, partaking of the amusements of the field, and writing for her own use a commonplace book on various subjects. Then retiring through disappointment (doubtless a love affair) to a cloister, her rank raised her to the position of prioress. There in her seclusion, writing amidst the solitude of listless hours and vain regrets, she versified the general rules of sport from her own pleasant recollection, and from the diaries of her youthful happiness, which fortunately she had preserved. If we remember the mania which seized all classes for diary-keeping at the beginning of the century, when Haslewood wrote this, it will deepen our sense of humour to note that he attributes private diary-keeping to a young lady who lived *ante* 1450."[30]

Haslewood, as we have seen, in fact allowed Dame Juliana not all four works but only the hunting treatise, and parts of others. The "difficulty of accounting for a lady so placed writing upon such subjects" had been raised first by Oldys and again by Haslewood and not incidentally but as a central part of their reflections. For Oldys—as later for Blades—the difficulty was insuperable. Haslewood offered a reconciliation of the conflict. "But why," said Haslewood, "should it be believed that our authoress passed her whole life immured in a cloister?" To eliminate the nun and her pedigree, one has to dispose not merely of Haslewood's conjectures but of the basic elements of the "biography" as set forth in the Burton notes and Chauncy. Haslewood obtained the pedigree of the Berners family from Chauncy, and developed the Sir James Berners branch, entering Juliana in the specified place in dotted lines. The place was specified neither by Chauncy nor by Haslewood, but by the Burton notes. Blades incorrectly states that Chauncy united Dame Juliana with the Berners family. Blades does not deal with the Burton notes, upon which Haslewood chiefly rested. Finally, Blades describes Haslewood's Juliana as keeping a diary, when in fact Haslewood supposed her "forming a common-place book." Blades appears not to have been aware of the difference between a diary and a common-place book (a collection of passages and reference notes), or that forming common-place books was in fact a popular pastime before 1450.

It is difficult to account for the low level of Blade's attack. For although Haslewood asked for trouble when he brought Juliana to life with imaginative detail, he did not distort the materials in support of his thesis. Possibly the "scientific" bent which in crude form was the fashion in Blades's time gave him such contempt for Haslewood's temporizing with the centuries of antiquarian gossip about Dame Juliana that he was carried away by the emotion. His conclusion—like that of Oldys—was reasonable. He also expressed it well: "She [Dame Juliana] probably lived at the beginning of the fifteenth century, and she possibly compiled from existing MSS some rhymes on Hunting" (p. 13).

Blades's ironic aside concerning Dame Juliana's supposed retirement through disappointment: "(doubtless a love affair)," suggests a new possibility for the legend that should make Blades turn over in his grave. If

[30] *The Boke of Saint Albans,* ed. by William Blades, 1881, p. 10.

Juliana had a love affair, who was her lover? A plot for Juliana could be imagined as follows: The daughter of Sir James Berners and Anne Berew would have had to be born no later than 1388, since Sir James was executed in that year for conspiracy against Richard II, son of the Black Prince and grandson of Edward III. A few years later her mother married Sir Roger Clarendon, bastard son of the Black Prince and so half-brother of the king who executed her father. In 1399 Henry IV deposed his cousin Richard II and seized the throne. Three years later Henry IV executed Juliana's stepfather, Sir Roger, as a possible pretender to the throne. Although her natural father had lost his head on behalf of Henry IV and her stepfather had been hanged by Henry IV, let us presume that the remaining family was in favor at court. In and out of this court and its prison was Edward, the second Duke of York, author-translator of *Master of Game,* the first book on hunting in the English language. In it he praised hunting as a good sport for warriors. Edward, cousin of Henry IV and arch-conspirator against both kings, managed to keep his head and almost wore the crown; he had a blood claim to the throne and at one time his cousin Richard II considered abdicating in his favor. As it was, he held some of the highest offices in England, including that of Master of Game. Suppose that Juliana as a girl hunted and fished with him. For various reasons—lack of dowry or the exigencies of the court—she did not marry. After Edward died in battle at Agincourt in the year 1415, at the age of forty-two, a hero, Juliana, sorrowing, entered the nunnery. There she reflected and wrote on sport. In the fishing treatise she wrote, with a touch of humor, that the right noble Duke of York, late called Master of Game, had described the joys of hunting; she, however, would describe its griefs. Turning from the pursuit of glory, she finds peace in the art of angling. This fantasy unites the first fishing writer and the first hunting writer in English as tragic lovers, with a certain symbolic merit.

The legend of Dame Juliana as it was actually created by that line of eminent antiquaries, Bale, Holinshed, Pits, Burton, and Chauncy, and believed by Hearne, Middleton, and Haslewood, is not much believed by their professional descendants. The hunting treatise, taken as a compilation, is not denied her; so, we presume, she lived. Bale, Holinshed, and Pits, living in the century after hers, celebrated her, but we do not know for certain that they knew any more than a person walking into a library and taking down the *Book of St. Albans* today. The Burton notes in which she becomes a nun and a Berners fade into the mystery of their origin, with implications about Leland, and the faint possibility of a discovery being made some day. Chauncy, taken at his word, corroborates her presence at Sopwell; but he might also have seen the catalogue of Bishop Moore's library and changed "Prioress" to "Abbess." In a sense it seems we owe the riddle of Juliana to Henry VIII; the gap in knowledge created in the disorders of the Reformation is the basis of the antiquaries' suspicion that the record of the nun existed and was lost.

But whatever one chooses to believe about the Dame Juliana legend and the hunting treatise, the authorship of the fishing treatise is a different matter. For their connection we have only the unsupported remarks of Bale and Pits. Against it are Wynkyn de Worde's notice that he only included the fishing treatise in the *Book of St. Albans* for social reasons, and the fact that he attached no author to it. Against it too is the opposition of antiquaries from Oldys to the present. Even more formidably in the way is the text of the *Book of St. Albans* itself. Assuming Dame Juliana wrote the hunting treatise, how could the same person be supposed to have written the fishing treatise? The styles of the two treatises, as Haslewood and others have noticed, are very different.

The opening passages of the two treatises illustrate their differences. The angler begins with an English quotation from the Book of Proverbs, which is presently supported by a Latin medical aphorism. So far from being mere ornament, these quotations serve to announce the main themes of the introductory section: a long life and a flourishing one, the importance of a cheerful spirit, sobriety, and moderation. These are fully developed in the introduction, the angler never losing sight either of Solomon or of the teachings of medicine. In a very different manner, in the hunting treatise, Dame Juliana begins:

> Wheresoeuere ye fare, by fryth or by fell,
> My dere chylde, take hede how Tristram dooth you tell;
> How many maner beestys of venery ther were,
> Lystyn to yowre dame, and she shall yow lere.

Tristram, never mentioned after the second line of Juliana's book, appears, as we have seen, to serve as the announcement of a lesson in chivalry. Alternatively, he serves a purely decorative function. In any case, the knight is quickly lost sight of, and the real instructor in hunting is "your dame" (referred to three times), who addresses herself to "my child, my dear child, child, my children, my lief children, my son, sons, my sons, dear sons, my dear sons" (twenty-eight times outside the dialogue of the master huntsman and his man). Although this conceit, or formalism, of the "dame" and "children" is maintained throughout most of the hunting treatise, it contributes nothing to the discussion of hunting. At times her phrases, "my dear sons" and the like, seem to be mere padding, and such padding is the most striking feature of Juliana's style, unlike the economical style of the fishing treatise. The hunting treatise is sprinkled with tags, like "by fryth or by fell" in the first line. The technical distinction between "enclosed woodland" and open country is important, yet the only function of the words here seems to be to complete the line and perhaps give a rhyme for "tell." All medieval poets resorted to such tags (even Chaucer occasionally), but it is difficult to find a poet whose verse is so full of them as this one. Everywhere are lines ending with "as I you tell," "as I you bid," "as I you say," "as I you ken," "so tell I my tale," "the sooth for to say," "the sooth I thee say," "I thee pray," "as ye may," "as ye see," "as thou mayst see," "so shall ye say," "all have I bliss," "that is no leas [i.e., lie]," "in frith or in field," and the like. There are many other tags like these in the hunting treatise, which anyone familiar with English poetry of the fourteenth and fifteenth centuries will recognize at once. There are long stretches of the hunting verse in which almost every couplet is eked out by some invention of this sort; and the rhymes for dozens of other couplets are provided by the addition of an otherwise functionless "also," "echone [each one]," "anon," "so free," or the like to one of the lines. Somewhere between a quarter and a third of the work consists of such verbal padding.

In the matter of organization the two works are altogether different. The author of the *Treatise of Fishing* had a great deal of information to impart concerning the methods and instruments of angling, the times, seasons, places, baits, flies, and all the rest. Some of it is of a miscellaneous and fragmentary nature, consisting of brief hints to the angler as to the best procedures to follow under certain circumstances. Although it does not always follow a strictly logical form of presentation, its materials are nevertheless set forth in an orderly manner, each subject being presented, concluded, and left for the next; closely related matters are grouped for discussion. Without exaggerating this feature of the treatise, it is clear that the angler's mind was basically systematic and orderly in its operations. In contrast, the hunting treatise, viewed as practical instruction in hunting, is a hotchpotch having no discernible guiding principle in its arrangement. It begins with a miscellaneous group of stanzas explaining nine different sets of hunting terms; tells how to cut up a roe; gives correct names for boars of different ages and tells how to reward the hounds after the killing of the boar; describes and discusses the hare; gives some general instructions in hunting; explains two more sets of terms; describes the roebuck, hart, and hind; gives the seasons for hunting various beasts; tells how to hunt the hare; gives the dialogue of the master huntsman and his man; tells how to cut up the boar and the hart. This summary is considerably simplified; if it seems chaotic, the hunting treatise itself is much more so. There is no organization by beasts; the hart is dealt with in three widely separated places, the roebuck in two, the hare in two, and the boar in two. There is no organization by techniques or subjects; the cutting up of animals is discussed in three separate places, proper terms for horns and antlers of different sorts appear in two places, and terms for animals of different ages are given in four places.

The most obvious flaw in the arrangement of the hunting treatise has already been noted by several writers. It is a seven-page dialogue of the master huntsman and his man, which interrupts the monologue of the dame to her children. Following it, we find the discussions of the cutting up of the boar and of the hart (four pages), which clearly belong somewhere among the matter preceding the dialogue. The printer may have mislaid this and set up the dialogue in the belief that the amorphous dame and children part was finished; then perhaps he discovered the missing item and tacked it on at the end. The dialogue seems, however, to have been put into its present form by Juliana; it is very similar in style and organization (or lack of it) to the rest of the treatise.

The two treatises differ also in content and in spirit. The fishing treatise begins with a sophisticated and rather philosophical defense of the special claims of angling as a sport—its physiological and spiritual values. The hunting treatise shows little interest in the values of hunting to the hunter's body or soul. After the introduction, the fishing treatise is concerned with the tools and the techniques of the angler (presented with at least an attempt at completeness), hardly at all with matters of terminology. The chief difficulty in interpreting the fishing treatise stems from the way in which the author takes the terms for granted, as though everyone would know what a "dor worme" is and what is the "bayte that bredyth on an oke leyf." The hunting treatise seldom bothers to describe the animals or their habits (two passages, three animals briefly dealt with) or give instruction in the art of hunting (two passages, only the hunting of the hare treated at any length). Dame Juliana's interests lay, not in the animals or the hunting as such, but in the words and phrases connected with them. The hunter must never speak of "a fair hart"; he must learn to say "a great hart" and "a fair doe." In referring to groups of animals he must take care to say "a herd" of harts or hinds or bucks or does, but "a bevy" of roes, "a sounder" of boars, "a route" of wolves. He must know when to say that the hart "profers," when he "reprofers," and when he is "defoulant." The hare may "sore" or "resore," "prick" or "reprick," and the well-bred huntsman must know when to use each term. He must also learn how to use words like "allay," "relay," and "vauntelay"; and he should know which animals are "beasts of venery," which "beasts of chase," and which merely "rascaille." In a word, the hunting treatise is snobbish; it presumes a hierarchic scheme of society in which the higher orders are marked by a codification of expression; whereas the fishing treatise is natural, plain, philosophic, and a manual of angling operations.

A number of the hunting terms have a distinctly foreign cast. The fishing treatise uses homespun terms, for the most part words which had long been familiar to ordinary Englishmen. Many are of strictly native origin ("staff" and "crop," "smite" and "strike"), while others are thoroughly naturalized borrowings from Latin, French, or Scandinavian ("trout," "tench," "bleak"). But the hunter setting his hounds on the track must say three times, "So ho, so ho"; and after that, "Sa, sa, cy avaunt, so ho." If the hounds run too fast and get too far ahead of him, he shall say, "How amy" and then "Sweff, mon amy, sweff." If a particular hound, let us say Bemounde, picks up the scent, the hunter cries: "Oyes a Bemounde le vallant" and "Que guide trouers la cowarde ou la court cowe." And so it goes. The French terms are usually spelled according to the conventions of Anglo-French, the French of England rather than that of France. Parisian-French, which could be learned abroad, would not have served the social purpose.

The foreign terminology is due as much to the sources used by Dame Juliana as to her own linguistic preferences. As we have seen, she compiled her hunting treatise from French sources, chiefly Twici, which was written in England in Norman-French, and the *Master of Game,* which was largely translated from the French of France. Perhaps she used translations rather than the sources themselves, since these works had been turned into Middle English shortly before her time, and in the translations the French hunting cries and much French terminology are retained intact.

The terminology in the hunting treatise may be explained through its social aspect. The education of a noble youth, serving his apprenticeship as a page, would require knowledge of this terminology, whether or not he actually hunted; and the children of merchants would at least want to know the terminology. Juliana's hunting treatise, which lacks practical organization, may have been designed not for practical instruction in hunting but only for instruction in the language of the sport. From that point of view the hunting treatise might be said to have linguistic organization. This theory would make some sense too out of the constant reiteration of expressions that otherwise appear only as padding. The hunting treatise thus may be conceived as a treatise on the conversation of a gentleman. This too would explain its French character. A noble English family of the time would have an Anglo-Norman tradition. The difference between the styles of the hunting treatise and the fishing treatise in the *Book of St. Albans* may be explained on the grounds that the fishing treatise was not part of a traditional corporate dignified way of life hardening into formalized literary convention as the hunting treatise was. The *Treatise of Fishing* may show the new class of merchants and others turning away from the courtly past, as reflected in purely chivalric literature, to a more individual and empiric approach to recreation.[31]

The plain English of the *Treatise of Fishing* suggests that there never was—as has sometimes been thought—a foreign original of that treatise, although, as we have seen in Chapter 1, its aesthetic structure appears to have been drawn from earlier continental hunting models. Juliana's hunting treatise, with its detached linguistic bias, is decadent by comparison with the older hunting treatises.[32] With respect to authorship, the difficulty here is in imagining the Juliana of the hunting treatise changing her spots to write the fishing treatise, a not impossible but not likely happening.

If it was not Juliana, what kind of person might have written the fishing treatise? There is no good reason to exclude the possibility of either a priest or a nun. Yet there is nothing to suggest monastic or priestly authorship; the tone is not even that of an especially devout layman. The writer evidently had a rather good education; at least he had an orderly mind, and he could quote a Latin couplet and interpret it correctly. His education

[31] A line of thought suggested by A. L. Binns.

[32] See Chapter 1 for the identical firm structure to be found in Xenophon's treatise on hunting (c. 400 B.C.?), the *Art of Falconry* (c. 1240–50), *La Chace dou Cerf* (c. 1245?), *Livre de Chasse* (c. 1387), and *Master of Game* (c. 1406).

would be exceptional for a country squire of the fifteenth century, and it is a question whether any squire of that day could have resisted the social pressure in favor of the fashionable sports of hunting and hawking. Although the tone and spirit of the treatise do not suggest a priest, it is possible that the author was a clerk in minor orders. A lawyer or a schoolmaster could have written it. Two small points suggest a physician. The treatise quotes from a highly regarded medical authority, the *Regimen Sanitatis Salernitanum,* treating it with almost as much respect as the Bible. It also echoes the common *probatum est* formula of the medical books, when it remarks that "thyse baytes ben well prouyd baytes for the samon." There is nothing in the treatise that could not have been written by a country doctor in the fifteenth century. However, until evidence for a new author is discovered, our legendary nun and sportswoman, Juliana Berners, doubtless will continue to serve.

CHAPTER 5

The First Modern Trout Flies

The *Treatise of Fishing* introduced the first modern trout flies. They were not the first known in history. Before the treatise, the artificial fly was described possibly twice in literature, once for certain by Aelian in the third century A.D., and once, less certainly—depending on your scholar—by Martial about two hundred years earlier. Before Martial the fly is without record. The twelve hundred years between Aelian and the *Treatise of Fishing* are the dark ages of the fly. Something went on but we do not know what until it turns up in the treatise, modern and almost complete. But the fly fishers of antiquity, who were not necessarily sport fishermen, had no influence in modern times—Aelian's fly was first noticed in the second half of the nineteenth century—and so the flies of the treatise stand alone as the ancestors of the modern trout fly.

As the author of the treatise calls these flies "the XII," we presume that they were entrenched in the fishing practices of the fifteenth century and earlier. This has long been the accepted interpretation. However, the authoritative ring of "the XII" could also be the author's own declaration of choice in flies. If the curse of classicism was not on them at the time they were first set down in writing, it came upon them afterward. For two centuries they ruled the sport, so far as writing is concerned. The trout fly is still subject to a constant pull between classicism and innovation. In recorded history the score now is even: three dominantly classical centuries, the fifteenth, sixteenth, and eighteenth, and three innovating, the seventeenth, nineteenth, and twentieth. The widespread search today for a small-number set of basic trout flies suggests the beginning of a new classicism.

The record of the rule of "the XII" is clear. Just seven books on angling, as we have seen in the first chapter of this book, are known to have been published from the *Treatise of Fishing* in the early fifteenth century to *The Compleat Angler* in the middle of the seventeenth century. Look at these again for their bearing on the development of the trout fly.

After the *Treatise of Fishing* came the recently discovered *The Arte of Angling* (1577) by an anonymous author, from whom Walton seems to have borrowed information on baits, keeping baits, and other matters. This long-lost and worthy writer mentions the trout and the fly only once and then surreptitiously: ". . . I dare not well deal in the angling of the trout, for displeasing of one of our wardens, which either is counted the best trouter in England, or so thinketh, who would not (as I suppose) have the taking of that fish common. But yet thus much I may say, that he worketh with a fly in a box." Another curious avoidance of trout flies occurs in an edition of the *Treatise of Fishing* published in 1586 and reprinted in 1614 under the title *A Jewell for Gentrie,* which omits the whole fly list. Other writers, however, used it freely.

The third book, Leonard Mascall's *A Booke of Fishing with Hooke and Line,* published in 1590, pirates and edits the twelve flies from the treatise.

The fourth book, John Dennys' *Secrets of Angling,* a treatise in verse published in 1613, treats of the trout but not of the fly; but the second edition of the poem, published in 1620, contains a remarkable observation, written by its felicitous editor, William Lawson, perhaps the only man to have been made famous by the writing of a single footnote.

Angle with a made fly, he says, and with a line of three hairs at least twice the length of your rod; counterfeit the May fly and change his color month by month from dark white to yellow. He gives a dressing, the first new trout-fly dressing after "the XII"—a period of about two hundred years, counting from the probable date of the original manuscript—as follows: "The head is of black silk or haire, the wings of a feather of a mallart, teele, or pickled hen-wing. The body of Crewell according to the moneth for colour, and run about with a black haire; all fastned at the taile, with the thread that fastned the hooke. . . ."

Lawson then offers an illustration of a trout fly—the first in angling history—but we can't count on it. It corresponds not to the dressing but to a natural that the engraver must have caught on his windowpane.

The fifth book on angling is Gervase Markham's *The Pleasures of Princes*, published in 1614. The trout flies in this prose version of *Secrets of Angling* are from the *Treatise of Fishing*, pirated, with revisions and additions, from Mascall. The historian John Waller Hills (*A History of Fly Fishing for Trout*) is inclined to believe that the editing of Markham's flies is the work of Lawson, and that by his work the flies of the treatise were brought to perfection, "complete and unambiguous, neither of which they originally were." Hills's high opinion of this version of the flies accounts for some of the differences between his conception of the original flies and ours presented here.

The sixth book, Thomas Barker's *The Art of Angling*, published in 1651, is the first to say how to tie a fly. His fly dressings are generalized.

The seventh is *The Compleat Angler* (1653). Walton seems not to have been much of a fly-fisher; he took his artificial flies from the *Treatise of Fishing* via Mascall. But Part Two of the fifth edition of *The Compleat Angler*, subtitled "Being Instructions How to Angle for a Trout or Grayling in a Clear Stream," written by his friend Charles Cotton and published in 1676, is a masterful specialized treatise on fly-fishing. Cotton published an original list of sixty-five flies with their dressings.

Three other works need to be mentioned here: *The Experienced Angler* by Robert Venables (1662), who, like Barker, gives generalized dressings; James Chetham's *The Angler's Vade Mecum* (1681); and Richard Franck's *Northern Memoirs* (written in 1658, published in 1694).

Thus from the *Treatise of Fishing* through Walton, with the minor exceptions noted, the only flies in print are "the XII." The revolution in fly-fishing, breaking this classicism-by-plagiary, was performed in the 1650s, '60s, and '70s by Barker, Cotton, and Venables.

So long as "the XII" ruled, the art of the fly scarcely moved. When their rule was broken, fly-fishing returned to firsthand imitation of nature, and a large variety of flies were invented. Barker and Venables introduced the idea of choosing flies for their relationship to weather and water. Fancy flies (flies imitative only of the generality of flies) came on, beginning with Cotton, and with him, too, fly-fishers entered the universe of minutely imitative fly dressings, where they have been ever since. Cotton fished fine and tied fine. For example, his fourth fly for March: "There is also for this month a fly called the THORN-TREE FLY; the dubbing an absolute black, mixed with eight or ten hairs of Isabella-coloured mohair; the body as little as can be made, and the wings of a bright mallard's feather. An admirable fly, and in great repute amongst us for a killer."

This killer is a simple fly, as simple as a treatise fly, except for the color of the mohair. Sir Harris Nicolas, who edited the most scholarly edition of *The Compleat Angler,* explains the reference as follows: "Isabella" he says, is "a kind of whitish yellow, or, as some say, a buff colour a little soiled." Soiled is the point.

A generation before Cotton, in the year 1602, the Infanta Isabella, daughter of Philip the Second, King of Spain, accompanied her husband the Archduke Albertus on a campaign. When he laid siege to Ostend, then held by heretics, she made a rash vow that she would not change her clothes until the city was taken. This happened to require three years. So Isabella's linen came to be the right color for the cavalier Cotton's trout fly.

The revolution steered by Cotton, Barker, Venables and, perhaps in some degree, Franck, ended in the seventeenth century. The eighteenth, like the fifteenth and sixteenth, with one exception, Richard (1747 edition) and Charles (1744 edition) Bowlker's *The Art of Angling,* went classical again so far as flies are concerned, though it was a lively century in what it did to create the modern rod, reel, line, and leader. Bowlker wrote off several of the treatise flies in "A Catalogue of Flies Seldom Found Useful to Fish with," and created a new list of "the most useful flies" which was promptly classicized for the second half of the eighteenth century. The nineteenth and twentieth centuries returned to the creation of new flies. Isabella buff had nothing on the body of the Green Drake by Alexander Mackintosh (*The Modern Angler or, Driffield Angler,* 1810): ". . . a little fine wool from the ram's testicles, which is a beautiful dusty yellow." That this tradition has not let up is shown by a dubbing for the Hendrickson Fly by our contemporary Art Flick (in his book *Streamside Guide,* 1947), which calls for belly fur of the vixen fox stained a little pink with urine burns.

The real work of the nineteenth century was in the creation of entomologies, the decisive shift to upstream fishing, and the invention of the dry fly, which together formed the greatest revolution in fly-fishing history since the sport has been known.

With the dry fly came a new brand of classicism, an effort led by Frederic Halford (*Floating Flies and How to Dress Them,* 1886, and other works) to create a definitive "scientific" set of imitation flies. But no action without a reaction. G. E. M. Skues, a great angling writer of a generation ago, successfully attacked dry-fly purism and the new classicism with the weapons of the old wet fly and the new nymph, and an urge to create. In the United States at about the turn of the century Theodore Gordon introduced the dry fly, with an impressionism like Monet's, and a streamside empiricism that altered forever the then American weakness for imitating not our own natural flies but the established English artificials. The tension between classicism and innovation is still with us, and, doubtless, always will be. Today in the United States, Easterners, with their perennial Quill Gordons and Cahills, usually are more classical than Westerners, with their experiments in new types as well as patterns of flies. But the issue is not sharp. Two innovators, Lee Wulff in the East and Dan Bailey in the West, both professionals who have invented many new flies—especially for fast rough water—may often be found fishing the old flies; and the traditionalist Sparse Grey Hackle ("angling is tradition"), who has given us idyls on sympathetic if fishless streams, will try any new fly so long as it is a May Fly.

There is reason for the coexistence of the old and the new in trout flies. A fly fisherman is likely to have conflicting desires for a small number of established patterns and for novelty. General Sory Smith, a talented contemporary amateur who knows enough about flies to invent new types as well as patterns, writes in a letter that he is "lost" in the hundreds of dressings. "If only," he says, "there was a box of floating flies containing the least possible number of patterns, a poor man's starting box of floaters." Having determined upon an effort to achieve simplicity, he made up a batch of "group" flies to the number of six, calculated as an optimum for the western United States. It does not matter here about the details of their construction, except that one was a Royal Coachman, one a Horner Bug, and four were his own creations. We submitted them to Bailey with a few words about Smith's intentions. "In principle," Bailey replied, "I agree. About two-thirds of the trout I have taken on dries have been on Adams, Quill Gordon, Light Cahill and Grizzly Wulff, the elements of which are in General Smith's group of six. The whole difficulty in simplifying flies comes from the other one-third of the trout. All of us would like to take trout all the time and a simplified list which will take them two-thirds of the time is not enough. This leads to carrying many patterns, most of which are only occasionally useful. From the fly tier's point of view there is nothing worse than the multiplicity of patterns. We only make money on the popular patterns which we can tie in thousands of dozens. So General Smith is right to seek a small number for the economy of the fisherman and the fly tier. But even if all fishermen felt that a half-dozen patterns were all that is needed, each fisherman would have a different small list and among all fishermen the variety would still be large."

Opinion on flies, however, has not always been so reconciled. In the wars between classicists and anticlassicists in times past, the *Treatise of Fishing* was sometimes held up as the bad example. Hewett Wheatley (*The Rod and Line*, 1849), a brilliant advocate of the fancy fly, "Water-Witches," and other new artificial baits, in the course of assailing all forms of classicism, said: "That the 'Jury of a dozen flies,' written about by our ancestors, may have condemned a few fins to death, I cannot dispute; but I believe they were mercifully pleased to acquit forty-nine out of every fifty that were arraigned before them. The moderns are not so merciful."

And Skues says, "The famous twelve flies for trout and grayling are described as if they were the laws of the Medes and Persians and altered not. . . ."

That the treatise flies were classicized to the absolute limit for perhaps two centuries is clear from the evidence, but it must be remembered that classicism is not the fault of the classic. It was an important moment for fly-fishers when the author of the treatise wrote down the twelve dressings in the first manual of the art. The great defense of the treatise flies is Hills's history, which traces eleven of the twelve down to the present. Our work in constructing the flies for the illustrations in this book would have been more difficult but for Hills, though we are forced to disagree with him in some important respects.

So much for the historical setting. We turn now to the business at hand, which is the actual tying of "the XII" trout flies. We present our argument (and travail) first as regards the general elements as they relate to all the flies, and then as regards each fly in particular.

The general elements:

Style. The treatise tells us the ingredients but does not tell us how the flies were tied, nor does it give a hint as to their general appearance. There is no known description of the act of tying a fly until Barker, Cotton, and Venables, and we have searched them and the other early writers for clues.

Markham, a little over a century away from the printing of the treatise, said this about their style: "Now for the shapes, and proportions of these flies, it is impossible to describe them without paynting, therefore you shall take of these severall flies alive, and laying them before you, try how neere your Art can come unto nature by an equall shape, and mixture of colours."

The assumption that the treatise flies were modeled on nature is our clue to size, but this only shifts the difficulty to one of identifying the naturals represented by these artificials. In only two of the flies is there certainty, namely, the Stone Fly and the Wasp Fly; these are the same today and there is no reason not to take fish with them now on the Beaverkill or the Madison. The Dun Fly No. 1 could be either the February Red or the March Brown. The coloration of the Shell Fly makes it acceptable as a caddis; the Shell Fly and Grannom are identified by Alfred Ronalds in *The Fly-fisher's Entomology,* 1836. For the rest we know of nothing better to do about the natural models than to present the often contradictory intuitions of Hills and Skues, two fly-fishers of one sensibility who spent their lives observing both English stream insects and their imitations. Our policy is to dress the fly to the size of a possible natural proposed by either or both of these masters.

It is not surprising that the treatise does not give us a word picture of the appearance of the flies. Modern fly dressings do not usually specify style in this respect, and most professional fly tiers today are not particularly conscious that their "exact imitation" imitates no fly in hand but may be a convincing impression of the fly on the water. We have concluded from its fur-and-feather materials that the treatise flies too are impressionistic, but that they were slightly rougher than modern flies; for the equipment was cruder, the professional was unknown, and the flies were tied by hand. To some extent the style is fixed by reverse wings. The most noticeable difference from the modern style is dictated by the shape of the hooks illustrated in the treatise. The shanks are so short and the bite of the hook so deep that the fly bodies must have extended well onto the bend.

The flies illustrated here vary in the "set" of the wings. This is partly intentional, partly chance, in the feathers used and random variations in the tying of each fly. We wished to avoid making a case for a uniform style.

Tying Thread. The treatise gives no directions. But in one instance, the Dun Cut, the wings are bound on with barked hemp, indicating that a dark effect was desired. A possible inference is that, unless, as in this case, something was done about it, tying off the fly ordinarily left a light or neutral effect. Venables says: "First, I begin to set on my Hook . . . with such coloured Silk as I conceive most proper for the Flie. . . ." Hence we suppose the rule for the treatise was merely to pick a harmonious silk.

Tails. Here the most obvious departure from most modern flies is in the absence of tails. The word *tail* is mentioned in two treatise flies (Dun Fly No. 2 and Stone Fly) but each time as a reference point. In the Stone Fly the reference is unmistakably to the insect; in the Dun Fly No. 2 the reference may mean part of the bird.

The argument *for* tails is this: (1) The treatise and later books counsel the fly maker to copy nature. Tails are conspicuous on many insects. (2) Venables specifically gives instruction on the point: "Let me add this only, that some Flies have forked tails, and some have horns, both which you must imitate with a slender hair fastened to the head or tail of your Flie . . . and in all things, as length, colour, as like the natural Flie as you can possibly." (3) Cotton dressed one of the treatise flies (the Stone Fly) with tails. (4) The earliest illustration of a fly (*Secrets of Angling*, 1620) has a tail, although the text doesn't specifically ask for one.

The argument *against* tails is this: (1) No directions to this effect are specifically given, and if one construed tails to be implied, what material should be used? (2) Neither Mascall nor Markham adds tails in their several changes of the treatise dressings. (3) In Cotton's list of sixty-five patterns, tails are specified in only three: the Green Drake (the whisks of the tails of long hairs of the sable or fitchet), the Grey Drake (the whisks of the tails of the beard of a black cat), and the Stone Fly (place two or three hairs of a black cat's beard on the top of the hook). The Dun Cut calls for horns. Since many of Cotton's flies must have simulated May flies, they should also have been tailed, but this does not seem to have been the fashion. Of one fly that is definitely a May fly he says: ". . . the Little Yellow May fly; in shape *exactly the same with the Green-drake* [our italics], but a very little one, and of as bright a yellow as can be seen, which is made of a bright yellow camlet, and the wings of a white-grey feather dyed yellow." No tails.

Our conclusion is that by tail the treatise means the hind or tail end of the fly. This is justified by the usage of the day, according to the *Oxford English Dictionary*.[1] But we must admit that the word could mean simply a tail-appendage.

Body. The basic body material for all flies is wool. Six of the patterns call for black; the others call for dun, ruddy, yellow, tawny, dusky, and

[1] The great classic of lexicography, otherwise known as *A New English Dictionary on Historical Principles* or the *O.E.D.*, deals with all periods of the English language (Oxford: Clarendon Press, 1884–1933).

green, respectively. To get ruddy, yellow, green, and perhaps tawny colors, natural wool must have been dyed. It could have been used as yarn or spun on as dubbing. The only problem is the black. Black could have been dyed or used natural. It seems strange that so many dressings call for black, as this is not a particularly common color for naturals. Natural black sheep's wool would be an off-black, even a dun, especially when held against sunlight, and so, we surmise that perhaps when dark hues were wanted, natural wool from the black sheep was used in the old flies.

In modifying the basic hue of the wool body, two flies call for ribbing of black silk, one for ribbing of yellow thread. Two call for peacock herl "lapped around" the body. The Dun Cut has a black body with a yellow stripe down either side. The Stone Fly has a bicolored body with yellow under the tail and wings of an otherwise black body. The problem lies in techniques for achieving mixed body colors.

Venables and Cotton give detailed directions on the techniques for tying some types of multicolor bodies, and these directions are clues. Venables says: "if your Flie be of divers colours, and those lying longways from head to tail, then I take my Dubbing, and lay them on the hook longwaies one colour by another (as they are mixt in the natural Flie from head to tail) then bind all on, and make it fast with silk of the most predominant colour."

Cotton's method was different: he spun his different furs first on the thread (as it is usually done today); for example, the Stone Fly: "the dubbing, of bear's dun with a little brown and yellow camlet very well mixt, but so placed that your fly may be more yellow on the belly and towards the tail, underneath, than in any other part."

There is no knowing how the author of the treatise dubbed, but it is plausible to suppose that it was done as either Venables or Cotton did it. Cotton's method gets more blending and is more suited to the Stone Fly than the Dun Cut, for the latter suggests a precise yellow stripe along the body.

As to the Stone Fly, we are indifferent between the two techniques, except for intuition that Venables' technique is the older. We therefore tied this fly more or less along his lines. For the Dun Cut, the mechanics of the operation make Venables' the only reasonable one to follow.

Fly Wings. The plumage from at least seven birds is specified for dressing treatise flies: partridge, jay, the red cock (rooster), capon, drake, buzzard, and peacock. All except the peacock are given as fly-wing materials. Two birds, the drake and the buzzard, need explanation.

In fifteenth-century England and since then, the word *drake* has the special meaning of the male of the common waterfowl (and domesticated duck), the mallard. The word was also applied to males of waterfowl in general, but it is most likely that the word *drake* in the treatise is used in the restrictive sense, the male mallard. In two flies, Maure and Tandy, there is no contention. The treatise specifies for them "the wild drake," which unquestionably is the male mallard.

In another instance it specifies "black drake" (Drake Fly), but it is not explicit as to whether the meaning is feather color or species of bird. We conclude feather, and give our reasons later in the discussion of the twelve flies.

"Buzzard" means the common hawk (and closely related species) in Great Britain, whereas in the United States the term is often used for another group of birds, the vultures. The buzzard members of the hawk family were considered inferior because they were useless in falconry (suggesting why it is uncomplimentary to be called one). The red-tailed hawk is the closest North American species to the common European buzzard. The plumage of juvenile buzzards differs from the adults in being lighter on the breast and parts of the feathers. This increases the range of feathers that could be used in dressing the treatise flies. (The specimen used in our illustration—a juvenile—was provided by the well-known British angling writer Major Richard Waddington.) Two types of markings are found on the flight feathers, white mottled with dark, and dark mottled with darker. The various effects are illustrated in the flies tied.

The problem of the specific feather to be used in treatise flies is more often than not difficult to decide. Only three specific types of feathers are clearly mentioned: (1) herl of the peacock's tail, (2) mail, or light and dark breast feathers, from the drake, (3) hackle feathers from the red cock or capon. These feathers are easily recognized. The distinction between rooster and capon hackles, however, is puzzling. Capon hackles would of course be softer; but we do not know how meaningful such subtle distinctions were to the author.

In eight of the twelve flies, the author mentions no specific feather (at least by present-day usage). These all take the form of "wings of the partridge" (i.e., wings of the fly to be made from the partridge), wings of the buzzard, or wings of the drake. The treatise makes qualifications in two cases: "wings of the blackest drake" and wings "of the drake dyed yellow." The problem: what specific feather of the bird is intended for the fly wings in these eight patterns?

It is exasperating, and interesting, that the treatise should be vague on this point and so specific on the others. Perhaps in the language of the day this phrase was meaningful as it stands. Aside from breast feathers, wing or flight feathers are the common mallard feather called for in fly dressings since the seventeenth century. But even Cotton is vague on this specification. He says, for example, ". . . the wings, of the pale grey feather of a mallard." It was apparently understood to be a flight or wing feather; only one of Cotton's dressings specifies mail: ". . . the wings, of the male of a mallard as white as may be." (In the English of this period, "mail" and "male" were both used to designate "breast feathers.") Hills concludes as regards the treatise's mallard feather: ". . . I think [that the fly had] wings from the quill feather of a drake: not the dark mottled feather, usually called dark mallard; for I think (though it is only a matter of opinion) that when the mottled feather, light or dark, is intended, the *Treatise* uses the word 'mail,' which would be an appropriate word for a body feather" (p. 151). Hills consistently follows this interpretation, except for Dun Fly No. 1, where he assumes that the direction "wings of the partridge" means hackle or body feather.

The immediate successors of the treatise offer little assistance in this area, possibly because they too had trouble in interpreting treatise dressings and thus improvised; or they were drawing on the experience or practice of their times, which would not necessarily correspond with those of the treatise.

Reading flight feathers into the vague treatise instruction, as we do, is purely deductive, but there is no strong argument against it and no satisfactory alternative.

Dual wings follow from one interpretation of three treatise flies (Dun No. 2, Ruddy, and Yellow Fly). Venables makes it clear that multiple-winged flies existed in his time: "Flies made for the Salmon are much better being made with four Wings, than if of two onely and with six better than them of four. . . ."

Hills, in his analysis of early fly construction, points out that in the first description, wings made of quill feathers were not matched slips of feather cut from right and left quills as they are today. Rather a section from one feather was folded over or rolled into a tube and then attached to the hook.

In the matter of attaching wings one is completely at the mercy of writers after the treatise. Barker, Walton, and Venables are consistent in that they attach the wings in reverse fashion; that is, they put on their wing materials with the ends of the feathers pointing away from the end of the hook. Then when the body was completed, they pulled the wings up and bent them back—how far back is not specified—and wedged them into place with a few turns of the working silk. Hills at best is obscure in his interpretation of the way Barker bent back his wing.

Barker is the first writer in history to provide any instruction on attaching wings, and we would have appreciated more lucidity from him. Read for yourself what he says: ". . . Cut so much of the browne of the Mallards feather as in your owne reason make the wings, then lay the outermost part of the feather near the hook, and the point of the feather next toward the shank of the hook, so whip it three or four times about the hook with the same silk you armed the hook with. [Instructions for adding body and hackle, palmer-tied, given here.] Then you must take the hook betwixt your fingers and thumb in the left hand, with a needle or pin part the wings in two, so take the silk you have wrought with all this while, and whip once about the shank that falleth crosse betwixt the wings; then with your thumb you must turn the point of the feather towards the bend of the hook, then whip three or four times about the shank of the hook, so view the proportion."

The rule of imitation suggests offhand that some wings should be up and some down, as they are in nature. But we do not assume that the rule is liberal, and here we are stymied by our decision on other grounds, mentioned above, to tie reverse wings, and therefore up wings. Conceivably reverse wings could be shaped down, but it would be a difficult and a backward way to get down wings. An argument against down wings is given by Venables: ". . . If you set the points of the wings backwards, towards the bending of the hook, the stream (if the feathers be gentle as they ought) will fold the points of the wings in the bending of the hook, as I have often found by experience. . . ."

We expect this to remain a controversial subject, but the act of tying the flies forces a conclusion. Venables' disapproval of down wings, and the logic of reverse-wing tying, lead us to conclude that the treatise fly wings took on a more or less upright form.

To Hackle or Not to Hackle. The treatise seems to regard hackle feathers as wings. The phrasing of both dressings is alike. It says "wings of the

THE BERNERS TROUT FLIES

Tied by Dwight A. Webster—Painted by John Langley Howard

DUN FLY (March)

First Choice

Alternative One

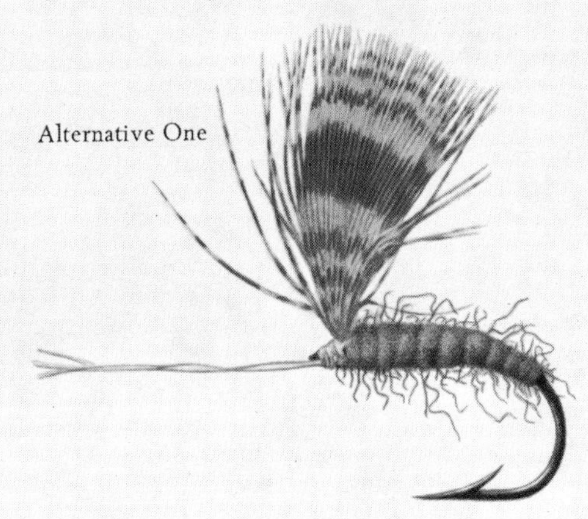

Alternative Two

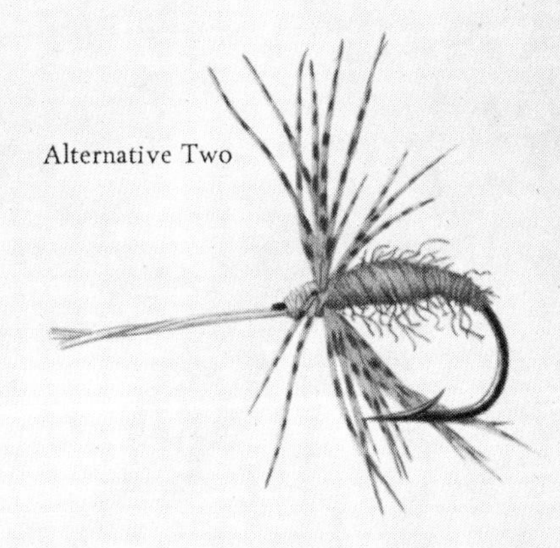

The donne flye the body of the donne woll & the wyngis of the pertryche

ANOTHER DUN FLY (March)

A nother doone flye. the body of blacke woll: the wynges of the blackyst drake: and the Jay und the wynge & under the tayle.

THE STONE FLY (April)

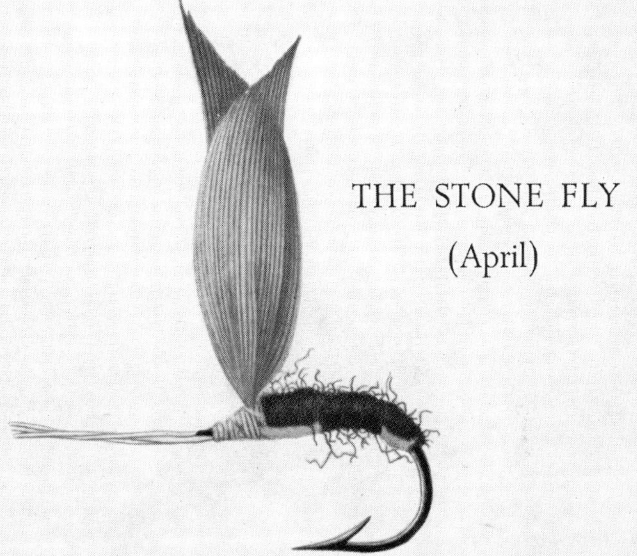

The stone flye. the body of blacke wull: & yelowe under the wynge. and under the tayle & the wynges of the drake.

RUDDY FLY (May)

First Choice

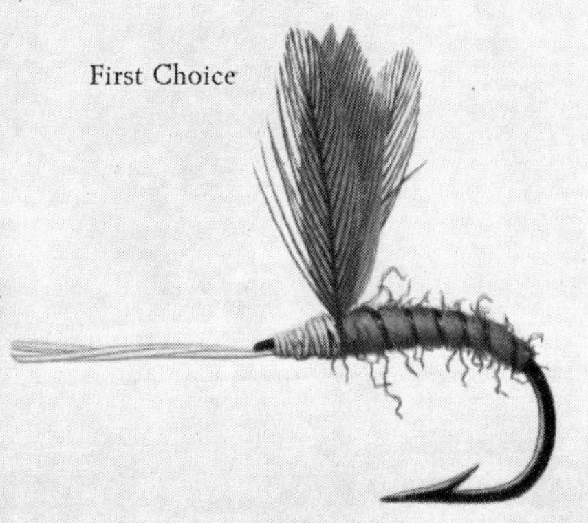

Alternative One

Alternative Two

In the begynnynge of May a good flye. the body of roddyd wull and lappid abowte wyth blacke sylke: the wynges of the drake & of the redde capons hakyll.

THE YELLOW FLY (May)

First Choice

Alternative One

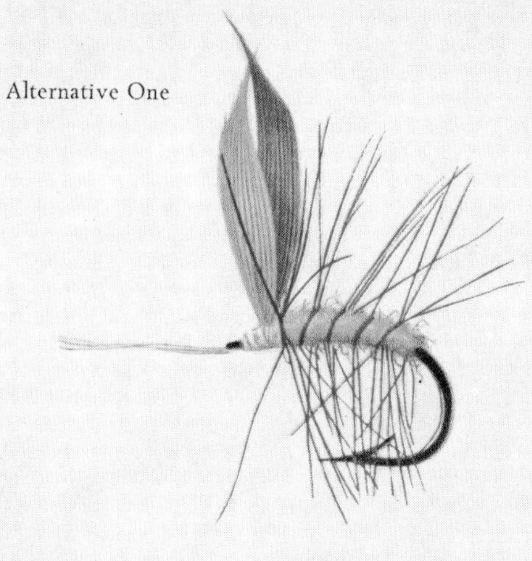

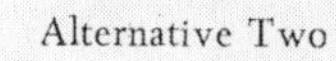

Alternative Two

The yelow flye. the body of yelow wull: the wynges of the redde cocke hakyll & of the drake lyttyd yelow.

THE BLACK LEAPER (May)

First Choice

Alternative

The blacke louper. the body of blacke wull & lappyd abowte wyth the herle of y^e^ pecok tayle: & the wynges of y^e^ redde capon wt a blewe heed.

DUN CUT (June)

The donne cutte: the body of blacke wull & a yelow lyste after eyther syde: the wynges of the bosarde bounde on with barkyd hempe.

MAURE FLY (June)

The maure flye. the body of dolke wull the wynges of the blackest mayle of the wylde drake.

TANDY FLY (June)

The tandy flye at saynt Wyllyams daye. the body of tandy wull & the wynges contrary eyther ayenst other of the whitest mayle of y^{e} wylde drake.

WASP FLY (July)

First Choice

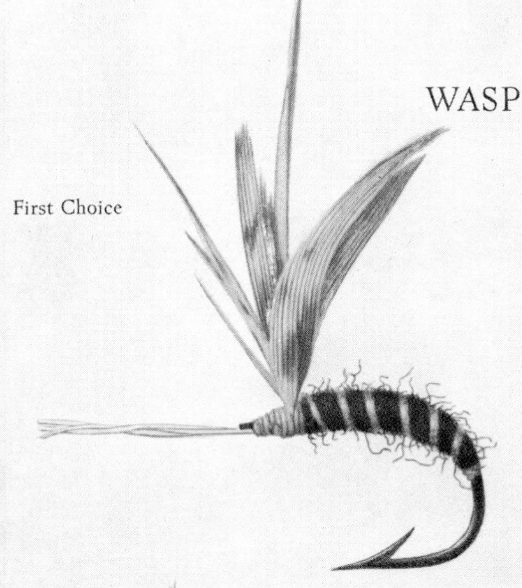

Alternative (down wing)

The waspe flye. the body of blacke wull & lappid abowte wt yelow threde: the winges of the bosarde.

SHELL FLY (July)

First Choice

Alternative

The shell flye at saynt Thomas daye. the body of grene wull & lappyd abowte wyth the herle of the pecoks tayle: wynges of the bosarde.

DRAKE FLY (August)

The drake flye. the body of blacke wull & lappyd abowte wyth black sylke: wynges of the mayle of the blacke drake with a blacke heed.

THE BERNERS FEATHERS AND HERL

RED CAPON

DRAKE MALLARD
Dyed Yellow

DRAKE

JAY
(From Under Wing)

PARTRIDGE BODY
FEATHER

BLACKEST MAIL OF MALLARD

WHITEST MAIL OF MALLARD

RED CAPON'S HACKLE

RED COCK'S HACKLE

ENGLISH PARTRIDGE

PEACOCK

BUZZARD

SUMMARY OF THE TREATISE FLY DRESSINGS

'TREATISE' NAME	POSSIBLE IDENTIFICATION	BODY	WINGS AND/OR HACKLE
Dun Fly No. 1	March Brown—Skues February Red—Hills	Dun wool	a) Wings: Section of partridge quill feather b) Wings: Partridge body feather c) Hackle: Partridge body feather (Hills)
Dun Fly No. 2	Olive Dun —Skues & Hills	Black wool	Wings: Dual, section dark mallard quill veiled with feather from under wing of Jay
Stone Fly	Stone Fly —Skues & Hills	Black wool made yellow under wing and tail	Wings: Section mallard quill
Ruddy Fly	Red Spinner—Hills Great Red Spinner —Skues	Ruddy wool ribbed with black silk	a) Wings: Dual, section mallard quill veiled with red capon hackle b) Wings: Section mallard quill Hackle: Red Capon, tied palmer c) Wings: Section mallard quill Hackle: Red Capon, under wing only (Hills)
Yellow Fly	Little Yellow May Dun—Hills; and, with some uncertainty, Skues	Yellow wool	a) Wings: Dual, section mallard quill dyed yellow veiled with red cock's hackle b) Wings: Section mallard quill dyed yellow Hackle: Red cock, tied palmer c) Wings: Section mallard quill dyed yellow Hackle: Red cock, under wing only (Hills)
Black Leaper	Caddis	Black wool ribbed with peacock herl	a) Wings: Red capon quill feather Head: Blue silk (or wool) b) Hackle: Palmer-tied dun
Dun Cut	Yellow Dun—Hills Sedge Fly—Skues	Black wool with yellow stripe down side	Wings: Section mottled buzzard quill whipped with barked hemp
Maure Fly	Green Drake—Hills Alder—Skues	Dusky wool	Wings: Brown mallard breast
Tandy Fly	Gray Drake—Hills Oak Fly—Skues	Tawny wool	Wings: Light gray mallard breast tied back to back
Wasp Fly	Wasp—Hills Crane Fly—Skues	Black wool ribbed with yellow thread	a) Wings: Section mottled buzzard quill b) Tied natural
Shell Fly	Grannom—Hills Sedge—Skues	Green wool ribbed with peacock herl	a) Wings: Section mottled buzzard quill b) Smaller, like a Grannom, down wing
Drake Fly	Alder—Hills	Black wool ribbed with black silk	Wings: Brown mallard breast feathers Head: Black silk (or wool)

Key: a) first choice; b) alternative one; c) alternative two.

FEATHERS IN TOP AND BOTTOM COLUMN ON OPPOSITE PAGE ARE ONE-THIRD ACTUAL SIZE, THE SNIPS TWO-THIRDS ACTUAL SIZE. IN MIDDLE COLUMN THEY ARE SHOWN ONE-QUARTER AND ONE-HALF ACTUAL SIZE, RESPECTIVELY

drake and of the red capon's hackle." It does *not* say wings of the drake and hackle of the red capon. In two patterns (Ruddy and Yellow Flies) where hackle feathers are mentioned, the literal interpretation would be wings composed of two different wing materials. The alternative is that hackle feathers were wound on in the conventional modern way but were still classified as a sort of wing. Hills and Skues both apparently make this assumption.

There is no clue in Mascall or Markham that the hackle should be wound on, but Barker and Venables both describe the tying of palmer-type flies. In Cotton's list there are two types of flies, palmer and winged. Hills quotes without comment Franck's ambiguous directions to hackle: "And among the variety of your Fly-adventurers, remember the Hackle, or the Fly substitute, form'd without Wings, and drest up with the Feather of a Capon, Pheasant, Partridg, Moccaw, Phlimingo, Paraketa, or the like, and the Body nothing differing in shape from the Fly, save only in ruffness, and indigency of Wings."

Has he hackled only at the throat of the fly or all along the hooks, palmer tie?

It appears that, a century and a half after the treatise was printed, there is still no certain evidence of flies hackled only at the throat, as they are today. The first definite evidence of conventional hackling that we have found is Bowlker in mid-eighteenth century.

When Bowlker wants a palmer tie, he is explicit; for example, his Black Palmer: "The body is made with the black ostridge's feather, ribbed with silver twist, with a black cock's hackle *over the body*" [our italics].

When he wants hackle around the neck of the fly, he says "hackle . . . for the legs" or "hackle wrapt twice or thrice under the but of the wing. . . ."

We conclude that the treatise flies should be unhackled, Hills to the contrary notwithstanding.

Fly Heads. One treatise direction (Black Leaper) ends "with a blue head" and another (Drake Fly) "with a black head." These could refer equally to the head of the bird or to the head of the fly.

We know this much, that fly heads of different colors were known to later writers. Lawson gives his fly a head in the famous footnote. Cotton gives us flies with brown, black, and red heads. And Venables is clear on the subject: "The Head is made after all the rest of the body, of silk or hair, as being of a more shining glossy colour, than the other materials, as usually the head of the flie is more bright than the body, and is usually of a different colour from the body. . . ."

Mascall and Markham give us both interpretations of the treatise's ambiguity as between head of fly and head of bird. For the Black Leaper, Mascall modifies the text from "wings of the red capon with a blue head" to ". . . the winges are made of the winges of a browne capon, with his blew feathers in the head," an intent even less clear than the treatise's. And Markham changes the dressing further to ". . . his wings with the browne feathers of the Mallard, and some of his blew feathers on his head. . . ." Thus Markham inexplicably changes the bird, and, furthermore, implies a dual wing (the metallic iridescent green head feathers could be construed as blue). Neither writer gives us this fly with a blue head.

In the Drake Fly, Mascall inconsequentially adds a comma to the text, but Markham makes a drastic change: ". . . wings of the under mayle of the Mallard, and his head made blacke. . . ." So here we have a black-headed fly.

Note how one gets out of trouble if the interpretation of "head" is as head of the fly: two knotty ornithological problems are neatly solved. (1) The wings of the Black Leaper are from a red capon rather than an uncertain blue mongrel chicken. (2) The wings of the Drake Fly are brown mallard breast instead of some aberrant color phase or another species. The interpretation—fly head—is simplest and clarifies both dressings. It makes sense, and we adopt it.

As to the treatise flies being wet flies there is no question. But some critics have believed that the dry fly is indicated in some of those who adopted the treatise flies. We don't think we can improve much on Hills's interpretations and discussion of this subject. With one exception, all the passages in the old literature leave considerable room for subjective interpretation. Therefore, when Mascall says the Ruddy Fly is good to use "aloft on the water," or Barker that "hogs wool floats best" or "fly at the top of the water" etc., we don't think one can go any further than admit a direction to fish in an upper stratum of water, including the surface. This certainly would not have been difficult by raising the rod and even using a dapping technique. The point is that this is a far cry from what we imply by dry-fly fishing, starting with the specialized construction and all the rest. It is only by the wildest stretch of the imagination that one could envision the existence of the dry fly in the seventeenth and eighteenth centuries and not have something more specific said about it.

The troublesome "exception" often mentioned is the cork-bodied flies of Barker. There is no way to get away from the implications here, even though the result is more like a bass bug than a dry fly. However, this is immaterial insofar as the treatise flies are concerned and is only a Mascall innovation, as there is no hint of it later. Hills's interpretation is as good as any.

Difficult Renditions. In the present stage of knowledge, secure conclusions cannot be made on several critical points. In instances where it is impossible to render a logically strong judgment between choices, we present our first choice as the most likely, and alternatives as possible but less likely. The alternatives are presented in the illustrations and the table of our dressings.

Now look at the flies and our argument for the dressing of each.

No. 1 Dun Fly (March)

The treatise: "The donne flye the body of the donne woll & the wyngis of the pertryche."

Does "dun" imply May fly? The *Oxford English Dictionary* indicates that *dun* was a descriptive adjective in the fifteenth century. The *Middle English Dictionary*[2] has the adjective *don,* "dun," but no example referring to flies. Reference to *dun* meaning subimago May flies seems to have come later in history through association with the fly's general hue. Our assumption is that *dun* refers to color only and does not imply a life stage of a May fly.

"Partridge" we assume to refer to the common (Hungarian) partridge. Is a wing or body feather intended? Markham specifies "male," and Hills must thus have got his body feather from Markham, and not the treatise; Hills further suggests that the feather was tied on as hackle. Since we assumed that a wing feather is implied if mail (breast) is not specified by the treatise, we make the partridge wing feather first choice.

[2] Edited by Hans Kurath, Sherman Kuhn, and staff (Ann Arbor: University of Michigan Press, 1952–). This is a more specialized dictionary than the *O.E.D.* and is designed to give a fuller treatment of the language of the Middle English period (i.e., from about 1100 to about 1500, excluding the early printed books). Thus far, the letters *A–F* have been published, and the files of the *M.E.D.* contain the materials which are now in process of becoming the published letters *G–Z*. The *M.E.D.* includes the vocabulary of the manuscript *Treatise of Fishing with an Angle* (1450), but not that of the 1496 print.

Hills believes that this fly is an imitation of the February red, a stone fly; Skues says March brown, a May fly. Either of these insects could readily be the prototype. Hills seems to have been influenced by the connotation of the modern fly "Partridge and Orange," a hackle fly, even though the use of partridge as hackle in the treatise fly is not apparent.

No. 2 Another Dun Fly (March)

The treatise: "A nother doone flye. the body of blacke woll: the wynges of the blackyst drake: and the Jay vnder the wynge & vnder the tayle."

"Wings of the blackest drake" we construe to mean a dark section of flight feathers.

Two interpretations can be made of the phrase "and the Jay under the wing and under the tail." One is that the reference means jay feathers placed under wing and tail end of the *fly*. If this is followed (as Hills recommends), what feathers from the jay are used (blue feathers?) and how are they placed? There is no answer to this.

The alternative is that the text refers to the bird and not to the fly. That is, the fly wings are to be made from feathers from under the wing and tail of the jay, as well as from the drake. Thus, a dual- or multiple-winged fly would result. This makes more sense in terms of construction. Mascall changes the bird but understands the meaning to be "feathers under the wings of his taile."

We conclude to stay with the jay and take a feather from under his wing, and so make a dual-wing fly.

Both Hills and Skues believe Dun Fly No. 2 is the olive or blue dun.

No. 3 The Stone Fly (April)

The treatise: "The stone flye. the body of blacke wull: & yelowe vnder the wynge, and vnder the tayle & the wynges of the drake."

This fly and its dressing have an unbroken history to modern times. It is one fly that is unmistakable in identification and one where the directions show the treatise to be clearly imitative of nature.

Making the black-wool body yellow under wing and tail pinpoints a conspicuous feature in the color pattern of some of the larger stone-fly adults. This interpretation seems inconsistent with our interpretation of the text of Dun Fly No. 2; if it is, in fact, inconsistent, then the error lies with Dun

Fly No. 2 rather than here; for this fly is known without question. However, order of directions differs: in the case of the Stone Fly the phrase "and yellow under wing and tail" follows "body" and hence should be related to the body in some way. In the case of Dun Fly No. 2 the phrase "and the Jay under wing and tail" follows the wing instruction and so seems to call for jay feathers in the fly wing.

"Wings of the drake" we again construe to mean sections of flight quills. The wings of the stone fly (in flight) are large and conspicuous. They could have been dressed large. Cotton gives this specific instruction and we follow it.

No. 4 Ruddy Fly (May)

The treatise: "In the begynnynge of May a good flye. the body of roddyd wull and lappid abowte wyth blacke sylke: the wynges of the drake & of the redde capons hakyll."

The archaic word *roddyd,* probably the past participle of the verb *rud* (*O.E.D.*), meant red or ruddy; and the word is clarified by Mascall, who gives the fly the title "Ruddy Fly."

"Wings of the drake and of the red capon's hackle" can be interpreted as a dual wing, and "wings" could be conventional wings of hackle wound on. If they are hackle wings, they could be conventional hackle or palmer. Hills does not say so outright, but implies a conventional hackle for this fly as well as for the others where hackle is mentioned: ". . . the basis of the fly, red hackle, is the same in both: the wings are not different."

This is a critical point. If the fly is tied with a conventional hackle, this must be done without specific instruction from the treatise to do so. If it is a hackle fly, it seems more likely to be a palmer, since the palmer tie appears to be the only hackle fly known to the seventeenth century.

If, on the other hand, it is a dual-wing fly, the order of placing the materials is important. It makes sense to veil the mallard quill sections with red-hackle points.

Hills considers the Ruddy Fly to have a modern counterpart in the Red Spinner (imago of the blue dun); Skues in the Great Red Spinner (imago of the March brown).

No. 5 The Yellow Fly (May)

The treatise: "The yelow flye. the body of yelow wull: the wynges of the redde cocke hakyll & of the drake lyttyd yelow."

The instruction "wings of red cock's hackle and of drake dyed yellow" again presumably refers to a dual wing. Some of Cotton's flies call for this dyed quill. The order of hackle and quill is reversed from that of the Ruddy Fly, but we assemble the materials as before: dyed quill veiled by hackle points. Hackle points on the inside are useless, as they would be obscured by the more opaque mallard quill.

No. 6 The Black Leaper (May)

The treatise: "The blacke louper. the body of blacke wull & lappyd abowte wyth the herle of þe pecok tayle: & the wynges of þe redde capon wt a blewe heed."

Does "with a blue head" refer to the bird (red capon) or the fly? As noted previously, if it refers to the fly an ambiguous direction becomes quite clear.

Taking the alternative interpretation, that it is the red capon that has the blue head, what feather and what color feather is implied? Both Hills and Skues take this alternative (without explanation), and both adopt hackle feathers. They do not specify the color of the hackle, although Skues implies red (Red Palmer). The argument could be advanced that a blue feather was intended. But the case for any hackle feather is weak in the absence of the word *hackle* in the directions. It is specified in two other dressings, so why not here, too, if it is actually intended?

All in all, a blue-feather interpretation is very subjective and seems to be tinged with wishful thinking from the fly tier's point of view. A blue-headed fly is not the most satisfying creation for a purist to contemplate. But a blue-headed fly is not much more startling than a yellow stripe down the side of a body, yellow under wing or tail, or wings tied on with brown hemp.

No. 7 Dun Cut (June)

The treatise: "The donne cutte: the body of blacke wull & a yelow lyste after eyther syde: the wynges of the bosarde bounde on with barkyd hempe."

The yellow stripe down the side and wings wrapped with barked hemp are, doubtless, clues to the identity of this fly. The bodies of many insects give the impression of being divided by a lighter line in the distribution of the back and belly color patterns.

"Wings of the buzzard" we take to mean sections of flight feathers. These are specified in Markham (and likewise by Mascall) as "the wings of the wings of a *Buzzard*."

"Barked hemp" is a rope cord steeped in a dye made of the bark of certain trees (for the preservative action).

Hills thinks the Dun Cut is a May fly, the yellow dun; Skues, "beyond question" the sedge fly or Welshman's Button of Halford.

No. 8 Maure Fly (June)

The treatise: "The maure flye. the body of dolke wull the wynges of the blackest mayle of the wylde drake."

Dolke does not appear in the *Oxford English Dictionary*. Dusky is the interpretation evident or implied in Mascall and Markham.

Maure, for them, becomes "moorerish" and "morish." Hills believes Mascall misread *maure*. Actually, *maure* and *moor* are legitimate synonyms in fifteenth- and sixteenth-century English. The *O.E.D.* gives *maure* and *moure* as obsolete forms of *moor* and the connotation of the word as dusky, with a 1489 example of usage: ". . . he became as blacke as a moure." *Maure* also meant "ant," but elsewhere in the treatise the word *pysmire* is used for ant.

Hills seems to make a good case here for the subimago of the May fly (green drake, *Ephemera danica*) as the natural meant by the treatise. Skues thinks it is the alder fly.

No. 9 Tandy Fly (June)

The treatise: "The tandy flye at saynt Wyllyams daye. the body of tandy wull & the wynges contrary eyther ayenst other of the whitest mayle of þe wylde drake."

Tandy becomes "tawny" in Mascall and Markham.

This is the only fly with directions for the form, or forming, of the wing. The literal translation would be "wings opposite, one against the other." This Hills interprets as meaning feathers set "back to back," which seems reasonable. The implication of these instructions seems to be that the identity of the two light mallard breast feathers should be preserved after they are set on the hook.

As with the Maure Fly, Hills makes a case for the imago of the May fly (gray drake, *Ephemera danica*). Skues thinks it is the oak fly.

No. 10 Wasp Fly (July)

The treatise: "The waspe flye, the body of blacke wull & lappid abowte wt yelow threde: the winges of the bosarde."

This fly's name and dressing are obviously related and provide another example of the treatise copying nature. (Skues says "probably a crane fly.") The *O.E.D.* gives only a primary meaning of *wasp* as referring to the natural insect.

Should the body be formed in an hourglass shape? It would not take much ingenuity or imagination to tie it that way. Perhaps the wings would also have been tied flat. We have presented an alternate Wasp Fly tied this way. This fly and the following Shell Fly will give the reader examples of the down-wing interpretation which generally we have rejected.

"Wing of the buzzard" is presumed to refer to flight feathers. By Markham's time the directions called for "wings of the downe of a Buzzard."

No. 11 Shell Fly (July)

The treatise: "The shell flye at saynt Thomas daye. the body of grene wull & lappyd abowte wyth the herle of the pecoks tayle: wynges of the bosarde."

This fly has a history that may be associated with the present grannom. The color and material fit this insect rather well. As Hills points out, the treatise date of the fly (July) is late for the actual emergence dates, but many of the caddis would be grannomlike in general appearance. Skues says the Shell Fly is "probably one of the green-bellied sedges."

The name Shell Fly is curious. If it is the grannom, or other caddis, could this refer to the case or "shell" or the larva?

Wings of buzzard flight feathers would be tied-down wings if the fly were a strict imitation, but we have not assumed such strictness, and, as we said above, we find that the weight of the evidence is for uprights.

No. 12 Drake Fly (August)

The treatise: "The drake flye. the body of blacke wull & lappyd abowte wyth blacke sylke: wynges of the mayle of the blacke drake wyth a blacke heed."

Drake (like *dun*) has a specialized meaning in fly-fishing. It refers to adult May flies. As in the case of *dun*, it seems likely that *drake* in the entomological sense was not intended in the treatise. The earliest *O.E.D.* example of this usage is in 1658 (Franck's *Northern Memoirs*): "It was only with dracks that I killed these trouts." The *O.E.D.* also gives *Drake-Fly*, meaning "an artificial fly dressed with breast feathers of a drake," and cites the treatise as an example.

Cotton gives another plausible reason for the association of ornithological and entomological meanings: ". . . and his [green drake] tail turns up towards his back, like a mallard, from whence, questionless, he has his name of the Green-drake." *Drake*, as synonymous with the May fly, or May flies in general, was evidently well established by the mid-seventeenth century.

One has to dispose of precisely what is meant by "mail of the black drake with black head." There seem to be at least four possibilities:

(1) As proposed by Hills: "some specially coloured dark mallard feather, only to be found on a black headed drake."

(2) Also by Hills: "black head refers not to the bird but the feather, and means one with a black or dark base."

(3) The reference was to the drake of another species of duck that had a black head.

(4) "With a black head" refers to the fly, not the bird (the interpretation spelled out in Markham: ". . . and his head make blacke").

Of these, No. 2, favored by Hills, seems a far-fetched interpretation. Hills apparently intuitively assumes that "black drake" means "black mail of the drake," and this would not be unreasonable if one could dispose of "with a black head." The fourth alternative above can be considered on the same basis as "red capon with a blue head" (Black Leaper), and we have followed it with a black-headed fly. Alternatives 1 and 3 are in effect the same except that Hills held to a variation of the mallard rather than a different species of duck.

The problem with changing the species of bird is that *drake* has the special meaning of male of the mallard, and it does not seem reasonable that the treatise would expect breast feathers from a different duck to be used. *Drake* does have the more generalized meaning of males of any species of duck. In British fauna the choice of alternative species is not great, and narrows to two alternatives, and of these, the tufted duck is an easy first choice. But because the fly is named Drake Fly, one needs to be cautious about going against the primary connotation of the word as used elsewhere in the treatise.

One last question. The trout-fly dressings are taken from the first printed version of the *Treatise of Fishing*, published in 1496. They occur near the end of the treatise. The earlier manuscript version of the treatise, about 1450, has no trout flies. This is not surprising, for the manuscript version is only a large fragment of the whole; its last several pages have not survived. The question is, were the flies in the original treatise? There are three possibilities: (1) Wynkyn de Worde copied the list from the original manuscript exactly, except for his usual changes in spelling, punctuation, syntax, etc.; (2) he took a simpler list from his original and added to it from other sources; (3) he got the entire list somewhere else. We are inclined to accept the first because the descriptions of the flies sound like the writer of the manuscript, and the printed text contains abbreviations which de Worde might copy but which he would be less likely to write himself. There are also indications in the manuscript that the writer intended to describe the dubbing of hooks. On page 7, after listing all the things that an angler must know (including how to dub the hooks), the author promises that they will be depicted: "All þese ȝe schall fynd expressed openly to your ye." From this one might conclude that it is possible that the original manuscript contained not only descriptions of the flies but also pictures of them. In the Middle Ages *dub* meant "disguise."

PART TWO

CHAPTER 6

Facsimile, with Transcript, of the Yale Wagstaff Manuscript of the Treatise

This is the first printing of a facsimile of the manuscript of the *Treatise of Fishing.**

On opposite pages, line for line, is printed a transcript of the treatise, to help with reading the hand.

In the transcript the text of the manuscript has been preserved as faithfully as is practicable. Punctuation has been modernized, and capitals have been added to supplement those of the manuscript. As one may see in the facsimile, the original punctuation and capitalization are of little value for interpretation of the text. All abbreviations have been expanded in italics, and suprascript letters have been brought down to the line. Any letters added to restore parts of words that have faded completely or been cut off by the binder are enclosed in square brackets. Obviously redundant words or letters, whether stricken through in the manuscript or not, are in diamond brackets. Doubtful readings are queried in the footnotes, where they are preceded by "Read:" or "R:". In a very few instances, the transcript contains a letter or two not visible in the facsimile, either because these letters are partially faded and can be read only when the manuscript is held at a certain angle to the light or because they are too close to the binding at the center margin to be photographed. These readings are usually unmistakable in the manuscript.

* Considering that the Yale Wagstaff manuscript is more than 500 years old, it has remained in remarkably good condition. However, portions of the text, particularly in the corners, have faded somewhat. In photographing the manuscript for the facsimiles in this volume, a film was used which would reproduce as accurately as possible the manuscript in its present condition, while, at the same time, making the faded portions as legible as possible.

Salamon in hys parabolis seith þt a glad spyryt makyt a flowryng
age That ys to sey a feyr age & a longe and sith hyt ys so
I aske þis question wyche bynne þe menys & cause to
reduse a man to a mery spyryt Truly vn to my symple
discrecion it semyth me that good & honest disportis and
gamez yn wyche a man ioyth wt owt any
repent and Then it folowyth þt gode & honest disportis
by cause of mannys fayr age and longe lyfe Ther for
now woll y chese of iiij good disportis and honest
gamys þt ys to sey of huntyng hawkyng fowlyng
and fysshyng namely anglyng wt a rod or a yerde
a lyne and a hoke and þer of to treyt as my symple
wit may suffice both for the seyde reson of Salomon
And also for the reson of physyke makyd yn þis wyse

Si tibi deficiant medici medici tibi fiant
Hec tria mens leta labor & moderata dieta

That ys to sey yf a man lak leches or medicyne he
schall make iij thynges his medicyne or leches and he
schall neu nede no mo The first of theym ys mery
thowght The ij is labur mesurably The iij ys
good dyet of clene mete & drynkes sesonable
First then yf a man wyl be mery & haue a glad

1

Salomа*n* in hys p*ara*boles seith þ*at* a glad spirit maket a flowry[n]g
age—That ys to sey, a feyr age & a longe. And sith hyt ys so,
j aske þis questyon, "Wyche bynne þe menys & cause to
reduse a man to a mery spryte?" Truly, vn-to my sympul
5 discrescon, it semyth me, <god> good & honest dysport*es* and
games jn wyche a mans hert joythe w*ith*-owt any
repentans. Than þis folowythe, þ*at* good & honeste disport*es*
by cause of mennys far age and longe lyfe. Ther-for
now will y cheys of iiij good disport*es* and honest
10 gamys, þ*at* ys to sey, of huntyng, haukyng, fowlyng,
and fyschyng, namely anglyng w*ith* a rod or a yarde,
a lyne, and a hoke; and þ*er*-of to treyt as my sympul-
nes may suffice, boith for the seyde reson of salonon
and also for the reson of physyke mayd yn þis wyse.
15 Si tibi deficiant medici, medici tibi fiant
H*ec* tria—mens leta, labor & moderata dieta.
That ys to sey, yf a man lak leches or medicens, he
schall make iij thyng*es* hys medicens or leches, and he
schall neu*er* neyd to mo. The fyrst of them ys mery
20 thowght. The ijd is labur mesurably. The iijd ys
good dyet of cleyn met*es* & drynkes sesenable.[1]
ffyrst þen yf a man wyl be mery & haue a glad

[1] Or: sesonable.

hys spyryt he must eschewe all othyrs copulynge and all
places of deth and sykenes where he myght haue caus
seen of malencoly and yf he wyl haue a labour not
ouer grete. he must the orden hym to hys herte
plesens in swet study pensyfulnes of trauel & mo
preocupacion occupacion wyche may greue hys
herte and hys spyrit in honest maner and yf he
wyl dyet hym selfe mesurably he must eschew all
places of fest wyche is cause of surfett and seknes
and he must drawe hym to a place of swete eyr
and therfore to ete norysshynge mete & desyrabel
I wyl now descryue the seyd iiij dysportes and shewe
to fynd the best of them as wyll as I can. All
be it that the worthy nobul duke of yorke late calle
mayster of the game hathe descryued the myrthes
of huntynge lyke as I thynke to schewe of it and
all the other the game for huntynge as to myne entent
is to grete labour the hunter must all day renne
& folow hys houndes trauelyng & swetyng ful
sore he blowethe tyl hys lyppes blyster and
when he wenyt hyt be an hare ful often hyt is
an hegge hogge thus he chaset and when he
cumes home at euen. hys beton sore prykud

2

<spry> spryt, he must eschew all *contra*ryus *com*panye and all
places of debat*es* and stryves, wher he myȝt haue occasyon of malencoly. And yf he wyl haue a labur not
outrages, he must the[2] orden hym to hys hert*es*
5 plesens, w*ith*-owt stody, pensifulnes, or trauel, a mery <ocupocon> occupacion wyche may reioyse hys
hert and hys spryit in honest man*er*. And yf he
wyl dyet hym selfe mesurably, he must eschew all
places of ryot, wiche is cause of surfett*es* and seknes,
10 and he must draw hym to a place[3] of sweyt <er> eyr
and hungre, & ete norysching met*es* & defyabul.
Y wyl now dyscryve the seyd iiijor disport*es* and gamys
to send[4] the best of them as wyll as y can. All
be it þat þe ryȝght nobul duke of ȝorke, late calde
15 mast*er* of the game, hathe dyscryved the myrthes
of huntyng, lyke as y thynke to scrywe (of it and
all þe other) þe greuys. ffor huntyng, as to myne ente*n*t,
is to gret labur. The hunter must all day renne
& folow hys hownd*es*, travelyng & swetyng ful
20 soyr. He blowythe tyl hys <lyf> lyppys blyst*er*, and
wen he wenyt hyt be a hare, fuloftu*n* <hys> h*i*t
ys a heyghoge. Thus he chaset, and wen he
cu*m*met home at even, reyn beton, soyr prykud

[2] Read: tho, (?) the*n*. [3] Altered to: plac*es*. [4] R: fend, i.e., find.

wt thornes and hys clothes tornes wet shod & ful myry
sū of hys howndes lost som surbatted suche greves
& many or to the hunter happeth which for dysples
sing of them yt lovyth hyt I dar not report All
Therfor me semyt that yt ys not the best disport
and game of the seyd iiij Hawkynge

The disporte and game of hawkyng is laborous
and noyous also as me semyth & it is very
thewth. The fawkener often tymes losyth hys
hawkes ye hunter hys howndes then all hys disport
ys gon and don. ffull often he cryeth & whyste
tyl he be ryght evyl a thurst hys hawke takyth a bowe
and lyst not onys to hym rewarde when he wolde
have hur for to fle. The wyl she bathe wt
wt mysfedyng she schall have the ffrownce
ye Rye ye crampe and many other sekenes that bryng
them to ye sowse. Thus me semyth be good
prefe but this be not ye best game of the seyd
iiij

ffowlyng

The disporte and game of fowlyng me semyth
most symplest for yn the season of somer ye fowler
spedyt not. But yn ye most hardest & coldest weder

with thornes and hys clothes tornes,[5] wetschod, fulwy,[6]
sum of hys howndes lost, som surbatted—suche grevys
& mony oþer to the hunter hapeth, wiche for disple-
sons of hem þat louyth hyt j dar not report all.
5 Trewly me semyt þat þis ys not the best disport[e]
and game of the seyd iiijor. Hawkynge
Thys disporte and game of hawkyng is laborous
and ryght noyous also, as me semyth, & it is very[7]
trowthe. The fawkner often tymes leseth hys
10 hawkes, þe hunter hys houndes; þen all hys dispor[tes]
ben gon and don. ffull ofton he cryethe & wyste[leth]
tyl he be sor a-thryst. Hys hawke <k> taket[8] a-bowe
and list not onys to hym reward wen he wolde
haue her for to fle. The wyl sche baythe. <with>
15 With mysfedyng þen schall sche haue the frounce,
þe Rey, þe Cray, and mony oþer seknes þat bryn-
get hur to þe souce. Theise me semyth be good
profet, but the be not þe best gamys of the seyd
iiijor. ffowlyng
20 The disporte and game of fowlyng me semyth
most symplvest,[9] for yn the season of somer þe fowler
spedyt not. But yn þe most herde & colde wedyr

[5] R: torn. [6] Or: fulwey. [7] Part of *y* cut off.
[8] Crossed out (by mistake?). [9] Or: sympleest.

4

he is sore greved for he wolde go to hys tymes he
may not for colde. Many a tym and many a fryday he
mysset a mele he loset yn þe mornyng he walket
yn the dew he geteth also wet schode and sore a colde
to dyner by the morow by the morow and sum tyme
to bed or he have wel souped for any thynge þt
he may gete by fowlyng. Many other suche I
can reherse but my mayster of anger maket me to
lef. Thus me semyth þat huntyng, hawkyng
and fowlyng be so laborous & grevous þat non of
them may perfourme to enduce a man to a mery
spryt þe whyche is cause of longe lyfe acordyng
to the seyd parabul of Salomon

Fysshynge

Dowtles then folowyth it þat it must nedys be
þe disporte and game of fyshyng wt an
angul rode for all oþer maner of fysshyng is also
ryght laborus and grevous often causyng men
to be ryght wete and colde whyche many tymes
hath be seyn the cheyf cause of infyrmytes and
sum tyme dethe. But the angler may have no
colde ne no disese ne angyr but he be causer hym

4

he is soyr greved, for he wolde go to hys gynnes; he
may not for colde. Many a gyn and many a snayr he
maket, & mony he leset. Yn þe mornyng he walket
yn the dew; he goyth also wetschode and soyr a-colde
5 to dyner by the morow, <by the morow> and su*m* tyme
to bed, or he haue wyl sowpud for any thynge þ*at*
he may geyt by fowlyng. Mony other syche y
can rehers, but my magyf or angr*e* maket me to
leyf. Thys me semyth, þat huntyng, haukyng,
10 and fowlyng be so laborous & greuous þat non of
them may p*er*forme to enduce a man to a mery
spryȝt, þe wyche is cause of longe lyfe acordyng
to the seyd p*ar*abul of salomon.

ffyschynge

15 Dowtles, then folowyth it þat it must nedys be
<b> þe disporte and game of <fyff> fyschyng w*ith* an
angul-rode—for all o*þer* man*er* of fyschyng is also
ryght laburs and grevous, often causyng men
to be ryght weyth and colde, wyche mony tymes
20 hathe be seyn the cheyf cause of jnfyrmyte and
su*m* tyme deythe. But the angleer may haue no
colde ne no disese ne angur but he be causer hym

selfe for he may not gretly lese but a lyne or an
hoke of wyche he may haue plente of hys owne
makyng or of oþer mennes as thys symple tretes
schall teche hym so then hys loste ys no greuous. And oþer greuous may he haue non but
yf any fysshe breke a way from hym when he
ys vp on hys hoke in londyng of the same fysch
or els þatt ye ta for þatt he catche not þe wych
be no gret greuans ffor yf he fayl of on he may
not fayle of a noþer yf he do as thys tretes folowyng sch
yn forme hym but yf þer ben non yn þe watur wyþ
he schall angul And yet at þe leste he schall haue hys
holsom walke & mery at hys owen ese And also many
a swete ayr of dyuers erbis & flowrs þat schall make
hym ryght hongry & well dysposid in hys body he
schall here þe ~~melodyus~~ melodious of þe armony of
byrde he schall se also þe yong swannys & sygnettes
folowyng þer damys Duckes Cootes herons & many
oþer fowlys wyþ þer brodys wyche me semyt bettur þan
all þe noyse of houndys & blastes of hornes & oþer gammys
þat fawkeners & hunters can make or els þe gammes
þat fowlers can make And yf þe angler take þe fysshe
surely þan ys þer no man merryer þan he ys in hys

selfe, for he may not gretly lose but a lyne or an
hoke, of wyche he may hayf plente of hys owyn
makyng or of oþ*er* mens, as thys sympul tretes
schall teche hym; so then hys loste ys no gre-
5 vons. And oþ*er* grevons may he haue non, But
yf any fysche breke a-wey from hym wen he
is vp-on hys hoke in londyng of the same fych[e],
or els þat ys to sey, þat he cache not, þe wich
be no greyt grevons. ffor yf he fayl of on, he may
10 not faylle of a-noþ*er*, yf he do as thys tretes folowys sch[all]
yn-forme hym—but yf þ*er* ben non yn þe watur wer[10]
he schall angul. And ȝet at þe leste he schall haue hys
holsom walke & mery at hys own ease and also mony
a sweyt eayr of dyuers erbis & flowr*es* þ*a*t schall make
15 hyt ryght hongre & well disposud in hys body. He
schall heyr þe <molodyes> melodieus[11] of þe Ermony of
bryde. He schall se also þe ȝong swanniys & signet*es*
folowyng þer Eyrours, Duck*es*, Coot*es*, herons, & many
oþ*er* fowlys w*ith* þer brodys, wyche me semyt bett*er* þen
20 all þe noyse of hound*es* & blast*es* of hornes & oþ*er* gamys
þ*a*t fawkners & hunters can make or els þe games
þ*a*t fowlers can make. And yf þe angler take þe fysche
hardly, þen ys þ*er* no man meryer þen he is in hys

[10] Half of *r* cut off. [11] Or: melodious.

6

spryte Also whoso woll use ye games and disportes of
anglynge he muste take hede to thys sentence of the
olde poete yt is thys wyse

Surgere mane mane si vis vivere sane

Sanctificat sanat ditat quoque surgere mane

That is to sey he must ryse erly ye wiche thing
is yt grett avayle to man yn thys wyse On
is for helthe of the sowyl for yt schall cause
hym to be holy & he schall be wel set to god
The secunde is yt schall cause bodely helthe and
schall cause hym to lyfe longe The thrydde yt
schall cause hym to be ryche wordly and gostly
yn goodys & goodnes That same I proved in myne
entent yt the disporte of anglynge is the
very meyn yt causeth a man to be mery spryte
wyche aftur ye sayd parabel of Salamon and the
doctryne of physyke maket a floryng age
and longe lyfe and therfor to all yo yt be vertuos
gentyls & fre borne I wryte and make thys symple tretes
folowynge by the wyche ye may have ye ful
crafte of anglynge to sport yow at yowr
luste to the entent yt yowr age may be mor
flore and ye lenger endure Then yf ye wyll

6

sprit*es*. Also whoso wol vse þe game and disporte of
angleyng, he muste take hede to thys sentence of the
olde p*rouer*be, þ*at* is, thise v*er*sus:
Surge, miser, mane *set* noli surger*e* vane;
5 Sanctificat, sanat, ditat quoq*ue* surger*e* mane.
This is to sey, he must ryse erly, þe wiche þing
<ry> ys ryght p*ro*phetabul to man yn thys wyse. On
is for helthe of the sowyl, for hyt schall cause
a man to be holy yf eu*er* he schall be wel set to god.
10 The ijd cause is it schall cause bodely helthe and
schall cause hym to lyfe longe. The iijd, hyt
schall cause hym to be ryche, wordly and gostly,
yn goodys & goodnes. þ*us* haue y p*ro*ued in myne
entent þat the disporte of angelynge is the
15 very meyn þ*at* causeth a man to be mery spyryt,
wyche, aftur þe seyd p*ar*abol of Salomo*n* and the
doctrine of physyke, maket a flowryng age
and longe lyfe. And þerfor to all þo þ*at* be v*er*tuose,
gentyle, & fre borne, j wryite þis sympul tretes,
20 folowynge by the wiche ȝe may haue þe ful
crafte of angelyng to sport ȝow wi*th* at ȝowr
luste, to the yntent þ*at* ȝowr age may be mor
flour*e* and þe lengur endur. Then yf ye wyll

be crafte yn angelyng ye muste fyrst lerne to make
your harneys that ys to sey yor rod yor lynes of dy
colors & yor hokes aft^r that ye muste knowe how
ye schall angel & yn what places of the wat
how depe & what tyme of the day for what ma
of fysche in what weder how many impedimen
ther ben yn anglyng and especially yn what bayt
to dyuers fyssches fysche yn eche moneth in y^e
yer how ye schall make your bayt bred wher ye
schall fynde hem & how ye schall fynde them &
how ye schall kepe them hem and for ye most
crafty thyng how ye schall make yor hokes of
steyl & of osmonde som for ye to dub & som for y^e
flote as ye schall here aftyr all thes ye schall fynd
expressed openly to youre ye

how ye schall make
your rodde

And how ye schall make yor rodde craftely I schall
tell how ye schall kytte be twene mychelmas and
candulmas a fayr staf euyn of a vj fote long
or more as ye lyst of hasyll wylowe or aspe and
bete hem in a hote ouen when ye bake & sette hem dry
right as ye can make them then let them cole &

7

be crafte yn angelyng, ye must furst lurne to mak[e]
ȝowr harnes, þat ys to sey, yo*ur* rod, yo*ur* lynys of dy[uerse]
colers, & yo*ur* hokes. Aft*ur* þat ye must know how
ȝe schall angel & yn wat places of the watu[r];
5 how depe & wat tyme of the daye for wat ma[ner]
of fysche in wath wedur; how many jmpedimen[tes]
þer ben yn anglyng; and especially w*ith* wat bay[tes]
to eu*ery*[12] dyu*er*se <fyssches> fysche yn yche moneth in þ[e]
ȝer; how ȝe schall make ȝowr bayt*es* brede, wher ye
10 schall fynde þem, & how ȝe schall fynde them, &
how ȝe schall kepe <them> þem; and for þe most
crafty þyng, how ye schall make yo*ur* hokes of
steyl & of osmonde, som for þe to dub & som for þe
flote, as ye schall her aftur. All þese ȝe schall fynd
15 expressed openly to your ye.

How ye schall make ȝowr rode

And how ȝe schall make yo*ur* Rodde craftely, j schall
tell ȝow. Ye schall kytte betwene mychelmas and
20 candulmas a feyr staf evyn of a vj fote long,
or mor as ye lyst, of hasill, wilowe, or aspe, and
beke hem in a ovyn when ye bake, & set hym evy[n]
ryght as ye can make hym, þen let hym cole &

[12] Inserted above.

ys a fayre wykes or mor Then take & bynd hym
fast wt a gud corde un to a forme or to an evyn squyr
tree & then take a plumers wyr yt is evyn & strong
& scharpe at ye one ende then hete the scharpe ende
in a charcol fyr tyl hyt be hote & perse ye staffe ye
wt therow ye pyth of the seyd staffe ffyrst at ye on
ende & sythen at ye other tyll hyt be therow & then
take a byrd spytte & bren hym as ye same tyll it
be to thyne entente in a man as a taper of wax
& wex them then let hym ly stylle two days aft
tyl hyt be therow colde then unbynde hym & let
hym drye yn a smoke hows or yn a hous rof tyl
hyt be therow drye In ye same seson take a yerde
of whyte hasel & bethe hym evyn & streyght &
let hym drye yn ye same wyse as hyt ys seyd of
the staffe and when they be drye make ye yerde mete
un to the hole of the seyd staffe yn to ye halfe
staffe lenkyt lyngth and to performe ye other halfe
of ye crop Take a fayr schoyt of blake thorne
crabtre medeler or Ienepr cut yn ye same seson
and wel bethed and streyght & bynd them to
gedyr fetely so yt ye crop may justly entyr all
in to ye seyd hole then schame the staffe ~~wt at~~

8

drye a fowr wykes or mor. Then take & bynd hym
fast *with* a good corde vn-to a forme or to an evyn squar
tree, & þen take a plumars wyr þ*at* is evyn & strong
& scharpe at þe oon ende. þen hete the scharpe ende
5 in a charcol fyr tyl hyt be hote & pers þe stafe þ*er*-
with thorow þe pith of the seyd stafe. ffyrst at þe oon
ende & sithen at þe other tyll hyt be thorow, & than
take a bryd spytte & bryn hym as ye seme tyll it
be to thyne entente in a man*er* as a tapur of wax,
10 & wax hym. Then let hym ly stylle two days aft*ur*
tyl hyt be thorow colde, tan vn-bynde hym & let
hym drye yn a smoke howse or yn a howsroyf tyl
hyt be thorow drye. In þe same seysen take a yarde
of white hasil & beth hym even & streighte, &
15 let hym drye yn þe same wyse as hyt ys seyd of
the stafe; and wen they be drye, make þe yarde mete
vn-to the hole of the seyd stafe yn-to þe halfe
stafe lynket lyngh. And to p*er*forme þe other halfe
of þe crop*pe*, Take a feyr schoyt of blake thorne,
20 crabtre, medeler, or genep*er*, cut yn þe same sesun
and wyl bethed and streyght; & bynd hem to-
gydur fetely so þ*at* þe cropp*e* may justly entur all
in-to þe seyd hole. Then schaue the stafe <wel at>

bothe endes And make hyt tapur wyse whenne
then whyte þe staff wel at bothe endys wt hopis
of yron or laton wt a pyke yn þe nether ende festnyd
wt a remevyng wyse to take in & out þe crop
Then set your crop an honful wt yn þe over ende
of your staffe in suche wyse þt it be als bigge
ther as any other place a bove Than arme your
crop at þe over ende down to the frete wt a lyn
of vj heres & double the lyne & frete hyt fast
yn þe top wt a bowe to fasten on an yor lyne And þus
shall ye make you a rode so prevy & fete þt ye
may walke þer wt And ther shall no man wyt
wher a bowt ye go And hyt wyl be lyȝt &
nemyll to fysshe wt at your plesur & devyce

To colo your lynes

After that ye have made your rodde ye must lern
to colour your lynes of here in thys wyse Fyrst ye
must take of a whyte horse tayle þe longest here
that may be had & ever the rounder ye better it
is & whan ye have departyd it at vj partes then
colour ever parte by hyt selfe in dyvers colours as yn
to yelow grene browne tawny russet and dusky

9

<bothe endes> and make hyt tapur-wyys waxing.
þen virell þe staff wel at bothe endys *with* hopy[s]
of yren or laten, *with* a pyke yn þe neþ*er* ende festnyd
with a remevyng vise to take in & owt þe crop*pe*.
5 Then set your crop an honful *with*-yn þe ovir ende
of ȝowr stafe in suche wyse þ*at* it be also bigge
ther as any other place a-bove. Than arme ȝow*ur*
crop at þe ovir ende down to the frete *with* a lyn[e]
of vj herys & double the lyne & frete hyt fast
10 yn þe top *with* a nose to fasten an yo*ur* lyne. And þ*us*
schall ye make yow a rode so p*er*fet & fete þ*at* ȝe
may walke þ*er*-*with*, and þer schall no man wyt
wer a-bowt ye go, and hyt <b> byl[13] be lyȝt &
nemyll to fysche *with* at yowr plesur & devyce.

15 To colo*ur* your lynes

Aftur þat ye haue made ȝowr rodde, ye must lern
to colur your lynys of heyr in þys wise. ffyrst y[e]
must take of a wyht hors tayle þe lengest her
þat may be had, & evyr the rounder þe better it
20 is. & when ye haue dep*ar*tyd it at vj p*ar*tes, þen
coler eu*er*y p*ar*te by hyt selfe in dyu*er*s colers, as yn-
to yelow, Grene, Broune, Tawny, Russet, and duskyn

[13] R: wyl.

colour. ffyrst to make yowr yelo ger. Take smale ale
a potell and stamp it wt an handful of walnot leves
and a quart of alom & put them all to geder
in a clene panne & boyle them wel to geder & when
it ys colde put yn yowr ger that ye wyll have
yelow tyl hyt be as derk as ye wyl have it &
then take hyt owte

To make grene colour

ye schall take smale ale the quantyte of a quarte
& put it yn a lytul panne and put therto halfe an
alom & do yowr ger therto & let hyt boyl halfe a
nowyr then take yowr ger & let hyt drye then
take a potell of watyr and put hyt yn a panne
& put therto of welde or woden the handful & presse
hyt down wt a presse and let hyt boyle soft by
halfe a nowyr and when hyt yelow in the flame
put the yn yowr ger and the worth halfe a lb of
copyrose wel beten yn to pondyr & let it boyle
halfe a myle wey and then set hyt down & let
hyt it cole v or vi myndes & then take owt yowr
ger & let hyt drye & yef ye schall have the
best grene that may be for the watyr and the more
that ye put to of the copyrose the grener hyt wyl
be

10

colur. ffurst, to make ȝowr ȝelo her: Take smale ale
a potell and stamp it w*ith* iij handful of walnot levys
and a quart*er* of alom, & put them all to-gedur
in a bras panne & boyle hem wel to-gedur; & wen
5 h*i*t ys colde, put yn ȝowr heyr þat ye wyll haue
ȝelow tyl hyt be as dyrk as ye wyl heue it, &
þen take hyt owte.

To make grene colour

Ye schall take smal ale þe quantyte of a quarte
10 & put it yn a lytul panne and put þ*er*-to halfe lb
alom, & do ȝowr her þ*er*-to & let hyt boyl halfe a
nowyr. Then take ȝowr her & let hyt drye. þan
take a potell of watur and put hyt yn a panne,
& put þ*er*-to of welde or waxen ijto handful, & presse
15 hyt down w*ith* a peyse, and let hyt boyle softly
halfe a nowyr. And wen hyt ȝelow in the skome,
put þ*er*-yn yowr her and þ*er*-with halfe a lb of
coporose wel beton yn-to poudur, & let it boyle
halfe a myle wey. And then set hyt down & let
20 <byyt> it coyl v or vj owres, & then take owt y*our*
here & let hyt drye, & þer ye schall haue þe
best greyn þ*a*t may be for the watur. And þe moyr
þ*a*t ȝe put to of the cop*er*as, the grener hyt wyl
be.

11 85

Wyth how many heeres ye
schall angle wt for any fysshe

Ffyrst for the menewes wt a lyne of on heer for the
waxyn roche the bleke and the gogyn & the ruffe wt a
lyne of ij heres ffor the dace & the grete roche wt
a lyne of iij heres ffor the perche the flounder the
breme wt a lyne of iiij heres ffor the cheven chobe
the tenche the ele wt a lyne of vj heres ffor the
trowt the grelyng and the barbyl and the grete
cheven wt a lyne of ix heres ffor the grete
trowt the grelyng & the perche wt a lyne of xij
heres ffor a Samon wt xv ffor the pyke ye
schall take a good fyne lyne of silke twynde made
in maner of a chalke lyne made hoven wt ye
colour as ye a for sayd endurand wt wyre for by the
lyne & fynding then lynys must be plumed
wt lede and the next plumme to the hoke schall be
ther from a large fote & more and euery plumbe
of quantite of the gretnes of the lyne Ther
be iij maner of plumbyng ffyrst for a ground
lyne rennyng and for the flote set upon the

11

Wyth how many herys ye schall angle w*ith* for eu*er*y fysche

ffyrst for the menewes, w*ith* a lyne of on heyr. For þe
wexen Roche, the bleke, and the gogyn, & þe Roffe, w*ith* a
5 lynne of ij herys. ffor the Dare & þe greyt Roche, v*ith*
a lyne of iij herys. ffor the perche, the flounder, þe
breme, w*ith* a lyne of iiij herys. ffor the cheven chobe,
the tenche, the Ele, v*ith* a lyne of vj herys. ffor þe
trowyt, the grelyng, and þe barbyl, and þe greyt
10 <chevys> cheven, w*ith* a lyne of ix herys. ffor þe gret
Trowt, þe grelyng, & þe perche, w*ith* a lyne of xij
herys. ffor a Samon, w*ith* xv. ffor the pyke, ye
schall take a good fyne lyne of pak thryde, made
yn man*er* of a chalke lyne made browne w*ith* y*our*
15 colour as ys a-for seyd, enarmyd w*ith* wyre for by-<þ>
<tl> tyng a-sundur. Your lynys must be plomed
w*ith* leyd, and þe next plume to the hoke schall be
ther-from a large fote & more, and eu*er*y plu*m*be
of quantite of þe gretnes of the lyne. þer
20 be iij man*er* of plumbyng. ffyrst, for a grond[14]
lyne rennyng and for the floyt set vppon the

[14] Or: groond.

grounde lyne lyneth a x plummys rennyng all to gedyr
On the grounde lyne lyneth a xx or x smale plumbes
For the flote plumbe hym so hevy that the lest plukke
of any fysshe may pulle hym downe in to the
watyr and make them rounde & smothe that thei
stik not on stones or weedys whiche wolde let yow
gretly in the disporte of angelynge

How ye schall make your flotis

Ye schall make your flotis in this wyse Take a
fayr corke that ys clene withoute many holes
bory hit thorow with a smale hote yren & put
it yn a penne and the gretter hole Than.
schape them yn maner of a dove egge lesse and
mor as ye wylle & make them smothe a pon a
grynston and your flote for on heer be no byger
then a pese for xii heere as a bene for xx heer
as a walnot and so forthe euery lyne after the
rate All maner of lynes must have a flote
to angle withe save only the grounde lyne and the
rennyng grounde lyne must have a flote The
lyinge grounde lyne withoute floote

grounde lyne lying, a x plumys re*n*nyng all to-gedur.
On þe gronde lyne lying, a xx[15] or x smale plu*m*bes.
ffor þe floote, plumbe hym so hevy þ*a*t þe lest ploke
of any fysche may pluke hym doune yn-to þe
5 watur. And make hym rounde & smothe þ*a*t þei
fast not on stones or weedys, wyche wolde let yow
gretly in yo*ur* disporte of angelynge.

How ye schall make your flot*es*

Ye schall make ȝowr flot*es* in þys wise. Take a
10 feyr corke y*a*t ys clene w*ith*-oute many <hol> hoolys,
boyr hyt þorow w*ith* a smale hoyt yru*n*, & put
þ*er*-yn a penne at[16] þe gretter hoole. Then[17]
schap hem yn man*er* of a dove egge, lesse and
mor as ȝe wylle, & make hem smothe a-pon a
15 gynston. And yowr floyt, ffor on heyr, be no byg-
ger a pese; for ij herys, as a beyn; for xij her*es*,
as a walnot, and so forthe, eu*er*y lyne aftur hys
gretnes. All man*er* of lynes must haue a floyt
to angle w*ith*, saue only þe gronde lyne, and the
20 rennyng ground lyne must haue a floote. The
lying ground lyne w*ith*-ovte floyte.

[15] R: ix(?). [16] Corrected from: and. [17] Or: Than.

13 8 4

Here many man[er] of anglyng
þat þer bene

Now I haue lerned you to make yor harnes now wyll I tell
you how ye schall understonde þat þer be vj man[er] of anglyng
oon is at þe grounde for þe troute a nother at þe grounde at
an arche of a brydge or at a standyng wer þer it ebbeth
or floweth for bleke roche and darse the iij is wt
wt owt flote for all man[er] of fysche the iiijth is a menow
for the troute wt owte plumbe or flote the same man[er]
of roche and darse wt a lyne of j or ij herys batyd
wt a flye the vjth is wt a dubbed hoke for the troute
troute & graylyng and for the principall point of
anglyng kepe you ev[er] from þe water and from þe syȝt
of fysche for on the londe or els be hynde a busche
or a tre þt ye fysch see you not for yf the do
the wyl not byte and loke ye schadow not the watt[er]
as meche as ye may for þt ys a thynge wyche
wyl a fray þe fysche and yf the be a frayd the
wyl not byt a good wyle after ffor all man[er]
of fysche þt fedyt by the grounde ye schall
angle to them by the [illegible] in the myddes of the
water & som tyme mor be nerthe than a bone
for on þe most fysche the nor the bytte þe botom

13

How many man*er* of anglyng*es*
þat þer bene

Now j haue lerned ȝow to make yo*ur* hernes, now wyll j telle
ȝow how ye schall vnderstonde þat þer be vj man*er* of anglyng.
5 Oon is at þe grounde for þe troute. A-nother at þe gromde[18] at
an arche of a brydge or at a stondyng, wer hyt ebbethe
or flowethe, for <s> bleke, Roche, and Dare. The iijd is <w*ith*>
w*ith*-owt floote for all man*er* of fyche. The iiijth, w*ith* a meney
for the troute w*ith*-oute plumbe or floote; the same man*er*
10 of Roche and Darse w*ith* a lyne <ofj> of j or ij herys batyd
w*ith* a flye. The vth is w*ith* a dubbed hooke for the <troote>
troute & gralyng. And for the principall poynt of
anglyng, kepe you eu*er* from þe watur and from þe syȝt
of fyche, fer on the londe or els be-hynde a busche
15 or a tre, þ*at* þe <fyf> fysche see yow not; for yf he do,
he wyl not bytte; and loke ye schadow not the wat*ur*
as moche as ye may, for hyt ys a thynge[19] wyche
wyl a-fray þe fyche, and yf he be a-frayd he
wyl not byt a good while aftur. ffor all man*er*
20 of fyche þ*at* fedyt by the grownde, ye schall
angle to hym <by the gro> in the mydd*es* of the
watur, & som deyl moyr be-neythe þen a-boue;
for eu*er* þe gret*er* fyche, the ner he lythe þe botu*m*

[18] Or: groonde. [19] The g from half-formed *k*.

of þe watter and the smaller fyche comenly frequentyth
a bone. The iij good poynte ys when þe fyche
bytetth þt ȝe be not to hasty to smyt hym nor to
late ye must abyde tylle ye suppose þat þe bayte
and the hoke be welle yn the mowthe of the fyche
and then stryke hym and þys ys for the grounde
and for the flote when ȝe se hyt pulled softely
under the watter or ele caryed upon þe watter
softly then smyte hym and se þt ȝe neu(er) ou(er)
smyt þe strength of youre lyne for brekyng
and yf he hap to stryke a grete fyche wt a
smalle lyne ye must lede hym in the water
and labour þer tyll he be overcome and weryd
Than take hym as well as ye may and be ware
þat ȝe holde not ou(er) þe strenght of youre lyne
and yf ȝe may yn any wyse let not hym ou(t)
at the lynes ende streyght from yow but
kepe hym eu(er) ye rod and eu(er) holde hym
streyght ~~from ...~~ So þt ȝe may susteyne
hys lepys & hys plumbes wt the helpe of
youre handes

In what place is best
anglyng

of þe watur, and the smaler fyche comenly swy*m*myth
a-bove. The vjd good poynte ys, when þe fyche
byteth, þ*at* ȝe be not to hasty to smyt hym nor to
late. Ye must a-byde tylle ye suppose þat þe bayte
5 and the hoke be welle yn the mouthe <f> of the fyche,
and then stryke hym. And þys ys for the grounde.
And for the floot: wen ȝe thy*n*ke[20] hyt pulled softely
vndur the watur or els caryed vpon þe watur
softly, then smyte hym. And se þ*at* ȝe neu*er* ou*er*-
10 smyt þe strynght of ȝowr lyne for brekyng.
And yf he[21] hap to styke[22] a gret fyche w*ith* a
smayl lyne, ye must leyd hym in the wat*ur*
and labur þer, tyll he be ouercome and weryd.
Than take hym as well as ye may, and be war
15 þat ȝe holde not ou*er* þe strynght of ȝowr lyne.
And yf ȝe may yn any wyse, let not hym on
at the lynes ende stregiht from ȝow, but
kepe hym eu*er*[23] þe rod, and eu*er* holde hym
streight. <from yow> So þ*at* ȝe may susteyn
20 hys lepys & hys plumbes w*ith* the helpe of
yowr honde.

In wat place is best angleyng

[20] Written over original: ley. [21] R: ye. [22] R: stryke. [23] Omitted: vndur(?).

In wynter ye [illegible] in warme placess of the watir
ye schall angle to your best spede ye schall an-
~~gle~~ angle yn a pole or yn a standyng watir yn
any place that it is any thyng ~~depe~~ depe ther is no
grete chyse in a pole for it is but a preson
to fysche and thei have moste parte in preson and
hunger as a presoner therfor it is the lesse mastry
to take them But in ryvers ye schall angle
any place wher it is depe and clere by the
grounde as gravel or clay without ~~mudde~~
mudde or wedes and specialli yf ther be a whirly
~~whirly~~ pyt of watir or a coverte as an ~~holow~~
holow banke or grete rotes of trees or long
wedys flotyng abone the watir wher the fysche
may ~~cov~~ cover them at dyvers tymes Also in depe
stiff stremys and yn fallis of wateris and weris
flode gates and mylle pittes and wher the watir
resteth by the banke and the streme renneth nye
ther by and ys depe and clere by the grounde and
yn other places wher ye may se any fysche hov-
yng and fede abone

What tyme of the day
is best to anglynge

15

<In> Her y wyll declar in wat places of the watur
ye schall angle to yowr best spede. Ye schall <an>
<gh> angle yn a pole on[24] yn a stondyng watur yn
eu*er*y place þ*er* it is any-þyng <dop> depe. þer is no
5 grete choyse in a pole, for it is but a pryson
to fysche, and þei lyve moste p*ar*te in preson and
hungre as a presoner. þ*er*-for it is þe lesse mastry
to take hym. But in rewarde ye schall angle
eu*er*y place wher it is depe and clere by þe
10 grounde, as grauel or clay w*ith*-owtu*n* <mude>
mudde or wedes, and especiall yf þer be a werly[25]
Wherly pyt of watur or a couerte, as an <halow>[26]
holow banke or greyt rott*es* of treys or long
wedys flotyng a-boue þe watur, wher þe fysche
15 may <cu> cou*er* hym at dyu*er*se tymes. Also in depe,
stiff stremys and yn falles of watur[27] and weer*es*,
flode gates, and mylle pitt*es*, and weyr þe watur
restith by the banke & þe streme renneyth nye
þ*er*-by and ys dep & clere by the grounde; and
20 yn oþ*er* places wher he[28] may se any fyche how-
vyng and fede a-bove.

Facsimile, with Transcript, of the Yale Wagstaff Manuscript of the Treatise

Wat tyme of þe day is best to angleyng

[24] R: or. [25] Redundant(?). [26] Above: hol(?). [27] From: waturs. [28] R: ye.

ye schall wete yͤ best tyme is to angle from the
be gynnyng of may un to Septembyr the bytyng
tyme ys erly by the morow from iiij at cloke un
to viij at aftur none from iiij un to viij but not
so good as is in ye morow and yf hyt be a colde
westerne wynde and a derke lowryng day
then wyl yͤ fysshe comynly byte all day ffor
a derke day is moche better yen any oyer
clere wedyr from the be gynnyng of Septembyr
un to ye ende of Apryle spare no tyme of the
day also many pole fysshe wyl byte best in
none tyme and yf ye se any tyme of the
day ye trowt or the Grayling lepe angle
to hym wt a dub accordyng to the same moneth
and wer the watyr ebbyt and flowythe ye
fysshe wyll byte in some place at ye flode
all aftr yat yei same restyng by hynde pylys
or arches of bryggys and oyer suche places

In what wedyr is best
anglyng

ye schall angle as y seyde be for yn derke low-

Ye schall wete þe best tyme is to angle from the
be-gynnyng of May vn-to Septembr*e*. The byty*n*g
tyme ys erly by the morow from iiij at cloke vnto viij; At aftur none from iiij vn-to viij, but not
5 so good as is in þe morow. And yf hyt be a colde,
westeling wynde and a darke, lowryng day,
þan wyl þe fysche co*m*mynly bite all day. ffor
a darke day is moche betur þen any oþer
cleyr wedur. From the be-gynnyng of september
10 vn-to þe ende of apryle, spare no tyme of the
day. Also mony poyl fysche wyl bytte beste yn
none tyme. And yf ye se any tyme of the
day þe trowyt or the graylyng lepe, angle
to hym w*ith* a dub accordyng to the same moneth.
15 And wer the watur ebbyt and flowythe, þe
fysche wyll bite in some place at þe floode,
all aft*ur* þat þei haue restyng by-hynd pilys
or arches of brigg*es* and oþer suche places.

In wat wedur is best
20 angleyng

Ye schall angle, as y seyde be-for, jn darke low-

ynne mornyng when the wynde bloweth softely And
yn som season when hyt ys thonneryng hote [illegible]
from September vn to Aprill and yn a feyr sonne
day ys good to angle in And yf the wynde yn that
season haue any pte of ye oriente [nought] ye wedir then
ys good and wen hyt ys a grete wynde when
hyt ys snowyng reynet or hayleth thondryng or
tempest lightnyng or also warmyng hote then [it] ys not
to angle The xij impedymentis
Whyche causis men to take no fyshe wt oute oþer
comyn causes whyche may casuelly happe The
first yf your harnes be not good and well
made The ijd is yf ye angle not yn bytyng
tyme The iijd yf þe fyshe be afrayde wt
ye syght of any man The iiijth yf þe water be
very thykke whitte or rede as of ... lye of any
flood falle late The vth yf the fyshe stere
not for colde or fere The vjth is yf þe water [to]
be very hote The vijth yf it reyne The viijth

17

ryng wedur when the wynde blowethe softely and
yn som*ur* seasen when hyt ys brennyng hote. Jt is[29]
from September vn-to Apryl and yn a feyr sonne
day ys good to angle in. And yf the wynde þat se-
5 san haue any p*ar*te of þe northe,[30] þe wetur þen
ys good. And wen hyt ys a greyt wynde, when
hyt <ys> snowyt, reynet or haylyth, thonderyt or
<lent> lightneth, or also nimynge hoyt,[31] þ*at* ys not
to angle.

10 The xij jmpedyme*ntes*

Wyche cause men to take no fyche, w*ith*-oute oþir
co*mm*yn causes wyche may casuelly hap. The
fyrst, yf yowr harnes be not good and well
made. The ijd is yf ye angle not yn bytyng
15 tyme. The iijd, yf þe fyche be a-frayde w*ith*
ye syȝt of any man. The iiijthe, yf þe watur be
wery thikke, whitte, or redde as <of ley> lye of any
floyd falle late. The vd, yf the fyche styr
not for colde or feyr. The vjte is if þe watur
20 be wery hote. The vijte, yf it reyne. The viijth,

[29] Something omitted(?). [30] Written above (and as correction of): oriente. [31] Or: heyt.

of hyt hayl or snowe. The v. yf þer be any tempest of any
wyndes. The vi. yf hyt be a grete wynde by any coste.
The vii. yf hyt be by the northe or northe est or sowthe
est. For comenly nother by wynter nor by somer yf þe wynde
blowe any of thes costs the fysshe wyll not comenly
byte ne stere. The west and þe sowthe be ryght good
but of þe two þe sowthe ys þe better.

Baytis to angle with — Baytes et c.

And now y haue tolde yow how to make yowr harnes
And how ye schall fysshe þerwith. Then reson wyll þat
ye knowe with what baytys ye schall angle to euery maner
fresche fysche watyr of fysche in euery moneth of þe yer
whyche ys pryncypall effecte of the dysport of angleyng. And but whyche baytys knowen all yowr
crafte [illegible] worth a warlethe lytell or nowght
to þe purpose. For ye cannot bryng a hoke to a fysche
mowthe but yf þer be mete theron to hys plesyr.

Bayt for the samonde

And for be cause þe samond ys þe most goodly fysshe
þat man may angle to in freshe watyr, þerfor

18

yf hyt hayl or snowe. The ix, yf þ*er* be any tempest of any
<ver> ve*þer*. The x, yf hyt be a greyt wynde by any coste.
The xij, yf hyt be by the northe or northe Est or sowthe
est; for co*m*menly ne*þer* by wynt*ur* nor by som*er*, yf þe wynde
5 haue any p*ar*te of þys cost*es*, the fysche wyll not co*m*mynly
byte ne styre. The west and þe sowthe be ryght good,
ʒet of þe two þe sowth is þe bettur.

Baytis to angle w*ith*[32]

And now y haue tolde yow how to make ʒowr harnes
10 and how ʒe schall fysche þ*er*-w*ith*, then reson wyll þat
ye know w*ith* wat baytys ye schall angle to eu*er*y man*er*
<fyche> freche watur <f> fyche in eu*er*y moneth of þe ʒer,[33]
whiche ys pryncipall effecte of þys <dis>[34] disport of angleyng. W*ith*-owt wyche baytys knowen, all ʒowr
15 craft*es* heyr a-foyr wryton a-waileth litull or nowʒt
to þe porpos, for ye cannot brynge a hoke to a fyche
mouthe but yf þ*er* be mete ther-on to hys plesur.

Bayt for þe samonde

And for be-cause þe samond ys þe most goodly fyche
20 þ*at* man may angle to in fresche watur, þ*er*-for j

[32] In later hand: bayt*ess*, etc. [33] Or: ʒ*ere*. [34] Or: <dif> (?).

rosses to be tyme wt hym The Salmond ys a gentyll
fysche but he ys cumbrus to take for comynly he ys but
yn grett dep wateris and grete ~~ryue~~ Ryueris And
for the more pte he holdet the myddul of the streme that
a man may not cu to hym easly and he ys in seson
from the moneth of marche vn to mychelmas In which
seson ye schall angul to hym wt thes baytys when they
may be had fyrst wt a boke like as ye do to the trowt
wt a menowe and wt a red worme in the begynnyng
and the endyng of the seyde seson and also wt a worme
that bredyt yn a dounghyll and specially wt a
souerent bayt that bredyt yn the watyr sedul but
hyt bytyt not at the grounde but at the flote Also
ye may hap to take hym but hyt ys seldum
seyn wt a dub at the tyme lepyng lyke as ye do a
trowyt or a gralynge

ffor the trowte

The trowyt ys a deyntet fysche and a fre bytyng
he ys in the seson as the seson ys he wyl not be
but yn clene gravel grounde wattyr and yn a
streme and ye may angle to hym at all tymys

porpos to be-gynne w*ith* hym. The samond ys a gentyl
fyche, but he ys cu*m*burs to take, for com*m*ynly he ys but
yn ryght dep waturs and greyt <ryu*ers*> Ryu*e*res, and
for the moyr p*ar*te he holdet þe mydul of þe streym þ*at*
5 a man may not cu*m* to hym easly. And he ys in season
from þe moneth of marche vn-to mychelmas, jn wyche
seson ye schall angul to hym w*ith* þys bayt*es* when þey[35]
may be had. Fyrst, w*ith* a bleke, like as ye do to þe trowt
w*ith* a menows, and w*ith* a red worme in þe begynnyn*g*
10 and þe endyng of þe seyde season, and also w*ith* a worme
þ*at* bredyt yn a <b> donghyll, and especially w*ith* a
sou*er*ent bayt þ*at* bredyt yn þe watur sokul. But
hyt bydyt not at þe grounde but at þe floot. Also
ye may hap to take hym (but hyt ys seldim[36]
15 seyn) w*ith* a dub at hys leping, lyke as ye do a
trowyt or a gralynge.

ffor þe Trowte

The trowyt ys a deyntet fyche & a fre bytyng.
He ys in þe season as þe season ys. He wyl not be
20 but yn cleyn grauel grounde watur and yn a
streme. And ye may angle to hym at all tymys

[35] From: pe. [36] Or: seldun.

wt a grounde lyne lyinge and rennynge fisshynge yn lepyng
tyme a pon wt a dubbe and oyer wyse a oyer grounde
lyne and fossyr more yn ye day wt a flote lyne ye schall
angle to hym in marche wt a menew hangend on yor
howe hoke by ye nesse lyp wt owt flote or plumbe
drawyng up a down in ye streme tyll ye fele
hym fast In ye same seson angle to hym wt a
grounde lyne wt a red worme for ye most sur
In Aprylle take ye same bayte also ye same seson
take a pyppe also ye canker yt bredyt in a
doke yart and ye red snayle In may take a ston
flye and ye bob vndur ye cow torde and the
dew worme and a bayt yt bredyth on a fyrne
tre lefe In June take ye red worme & nyp
of ye hed & put on ye hoke a codworme by
forn In Julye take ye litle red worme and ye
codworme to gedyr In August take ye flye
ye lytyl red worme the fatte bakon & bynde ye
hoke In Septembyr take ye red worme &
ye menow In octobyr take ye same for yey
be speciall bayts for ye trowyt all tymys

20

w*ith* a grownde lyne lying and rennyng, sauyng yn lepy*n*g
tyme, a þen w*ith* a dubbe; and erly wyth a erly grounde
lyne, and forþ*er*-moyr yn þe day w*ith* a floyt lyne. Ye schall
angle to hym marche w*ith* a menew hangud by
5 yowr hoke by þe neþ*er* lyp, w*ith*-owt floote or plumbe,
drawyng vp & down in þe streym tyll ȝe feyl
hym fast. In þe same seson angle to hym w*ith* a
grownde lyne w*ith* a red worme for þe mor sur.
In a-pryle take þe same bayt*es;* also þe same seson
10 take a pryde, also þe canker wyche bredyt in a
doke royt, and þe red snayl. In may take a ston
flye, and þe bub vndur þe cow torde, and the
dor worme, and a bayt þ*at* bredyth on a pyne
tre lefe. In june take þe red worme & nyp
15 of þe hed, & put <of> on þe hoke a codworme by-
foyr. In <l> julye take þe litle red worme and þe
codworme to-gedur. In august take þe flye,
þe lytyl red worme, the herlesoke, & bynde þe
hooke. In september take þe red worme &
20 þe meneys. In octobr*e* take þe same, for þey
be especiall bayt*es* for þe trowyt all tymys. . . .

Facsimile, with Transcript, of the Yale Wagstaff Manuscript of the Treatise

CHAPTER 7

Description and History of the Manuscript

DESCRIPTION

The manuscript here shown in facsimile is a slender volume in a nineteenth-century binding, as it was when Mrs. David Wagstaff presented it to the Yale University Library. Without the modern added leaves (not reproduced here) the manuscript proper consists of ten paper leaves (twenty pages).

Thomas Satchell in his edition (Preface, p. i) described the manuscript as "written on five sheets of paper folded in quarto form." Precisely what he meant by this would be hard to say, for the manuscript was long ago taken apart into its individual leaves and mounted with modern paper. It has also been interleaved with paper sheets containing a transcription, presumably that mentioned by Haslewood in his prefatory note (Haslewood, p. 63). At some time the manuscript was rather severely trimmed by a binder, so that on several pages letters have been cut off at the outer margins. The leaves now measure about seven and one-half by five and one-half inches, the written area averaging about seven by five inches. The number of lines per page varies from twenty to twenty-four, as follows: 22, 23, 22, 22, 23, 23, 23, 23, 22, 24, 21, 21, 23, 23, 23, 21, 20, 20, 21, 21.

The manuscript proper is written on a smooth, heavy paper of the fifteenth century, which has yellowed somewhat but shows little sign of real deterioration. About the middle of the left side of pages 3, 7, 13, and 17 (reversed on pages 4, 8, 14, 18), parts of a watermark are visible in the manuscript but not in the facsimile. It can be seen in the manuscript only by holding it up to the light. From the portions remaining, the watermark appears to have been a gauntleted hand with a six-pointed star attached by a short line to either the index or the middle finger. The ink in which the body of the text is written has faded to a light brown but is still clear and legible. Writing, punctuation, and marks of deletion all appear to be in the same ink and are, no doubt, all by the same scribe. Page numbers at the tops of the pages are in a modern hand, and some letters (cf. especially pages 1, 2, 18, 19) may have been touched up, or traced over, in a darker ink sometime after the manuscript was written. A few marginal scribblings in Latin, apparently modern, may be seen in the facsimile; their significance, if any, is not easily discovered.

There is little decoration in the manuscript. Patterns of lines, rough parallelograms, have been drawn about a number of the section headings and around *þer* (page 11, line 19). These and the bracket linking the lines of the Latin quotation on page 1 are in red ink. Capitals in the manuscript have been decorated with red; parts of the letters are outlined or traced over in red ink, or open spaces in the letters are filled with red patches. This ornamentation is unsystematic, rather amateurish in appearance, and seems to have been added by the copyist as an afterthought or put in by a later hand. The first letter of a section heading or the first letter of text following it may (or may not) be so ornamented; similarly, the first letter of a line of quotation or the first letter of text following the quotation. First letters of certain words are apt to be decorated: *Solomon* (twice), *Trout* and *Salmon* (page 11), *May* (page 16, line 2), *September* (16, 2; 17, 3), *august* (lower case, 20, 17), colors in the list on page 9 (including lower-case *y* and *d*). Oddest perhaps is the decoration of the *l* and *s* of *Also* (16, 11). Apart from the words mentioned, initial *T* is most frequently reddened (more than thirty times); *A*, *B*, and *ff* are reddened occasionally; and *I* is reddened six times on page 20.

The script is a fifteenth-century informal hand, not a book hand and probably not the work of a professional scribe. The letter-forms, as may be seen in the facsimile, are normal for the fifteenth century, rather more typical of the first half than of the second. Certain letters (*e*, *o*, *r*, *s*) have two distinct forms each—apart from capitals. Although the manuscript distinctions between *i* and *j*, *u* and *v*, are retained in the transcription, they are not linguistically significant, these pairs being interchangeable in the text, both as vowels and as consonants. The pairs *n* and *u, c* and *t,* are frequently alike in form and can be distinguished only by their context. There are two letters which may be unfamiliar to a modern reader: þ, called "thorn" and pronounced like *th;* and ȝ, called "yogh" and pronounced like *y* in some words, like German *ch* in others. A double *f* is often used as a capital.

Ligatures, or combinations of two or more letters in which the letter-forms may be somewhat modified, occur sporadically; e.g., *re* in *repentans* (1, 7), *de* in *yarde* (1, 11), *st* in *fyrst* (1, 19), *ro* in *Eyrours* (5, 18). These are more easily recognized than described.

Abbreviations are frequent; e.g., those for *and* (1, 5; 1, 7); *con-* in *contraryus* (2, 1); *-er* in *þer-of* (1, 12), *master* (2, 15); *-es* in *dysportes* (1, 5); *hit* (2, 21); *pound* (10, 10); *par-* or *per-* in *paraboles* (1, 1) and *performe* (4, 11); *pro-* in *profet* (3, 18); *-ra-* in *contraryus* (2, 1); *þat* (1, 1) and *yat* (12, 10); *-ur* in *your* (7, 2), *aftur* (8, 10), *colour* (9, 15); *-us* in *þus* (6, 13); *with* (1, 6). Three abbreviations occur only in the Latin quotations; i.e., those for *haec* (1, 16), *-que* (6, 5), and *set* (for *sed,* 6, 4). A bar or macron may mean one of several things: an *m* as in *companye* (2, 1), an *n* as in *mens* (1, 16), an *e* as in *croppe* (8, 22), *pe* as in *croppe* (8, 19), or *c* as in *especiall* (20, 21). A curl over a final letter is usually a mere flourish, but occasionally it seems to have been intended as a macron; e.g., in *surgere* (6, 4) and *fuloftun* (2, 21).

There are frequent errors of an obvious sort (one reason for supposing that the copyist was not a professional) in which a letter, word, or phrase has been written twice, sometimes because the first writing contained an error, sometimes through careless double copying. There are also instances in which something has been copied from the wrong line of the exemplar; e.g., *by the gro* (13, 21), cf. *by the grownde* (13, 20). Such redundancies are not erased. Many, but by no means all, are deleted, apparently by the copyist himself. A word or phrase is scratched out with a horizontal line (or with two lines) drawn through it. One or two letters may be deleted by virgules, while the *s* of *waturs* (15, 16) is deleted with an *x*-mark.

The present manuscript is obviously copied, as is indicated by the scribe's occasionally taking the text from the wrong line. We have already noted *by the gro.* We may also compare *wel at bothe endes* (8, 23 to 9, 1) with *wel at bothe endys* (9, 2). Further instances will be found. Another indication of copying is the section headings on pages 14 and 15, which appear at the very bottoms of the pages, while the sections to which they belong begin at the tops of the following pages. In the original the size of leaves must have differed from the size in the copy, and presumably these headings appeared properly above their sections.

There are two places in which the manuscript has been altered in a different manner. In "he must draw hym to a place of sweyt eyr" (2, 10), *place* has been changed to *places,* giving "to a places," which was as incorrect in the fifteenth century as it is now. The 1496 print has "he must drawe him to places of swete ayre." The alteration in the manuscript could have arisen in one of three ways: (1) the copyist made a careless mistake, writing "to a place" where his exemplar had "to places," then corrected *place* to *places* but forgot to delete the *a;* (2) the copyist thought to improve upon his original, changed *place* to *places,* leaving it for some later copyist or an editor to make the grammar consistent, as it is in the print; (3) the author used our manuscript as a rough working copy, and hasty revisions were to be incorporated into a neater, fairer copy afterward. Of these, (2) is unlikely since the manuscript and the print appear to be independent of each other, separate developments from the original treatise. Either (1) or (3) could be the explanation; hence nothing can be concluded positively. But the possibility that we have in the manuscript a copy made for, or by, the author for the author's own use is an interesting one and well worth keeping in mind. Again, "euery maner fyche" (18, 11–12) is altered to "euery maner freche watur fyche"—a change which does not appear in the 1496 print. This is clearly not a correction, but a deliberate alteration. Fifteenth-century scribes were entirely capable of taking liberties with an author's text; some of them fancied themselves able to improve upon Chaucer's poetry. But again, there is the possibility that this is a change introduced by the author—one which did not get into the copy from which the print was made. The two alterations are not intrinsically significant. They add little or nothing to the value of the treatise on angling, and are important only in that they may perhaps point to the author revising the work.

The manuscript does not contain the complete treatise. Between page 10 and page 11 there is a gap which can be filled from the more complete text of 1496. This gap, assuming that nothing of consequence has been added to the later version, would be equal to about six pages (or three leaves) of the manuscript. The latter breaks off at the bottom of page 20 in the midst of the baits for the trout. If we assume that nothing of any length was added in 1496 except the "Order to anglers" ("Here folowyth the order," etc.), which differs in style and tone from the rest of the work, the loss would be a trifle less than fourteen pages or seven leaves. We may, therefore, estimate roughly that about half of the manuscript has survived.

HISTORY

The earliest modern reference to the manuscript is in Haslewood's edition of the *Book of St. Albans* (1810), pp. 63–64:

> There was a fragment of this treatise, in manuscript, in the possession of the late typographical historian, William Herbert. His own transcript therefrom, where he says "from a very ancient manuscript, penes W. H." I have inspected. It extends to the instructions respecting the trout, and stops with the bait to be used in September. Sig. h. vj *rev.*

He added that the transcript mentioned was at that time "in the possession of John Townley, Esq."

This is clearly our manuscript, which breaks off near the end of the baits for trout, at a point corresponding to about the middle of the verso of signature H.6 in the 1496 print. The short passages quoted by Haslewood (Haslewood, p. 64) contain things obviously copied from our manuscript, including the erroneous repetition of "by the morow" (4, 5). William Herbert (1718–95) was a bibliographer and the author of *Typographical Antiquities, or an Historical Account of the Origin and Progress of Printing in Great Britain and Ireland* (1785). He was a collector of early printed books and manuscripts. During the latter part of his life he resided at Cheshunt, Hertfordshire. At his death, part of his collection was held together and found its way to the British Museum, but our manuscript was in the portion of his library which was dispersed.

The transcript made by Herbert (not the manuscript itself) was acquired by John Townley and seen by Haslewood some time before 1810. This was not the transcript which is now interleaved with the manuscript. Haslewood's quotations indicate that the old transcript had some small errors where the later one is correct; and the quotations, on the other hand, give a few correct readings where the later transcript is in error or leaves a blank.

It thus appears that at the time Haslewood wrote his book he had seen only Townley's transcript and not the original manuscript. Later, however, he acquired the manuscript itself. In a note which he prefixed to the manuscript in 1821, and is now attached to the manuscript in the Yale library, Haslewood sheds further light on its history, as follows:

> The following twenty pages is the fragment of a manuscript of the earlier part of the xvth Century and forms a considerable portion of the "little pamphlet" first printed in the Book of St. Albans, anno 1496. It is the same manuscript as is noticed in the introduction to the reprint of that volume (p. 63.) as formerly in the possession of the typographical historian William Herbert who transcribed same and that copy is there referred to as then possessed by the late Mr. Townly. The original, here preserved, passed from the possession of Herbert to Mr. Brand and from him to the late George Isted Esq. who presented it to me a few months before he died. It was bound with other manuscripts of less interest and value. A paginary transcript was added for the convenience of reading, wherein it will be found the letter *y* is occasionally substituted for the Saxon compound character þ or th.

The Brand referred to is probably John Brand (1744–1806), an antiquary and author of *Observations on Popular Antiquities* (1777), who must have acquired the manuscript in 1795 or shortly thereafter. His library was sold at auction in 1807–8, after his death, the manuscript being purchased by George Isted, who gave it to Haslewood. The latter separated it from the manuscripts with which it had been bound, added three illuminations in gold and colors plus his own historical note, and had the whole rebound in calfskin by C. Lewis in 1823. The added leaves, which are modern imitations of medieval manuscript art and form no part of the original manuscript, consist of a coat of arms, a title page, and a painting of a fisherman. The last is a copy, considerably modified, of the woodcut prefixed to the 1496 print. The title page presents the manuscript as *A Treatise of Fishing with an Angle.* The coat of arms may be that of Joseph Haslewood, although it does not resemble the arms of any Haslewood family to be found in the better-known works on modern heraldry. The arms appear not to be those of any branch of the Berners family, nor do they seem to belong to William Herbert. At his death in 1833, Haslewood's library was sold.

The manuscript now passed from antiquarians to anglers and angling writers. We next find it in the hands of Edward Jesse (1780–1868), author of *An Angler's Rambles* (1836) and *Lectures on Natural History, De-*

livered at the Fisherman's Home, Brighton (1861) and editor of Isaak Walton and other writers on angling. His library was sold at auction in November 1868, at which time Alfred Denison purchased the manuscript for his extensive angling collection. According to Thomas Satchell (Preface, p. i), the price paid was forty-five shillings—a rare bargain. This paltry price was probably due to a belief, in spite of Haslewood's statements, that the manuscript was nothing more than a copy in longhand of a part of the 1496 print.

In 1883 Satchell edited Denison's manuscript in an edition of four hundred copies for the English Dialect Society "and others," with the title *An Older Form of the Treatyse of Fysshynge wyth an Angle* and as the first member of the series called "The Library of Old Fishing Books." Letters from Satchell to Denison in 1883 (now in the possession of the Yale University Library) reveal that the significance of the manuscript was at last beginning to be felt. On February 27 Satchell wrote that he had submitted the treatise to Mr. Sims of the British Museum Department of Manuscripts, who had "pronounced it to be a genuine manuscript of the first half of the 15th century: the time (say) of Henry 5th" [i.e., 1413–22]. On March 31 he wrote that W. W. Skeat had examined the manuscript and judged it to have been written in "1450 or even earlier." Skeat, after comparing the manuscript with the printed version, did not believe that the dialectal variations were of a sort to indicate a different place of origin for the manuscript. He was convinced, however, that the manuscript was completely independent and not a mere copy of the print. Satchell suggested that the treatise was probably a translation from French or Latin and that "the original treatise may be lurking in some library on the Continent or even here." "I am having a search made," he says, "through the Catalogues of manuscripts in the National French Library and elsewhere." The search referred to was apparently without result, and to this day no one has found any trace of a lost French or Latin original; nor does it read like a translation.

From Denison the manuscript passed to the great angling library of the late David Wagstaff of Tuxedo Park, New York. It was presented to the Yale University Library in 1946 by Mrs. David Wagstaff.

CHAPTER 8

Facsimile, with Transcript, of the First Printed Text of the Treatise

The treatise is reproduced here as it first appeared in print in Wynken de Worde's edition of the *Book of St. Albans* (1496).

On opposite pages, line for line, is printed a transcript of the treatise, to help with reading the print from the old fount.

¶ Here begynnyth the treatyse of fysshynge wyth an Angle.

SAlamon in his parablys sayth that a good spyryte
makyth a flourynge aege / that is a fayre aege & a
longe. And syth it is soo: I aske this questyon / Whi
che ben the meanes & the causes that enduce a man
in to a mery spyryte .: Truly to my beste dyscrecōn
it semeth good dysportes & honest gamys in whom a man Joy
eth wythout ony repentaunce after. Thenne folowyth it ẏ go=
de dysportes & honest games ben cause of mannys fayr aege &
longe life. And therfore now woll I chose of foure good dispor
tes & honeste gamys / that is to wyte: of huntynge: hawkynge:
fysshynge: & foulynge. The beste to my symple dyscrecōn why
che is fysshynge : callyd Anglynge wyth a rodde : and a lyne

Here begynnyth the treatyse of fysshynge wyth an Angle.

Facsimile, with Transcript, of the First Printed Text of the Treatise

Salamon in his parablys sayth that a good spyryte
makyth a flourynge aege/ that is a fayre aege & a
longe. And syth it is soo: I aske this questyon/, whi
che ben the meanes & the causes that enduce a man
in to a mery spyryte.: Truly to my beste dyscrecion
it semeth good dysportes & honest gamys in whom a man Ioy
eth wythout ony repentannce[1] after. Thenne folowyth it þ*a*t gode dysportes & honest games ben cause of mannys fayr aege &
longe life. And therfore now woll I chose of foure good dispor
tes & honeste gamys/ that is to wyte: of huntynge: hawkynge:
fysshynge: & foulynge. The beste to my symple dyscrecion why
che is fysshynge: callyd Anglynge wyth a rodde: and a lyne

[1] Read: repentaunce.

and an hoke/ And therof to treate as my symple wytte may suf
fyce: both for the sayd reason of Salamon and also for the reason that phisyk makyth in this wyse/ ¶ Si tibi deficiant medici
medici tibi fiant: hec tria mens leta labor & moderata dieta.
¶ Ye shall vnderstonde that this is for to saye/ Yf a man lacke
leche or medicyne he shall make thre thynges his leche & medy
cyne: and he shall nede neuer no moo. The fyrste of theym is a
mery thought. The seconde is labour not outrageo9. The thyr
de is dyete mesurable. Fyrste that yf a man wyll euer more be
in mery thoughtes and haue a gladde spyryte: he must eschewe
all contraryous company & all places of debate where he myghte haue ony occasyons of malencoly. And yf he woll haue a
labour not outrageous he must thenne ordeyne him to his her
tys ease and pleasaunce wythout studye pensyfnesse or traueyl
le a mery occupacyon whyche maye reioyce his herte: & in why
che his spyrytes may haue a mery delyte. And yf he woll be dy
etyd mesurably he must eschewe all places of ryotte whyche is
cause of surfette and of syknesse/ And he must drawe him to pla
ces of swete ayre and hungry: And ete nourisshable meetes and
dyffyable also.

Now thenne woll I dyscryue the sayd dysportes and ga
mys to fynde the beste of theym as veryly as I can/ alle
be it that the ryght noble and full worthy prynce the du
ke of Yorke late callid mayster of game hath discryued the myr
thes of huntynge lyke as I thynke to dyscryue of it and of alle
the other. For huntynge as to myn entent is to laboryous/ For
the hunter must alwaye renne & folowe his houndes: traueyl-
lynge & swetynge full sore. He blowyth tyll his lyppes blyster
And whan he wenyth it be an hare full oft it is an hegge hogge
Thus he chasyth and wote not what. He comyth home at euyn
rayn beten pryckyd: and his clothes torne wete shode all myry
Some hounde loste: some surbat. Suche greues & many other
happyth vnto the hunter/ whyche for dysplesaunce of theym yt
loue it I dare not reporte. Thus truly me semyth that this is
not the beste dysporte and game of the sayd foure. The dyspor
te and game of hawkynge is laboryous & noyouse also as me
semyth. For often the fawkener leseth his hawkes as the hun-

and an hoke/ And therof to treate as my symple wytte may suf
fyce: both for the sayd reason of Salamon and also for the reason that phisyk makyth in this wyse Si tibi deficiant medici
medici tibi fiant: Hec tria mens leta labor & moderata dieta.
Ye shall vnderstonde that this is for to saye/ Yf a man lacke
leche or medicyne he shall make thre thynges his leche & medy
cyne: and he shall nede neuer no moo. The fyrste of theym is a
mery thought. The seconde is labour not outrageous. The thyr
de is dyete mesurable. Fyrste that yf a man wyll euer more be
in mery thoughtes and haue a gladde spyryte: he must eschewe
all contraryous company & all places of debate where he myghte haue ony occasyons of malencoly. And yf he woll haue a
labour not outrageous he must thenne ordeyne him to his her
tys ease and pleasaunce wythout studye pensyfnesse or trauey
le a mery occupacyon whyche maye reioyce his herte: & in why
che his spyrytes may haue a mery delyte. And yf he woll be dy
etyd mesurably he must eschewe all places of ryotte whyche is
cause of surfette and of syknesse/ And he must drawe him to pla
ces of swete ayre and hungry: And ete nourishable meetes and
dyffyable also.

Facsimile, with Transcript, of the First Printed Text of the Treatise

Now thenne woll I dyscryue the sayd dysportes and ga
mys to fynde the beste of theym as veryly as I cann/ alle
be it that the ryght noble and full worthy prynce the du
ke of Yorke late callid mayster of game hath discryued the myr
thes of huntynge lyke as I thynke to dyscryue of it and of alle
the other. For huntynge as to myn entent is to laboryous/ For
the hunter must alwaye renne & folowe his houndes: traueyl-
lynge & swetynge full sore. He blowyth tyll his lyppes blyster
And whan he wenyth it be an hare full oft it is an hegge hogge
Thus he chasyth and wote not what. He comyth home at euyn
rayn beten pryckyd: and his clothes torne wete shode all myry
Some hounde loste: some surbat. Suche greues & many other
happyth vnto the hunter/whyche for dyspleysaunce of theym þat
loue it I dare not reporte. Thus truly me semyth that this is
not the beste dysporte and game of the sayd foure. The dyspor
te and game of hawkynge is laboryous & noyouse also as me
semyth. For often the fawkener leseth his hawkes as the hun-

cer his houñdes. Thenne is his game & his dysporte goon. Full
often cryeth he & whystelyth tyll that he be ryght euyll a thur
ste. His hawke taketh a bowe and lyste not ones on hym rewar
de. Whan he wolde haue her for to flee: thenne woll she bathe.
With mysfedynge she shall haue the Fronse: the Rye: the Cray
and many other syknesses that brynge theym to the Sowse.
Thus by prouff this is not the beste dysporte & game of the sa
yd foure. The dysporte & game of fowlynge me semyth moost
symple For in the wynter season the fowler spedyth not but in
the moost hardest and coldest weder: whyche is greuous. For
whan he wolde goo to his gynnes he maye not for colde. Many a gynne & many a snare he makyth. Yet soryly dooth he fa-
re. At morn tyde in the dewe he is weete shode vnto his taylle.
Many other suche I cowde tell: but drede of magre makith me
for to leue. Thus me semyth that huntynge & hawkynge & also fowlynge ben so laborous and greuous that none of theym
maye perfourme nor bi very meane that enduce a man to a me
ry spyryte: whyche is cause of his longe lyfe acordynge vnto yͤ
sayd parable of Salamon. ¶ Dowteles theñe folowyth it that
it must nedes be the dysporte of fysshynge wyth an angle. For
all other manere of fysshyng is also laborous & greuous: often
makynge folkes ful wete & colde/ whyche many tymes hath be
seen cause of grete Infirmytees. But the angler maye haue no
colde nor no dysease nor angre/ but yf he be causer hymself. For
he maye not lese at the moost but a lyne or an hoke: of whyche
he maye haue store plentee of his owne makynge/ as this sym
ple treatyse shall teche hym. Soo thenne his losse is not greuo
us. and other greyffes maye he not haue / sauynge but yf ony
fisshe breke away after that he is take on the hoke/ or elles that
he catche nought: whyche ben not greuous. For yf he faylle of
one he maye not faylle of a nother/ yf he dooth as this treatyse techyth: but yf there be nonght in the water. And yet atte the
leest he hath his holsom walke and mery at his ease. a swete ay
re of the swete sauoure of the meede floures: that makyth hym
hungry. He hereth the melodyous armony of fowles. He seeth
the yonge swannes: heerons: duckes: cotes and many other fou
les wyth theyr brodes/ whyche me semyth better than alle the

ter his houndes. Thenne is his game & his dysporte goon. Full
often cryeth he & whystelyth tyll that he be ryght euyll a thur
ste. His hawke taketh a bowe and lyste not ones on hym rewar
de. Whan he wolde haue her for to flee: thenne woll she bathe.
with mys fedynge she shall haue the Fronse: the Rye: the Cray
and many other syknesses that brynge theym to the Sowse.
Thus by prouff this is not the beste dysporte & game of the sa
yd foure. The dysporte & game of fowlynge me semyth moost
symple. For in the wynter season the fowler spedyth not but in
the moost hardest and coldest weder: whyche is greuous. For
whan he wolde goo to his gynnes he maye not for colde. Many a gynne & many a snare he makyth. Yet soryly dooth he fa-
re. At morn tyde in the dewe he is weete shode vnto his taylle.
Many other suche I cowde tell: but drede of magre makith me
for to leue. Thus me semyth that huntynge & hawkynge & also fowlynge ben so laborous and greuous that none of theym
maye perfourme nor bi very meane that enduce a man to a me
ry spyryte: whyche is cause of his longe lyfe acordynge vnto þe
sayd parable of Salamon. Dowteles thenne folowyth it that
it must nedes be the dysporte of fysshynge wyth an angle. For
all other manere of fysshyng is also laborous & greuous: often
makynge folkes ful wete & colde/ whyche many tymes hath be
seen cause of grete Infirmytees. But the angler maye haue no
colde nor no dysease nor angre/ but yf he be causer hymself. For
he maye not lese at the moost but a lyne or an hoke: of whyche
he maye haue store plentee of his owne makynge/ as this sym
ple treatyse shall teche hym. Soo thenne his losse is not greuo
us. and other greyffes maye he not haue/ sauynge but yf ony
fisshe breke away after that he is take on the hoke/ or elles that
he catche nought: whyche ben not greuous. For yf he faylle of
one he maye not faylle of a nother/ yf he dooth as this treatyse techyth: but yf there be nought in the water. And yet atte the
leest he hath his holsom walke and mery at his ease. a swete ay
re of the swete sauoure of the meede floures: that makyth hym
hungry. He hereth the melodyous armony of fowles. He seeth
the yonge swannes: heerons: duckes: cotes and many other fou
les wyth theyr brodes./ whyche me semyth better than alle the

noyse of houndys: the blastes of hornys and the scrye of foulis
that hunters: fawkeners & foulers can make. And yf the angler
take fysshe: surely thenne is there noo man merier than he is in
his spyryte. ¶ Also who soo woll vse the game of anglynge: he
must ryse erly. Whiche thyng is prouffytable to man in this wy
se. That is to wyte: moost to the heele of his soule. For it shall
cause hym to be holy. and to the heele of his body. For it shall
cause hym to be hole. Also to the encrease of his goodys. For it
shall make hym ryche. As the olde englysshe prouerbe sayth in
this wyse. ¶ Who soo woll ryse erly shall be holy helthy & zely.
¶ Thus haue I prouyd in myn entent that the dysporte & game of anglynge is the very meane & cause that enducith a man
in to a mery spyryte: Whyche after the sayde parable of Salomon & the sayd doctryne of phisyk makyth a flourynge aege &
a longe. And therfore to al you that ben vertuous: gentyll: and
free borne I wryte & make this symple treatyse folowynge: by
whyche ye may haue the full crafte of anglynge to dysport you
at your luste: to the entent that your aege maye the more flou
re and the more lenger to endure.

IF ye woll be crafty in anglynge: ye must fyrste lerne to
make your harnays. That is to wyte your rodde: your
lynes of dyuers colours. After that ye must know how
ye shall angle in what place of the water: how depe: and what ti
me of day. For what manere of fysshe: in what wedyr. How ma
ny impedymentes there ben in fysshynge yͭ is callyd anglynge
And in specyall wyth what baytys to euery dyuers fysshe in e-
che moneth of the yere. How ye shall make your baytes brede
where ye shall fynde theym: and how ye shall kepe theym. And
for the moost crafty thynge how ye shall make youre hokes of
stele & of osmonde. Some for the dubbe: and some for the flote:
& the grounde. as ye shall here after al thyse fynde expressed o-
penly vnto your knowlege.
¶ And how ye shall make your rodde craftly here I shall teche
you. Ye shall kytte betwene Myghelmas & Candylmas a fayr
staffe of a fadom and an halfe longe: & arme grete of hasyll: wy
lowe: or aspe. And bethe hym in an hote ouyn: & sette hym euyn
Thenne lete hym cole & drye a moneth. Take thenne & frette

h j

noyse of honndys:[2] the blastes of hornys and the scrye of foulis
that hunters: fawkeners & foulers can make. And yf the angler
take fysshe: surely thenne is there noo man merier than he is in
his spyryte. Also who soo woll vse the game of anglynge: he
must ryse erly. whiche thyng is prouffytable to man in this wy
se/ That is to wyte: moost to the heele of his soule. For it shall
cause hym to be holy. and to the heele of his body/ For it shall
cause hym to be hole. Also to the encrease of his goodys. For it
shall make hym ryche. As the olde englysshe prouerbe sayth in
this wyse. Who soo woll ryse erly shall be holy helthy & zely.
Thus haue I prouyd in myn entent that the dysporte & game of anglynge is the very meane & cause that enducith a man
in to a mery spyryte: Whyche after the sayde parable of Salomon & the sayd doctryne of phisyk makyth a flourynge aege &
a longe. And therfore to al you that ben vertuous: gentyll: and
free borne I wryte & make this symple treatyse folowynge: by
whyche ye may haue the full crafte of anglynge to dysport you
at your luste: to the entent that your aege maye the more flou
re and the more lenger to endure.

Facsimile, with Transcript, of the First Printed Text of the Treatise

Yf ye woll be crafty in anglynge: ye must fyrste lerne to
make your harnays/ That is to wyte your rodde: your
lynes of dyuers colours. After that ye must know how
ye shall angle in what place of the water: how depe: and what ti
me of day. For what manere of fysshe: in what wedyr How ma
ny impedymentes there ben in fysshyng þat is callyd anglynge
And in specyall wyth what baytys to euery dyuers fysshe in e-
che moneth of the yere. How ye shall make your baytes brede
where ye shall fynde theym: and how ye shall kepe theym. And
for the moost crafty thynge how ye shall make yours hokes of
stele & of osmonde/ Some for the dubbe: and some for the flote:
& the grounde. as ye shall here after al thyse fynde expressed o-
penly vnto your knowlege.

And how ye shall make your rodde craftly here I shall teche
you. Ye shall kytte betwene Myghelmas & Candylmas a fayr
staffe of a fadom and an halfe longe: & arme grete of hasyll: wy
lowe: or aspe. And bethe hym in an hote ouyn: & sette hym euyn
Thenne lete hym cole & drye a moneth. Take thenne & frette

[2] R: houndys.

hym faste wyth a cockeshotecorde: and bynde hym to a fourme
or an euyn square grete tree. Take thenne a plūmers wire that
is euyn and streyte & sharpe at the one ende. And hete the shar
pe ende in a charcole fyre tyll it be whyte: and brenne the staffe
therwyth thorugh: euer streyte in the pythe at bothe endes tyll
they mete. And after that brenne hym in the nether ende wyth
a byrde broche & wyth other broches eche gretter than other. &
euer the grettest the laste: so that ye make your hole aye tapre
were. Thenne lete hym lye styll and kele two dayes. Unfrette
hym theñe and lete hym drye in an hous roof in the smoke tyll
he be thrugh drye ¶ In the same season take a fayr yerde of gre
ne hasyll & beth hym euyn & streyghte. and lete it drye with the
staffe. And whan they ben drye make the yerde mete vnto the
hole in the staffe: vnto halfe the length of the staffe. And to per
fourme that other halfe of the croppe. Take a fayr shote of blac
ke thorn: crabbe tree: medeler. or of Jenypre kytte in the same se
ason: and well bethyd & streyghte. And frette theym togyder fe
tely: soo that the croppe maye iustly entre all in to the sayd hole. Thenne shaue your staffe & make hym tapre were. Thenne
vyrell the staffe at bothe endes wyth longe hopis of yren or la
ton in the clennest wise wyth a pyke in the nether ende fastnyd
wyth a rennynge vyce: to take in & oute youre croppe. Thenne
set your croppe an handfull within the ouer ende of your staffe
in suche wise that it be as bigge there as in ony other place abo
ne. Theñe arme your croppe at thouer ende downe to ẏ frette
wyth a lyne of. vj. heeres. And dubbe the lyne and frette it fast
in ẏ toppe wyth a bowe to fasten on your lyne. And thus shall
ye make you a rodde soo preuy that ye maye walke therwyth;
and there shall noo man wyte where abowte ye goo. It woll be
lyghte & full nymbyll to fysshe wyth at your luste. And for the
more redynesse loo here a fygure therof in example.:

After that ye haue made thus your rodde: ye must lerne
to coloure your lynes of here in this wyse. ¶ Fyrste ye
must take of a whyte horse taylle the lengest heere and

hym faste wyth a cockeshotecorde: and bynde hym to a fourme or an euyn square grete tree. Take thenne a plummers wire that is euyn and streyte & sharpe at the one ende. And hete the shar pe ende in a charcole fyre tyll it be whyte: and brenne the staffe therwyth thorugh: euer streyte in the pythe at bothe endes tyll they mete. And after that brenne hym in the nether ende wyth a byrde broche/ & wyth other broches eche gretter than other. & euer the grettest laste: so that ye make your hole aye tapre wexe. Thenne lete hym lye styll and kele two dayes. Vnfrette hym thenne and lete hym drye in an hous roof in the smoke tyll he be thrugh drye In the same season take a fayr yerde of gre ne hasyll & beth hym euyn & streyghte. and lete it drye with the staffe. And whan they ben drye make the yerde mete vnto the hole in the staffe: vnto halfe the length of the staffe. And to per fourme that other halfe of the croppe. Take a fayr shote of blac ke thornn: crabbe tree: medeler. or of Ienypre kytte in the same se ason: and well bethyd & streyghte. And frette theym togyder fe tely: soo that the croppe maye iustly entre all in to the sayd ho- le. Thenne shaue your staffe & make hym tapre wexe. Thenne vyrell the staffe at bothe endes wyth longe hopis of yren or la ton in the clennest wise wyth a pyke in the nether ende fastnyd wyth a rennynge vyce: to take in & oute youre croppe. Thenne set your croppe an handfull within the ouer ende of your staffe in suche wise that it be as bigge there as in ony other place abo ne.[3] Thenne arme your croppe at thouer ende downe to þe frette wyth a lyne of .vj. heeres. And dubbe the lyne and frette it fast in þe toppe wyth a bowe to fasten on your lyne. And thus shall ye make you a rodde soo preuy that ye maye walke therwyth: and there shall noo man wyte where abowte ye goo. It woll be lyghte & full nymbyll to fysshe wyth at your luste. And for the more redynesse loo here a fygure therof in example.:

Facsimile, with Transcript, of the First Printed Text of the Treatise

After that ye haue made thus your rodde: ye must lerne to coloure your lynes of here in this wyse. Fyrste ye must take of a whyte horse taylle the lengest heere and

[3] R: aboue.

fayrest that ye can fynde. And euer the rounder it be the better it is. Departe it in to .vj. partes: and euery parte ye shal colour by hymselfe in dyuers colours. As yelowe: grene: browne: taw-ney: russet. and duske colours. And for to make a good grene co lour on your heer ye shall doo thus. ¶ Take smalle ale a quar te and put it in a lytyll panne: and put therto halfe a pounde of alym. And put therto your heer: and lete it boylle softly half an houre. Thenne take out your heer and lete it drye. Thenne ta ke a potell of water and put it in a panne. And put therin two handfull of oldys or of wyxen. And presse it wyth a tyle sto-ne: and lete it boylle softly half an houre. And whan it is yelow on the scume put therin your heer wyth halfe a pounde of copo rose beten in powdre and lete it boylle halfe a myle waye: and thenne sette it downe: and lete it kele fyue or syxe houres. Then take out the heer and drye it. And it is thenne the fynest grene that is for the water. And euer the more ye put therto of copo rose the better it is. or elles in stede of it vertgrees.

¶ A nother wyse ye maye make more bryghter grene (as thus Lete woode your heer in an woodefatte a lyght plunket colour And thenne sethe hym in olde or wyxin lyke as I haue sayd: sa-uynge ye shall not put therto neyther coporose ne vertgrees.

¶ For to make your heer yelow dyght it wyth alym as I haue sayd before. And after that wyth oldys or wyxin wythout copo rose or vertgrees. ¶ A nother yelow ye shal make thus. Ta ke smalle ale a potell: and stampe thre handful of walnot leues and put togider: And put in your heer tyll that it be as depe as ye woll haue it. ¶ For to make russet heer. Take stronge lye a pynt and halfe a pounde of sote and a lytyll iuce of walnot le uys & a quarte of alym: and put theym alle togyder in a panne and boylle theym well. And whan it is colde put in youre heer tyll it be as derke as ye woll haue it. ¶ For to make a brow ne colour. Take a pounde of sote and a quarte of ale: and seth it wyth as many walnot leuys as ye maye. And whan they wexe blacke sette it from the fyre. And put therin your heer and lete it lye styll tyll it be as browne as ye woll haue it.

¶ For to make a nother browne. Take strong ale and sote and tempre them togyder. and put therin your heer two dayes and two nyghtes and it shall be ryght a good colour.

h ij

fayrest that ye can fynde. And euer the rounder it be the better
it is. Departe it in to .vj. partes: and euery parte ye shal[4] colour
by hymselfe in dyuers colours. As yelowe: grene: browne: tawney: russet. and duske colours. And for to make a good grene co
lour on your heer ye shall doo thus. Take smalle ale a quar
te and put it in a lytyll panne: and put therto halfe a pounde of
alym. And put therto your heer: and lete it boylle softly half an
houre. Thenne take out your heer and lete it drye. Thenne ta
ke a potell of water and put it in a panne. And put therin two
handfull of ooldys or of wyxen. And presse it wyth a tyle stone: and lete it boylle softly half an houre. And whan it is yelow
on the scume put therin your heer wyth halfe a pounde of copo
rose betyn in powdre and lete it boylle halfe a myle waye: and
thenne sette it downe: and lete it kele fyue or syxe houres. Thenn
take out the heer and drye it. And it is thenne the fynest grene
that is for the water. And euer the more ye put therto of copo
rose the better it is. or elles in stede of it vertgrees.

Facsimile, with Transcript, of the First Printed Text of the Treatise

A nother wyse ye maye make more bryghter grene/ as thus
Lete woode your heer in an woodefatte a lyght plunket colour
And thenne sethe hym in olde or wyxin lyke as I haue sayd: sa-
uynge ye shall not put therto neyther coporose ue[5] vertgrees.

For to make your heer yelow dyght it wyth alym as I haue
sayd before. And after that wyth oldys or wyxin wythout copo
rose or vertgrees. A nother yelow ye shal make thus. Ta
ke smalle ale a potell: and stampe thre handful of walnot leues
and put togider: And put in your heer tyll that it be as depe as
ye woll haue it. For to make russet heer. Take stronge lye
a pynt and halfe a pounde of sote and a lytyll iuce of walnot le
uys & a quarte of alym: and put theym alle togyder in a panne
and boylle theym well. And whan it is colde put in youre heer
tyll it be as derke as ye woll haue it. For to make a brow
ne colour. Take a pounde of sote and a quarte of ale: and seth it
wyth as many walnot leuys as ye maye. And whan they wexe
blacke sette it from the fire. And put therin your heer and lete it
lye styll tyll it be as browne as ye woll haue it.

For to make a nother browne. Take strong ale and sote and
tempre them togyder. and put therin your heer two dayes and
two nyghtes and it shall be ryght a good colour.

[4] Or: shall. [5] R: ne.

¶ For to make a tawney coloure. Take lyme and water & put
theym togyder: and also put your heer therin foure or fyue hou
res. Thenne take it out and put it in a Tanners ose a day: and
it shall be also fyne a tawney colour as nedyth to our purpoos
¶ The syxte parte of your heer ye shall kepe styll whyte for ly
nes for the dubbyd hoke to fysshe for the trought and graylyn
ge: and for smalle lynes for to rye for the roche and the darse.

Whan your heer is thus colourid: ye must knowe for whi
che waters and for whyche seasons they shall serue.
¶ The grene colour in all clere water from Apryll tyll
Septembre. ¶ The yelowe coloure in euery clere water from
Septembre tyll Nouembre: For is is lyke ẏ wedys and other
manere grasse whiche growyth in the waters and ryuers whan
they ben broken. ¶ The russet colour seruyth all the wynter
vnto the ende of Apryll, as well in ryuers as in poles or lakys
¶ The browne colour seruyth for that water that is blacke de
dysshe in ryuers or in other waters. ¶ The tawney colour for
those waters that ben hethy or morysshe.

Now must ye make youre lynes in this wyse. Fyrste lo=
ke that ye haue an Instrument lyke vnto this fygure
portrayed folowynge. Thenne take your heer & kytte
of the smalle ende an hondfull large or more; For it is neyther
stronge nor yet sure. Thenne torne the toppe to the taylle eue
ryche ylyke moche. And departe it in to thre partyes. Thenne
knytte euery part at the one ende by hymself. And at the other
ende knytte all thre togyder: and put ẏ same ende in that other
ende of your Instrument that hath but one clyft. And sett that
other ende faste wyth the wegge foure fyngers in alle shorter
than your heer. Thenne twyne euery warpe one waye & ylyke
moche: and fasten theym in thre clyftes ylyke streyghte. Take
thenne out that other ende and twyne it that waye that it woll
desyre ynough. Thenne streyne it a lytyll: and knytte it for vn
doynge: and that is good. And for to knowe to make your In=
strument: loo here it is in fygure. And it shall be made of tree
sauynge the bolte vnderneth: whiche shall be of yren.

For to make a tawney coloure. Take lyme and water & put theym togyder: and also put your heer therin foure or fyue hou res. Thenne take it out and put it in a Tanners ose a day: and it shall be also fyne a tawney colour as nedyth to our purpoos The syxte parte of your heer ye shall kepe styll whyte for ly nes for the dubbyd hoke to fysshe for the trought and graylyn ge: and for smalle lynes for to rye for the roche and the darse.

Whan your heer is thus colourid: ye must knowe for whi che waters and for whyche seasons they shall serue. The grene colour in all clere water from Apryll tyll Septembre. The yelowe coloure in euery clere water from Septembre tyll Nouembre: For is[6] is lyke þe wedys and other manere grasse whiche growyth in the waters and ryuers whan they ben broken. The russet colour seruyth all the wynter vnto the ende of Apryll/ as well in ryuers as in poles or lakys The browne colour seruyth for that water that is blacke de disshe in ryuers or in other waters. The tawney colour for those waters that ben hethy or morysshe.

Now must ye make youre lynes in this wyse. Fyrste lo- ke that ye haue an Instrument lyke vnto this fygure portrayed folowynge. Thenne take your heer & kytte of the smalle ende an hondfull large or more/ For it is neyther stronge nor yet sure. Thenne torne the toppe to the taylle eue ryche ylyke moche. And departe it in to thre partyes. Thenne knytte euery part at the one ende by hymself. And at the other ende knytte all thre togyder: and put þe same ende in that other ende of your Instrument that hath but one clyft. And sett that other ende faste wyth the wegge foure fyngers in alle shorter than your heer. Thenne twyne euery warpe one waye & ylyke moche: and fasten theym in thre clyftes ylyke streyghte. Take thenne out that other ende and twyne it that waye that it woll desyre ynough. Thenne streyne it a lytyll: and knytte it for vn doynge: and that is good. And for to knowe to make your In- strument: loo here it is in fygure. And it shall be made of tree sauynge the bolte vnderneth: whiche shall be of yren.

[6] R: it.

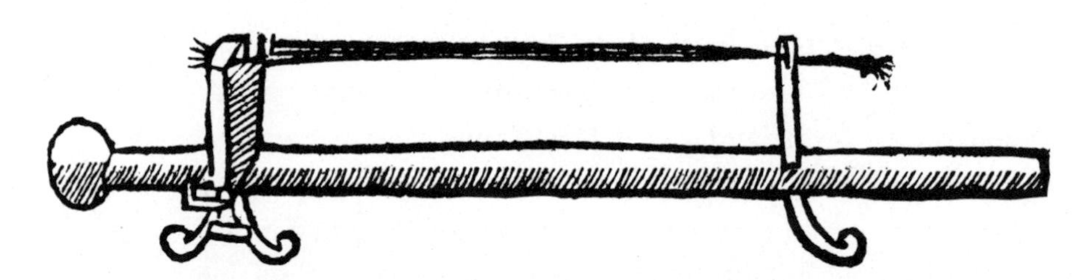

Whan ye haue as many of the lynkys as ye suppose wol suffyse for the length of a lyne :thenne must ye knytte theym togyder wyth a water knotte or elles a duchys knotte. And whan your knotte is knytte: kytte of ẏ voyde shorte endes a strawe brede for the knotte. Thus shal ye make youre lynes fayr & fyne: and also ryght sure for ony manere fysshe. ¶And by cause that ye sholde knowe bothe the water knotte & also the duchys knotte: loo theym here in fygure caste vnto the lykenesse of the draughte.

Ye shall vnderstonde that the moost subtyll & hardyste crafte in makynge of your harnays is for to make your hokis. For whoos makyng ye must haue fete fyles. thyñ and sharpe & smalle beten: A semy clam̄ of yren: a bender: a payr of longe & smalle tongys : an harde knyfe somdeale thycke: an anuelde: & a lytyll hamour. ¶And for smalle fysshe ye shall make your hokes of the smalest quarell nedlys that ye can fynde of stele: & in this wyse. ¶Ye shall put the quarell in a redde charkcole fyre tyll that it be of the same colour that the fyre is. Thenne take hym out and lete hym kele: and ye shal fynde hym well alayd for to fyle. Thenne reyse the berde wyth your knyfe: and make the poynt sharpe. Thenne alaye hym agayn: for elles he woll breke in the bendyng. Thenne bende hym lyke to the bende fyguryd herafter in example. And gretter hokes ye shall make in the same wyse of gretter nedles: as broderers nedlis: or taylers: or shomakers nedlis spere poyntes &

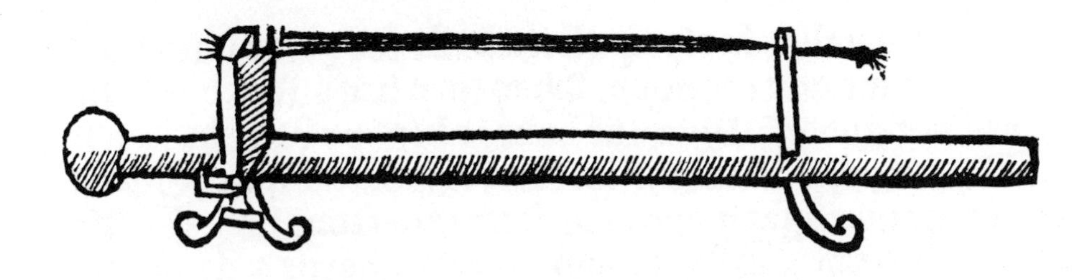

Facsimile, with Transcript, of the First Printed Text of the Treatise

Whan ye haue as many of the lynkys as ye suppose wol
suffyse for the length of a lyne: thenne must ye knytte
theym togyder wyth a water knotte or elles a duchys
knotte. And whan your knotte is knytte: kytte of þe voyde shor
te endes a strawe brede for[7] the knotte. Thus shal ye make you
re lynes fayr & fyne: and also ryght sure for ony manere fysshe.
And by cause that ye sholde knowe bothe the water knotte &
also the duchys knotte: loo theym here in fygure caste vnto the
lyknesse of the draughte.

Ye shall vnderstonde that the moost subtyll & hardyste
crafte in makynge of your harnays is for to make your
hokis. For whoos makyng ye must haue fete fyles. thynn
and sharpe & smalle beten: A semy clamm of yren: a bender: a payr of longe & smalle tongys: and harde knyfe somdeale thycke:
an anuelde: & a lytyll hamour. And for smalle fysshe ye shall
make your hokes of the smalest quarell nedlys that ye can fyn
de of stele/ & in this wyse. Ye shall put the quarell in a redde
charkcole fyre tyll that it be of the same colour that the fyre is.
Thenne take hym out and lete hym kele: and ye shal fynde him
well alayd for to fyle. Thenne reyse the berde wyth your kny-
fe/ and make the poynt sharpe. Thenne alaye hym agayn: for
elles he woll breke in the bendyng. Thenne bende hym lyke to
the bende fyguryd herafter in example. And gretter hokes ye
shall mabe[8] in the same wyse of gretter nedles: as broderers nedlis: or taylers: or shomakers nedlis spere poyntes/ &

[7] R: fro.
[8] R: make.

of shomakers nalles in especyall the beste for grete fysshe. and
that they bende atte the poynt whan they ben assayed/for elles
they ben not good ¶ Whan the hoke is bendyd bete the hynder
ende abrode: & fyle it smothe for fretynge of thy lyne. Thenne
put it in the fyre agayn: and yeue it an easy redde hete. Thenne
sodaynly quenche it in water: and it woll be harde & stronge.
And for to haue knowlege of your Instrumentes: lo theym here in fygure portrayd.

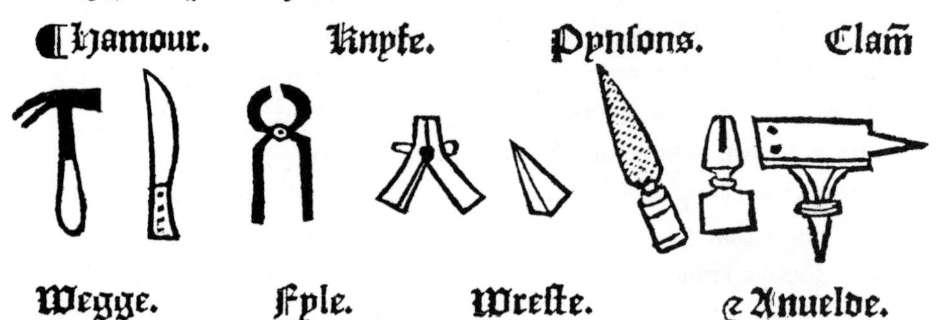

Whan ye haue made thus your hokis: thenne must ye set
theym on your lynes acordynge in gretnesse & strength
in this wyse. ¶ Ye shall take smalle redde silke. & yf it be
for a grete hoke theñe double it: not twynyd. And elles for sma
le hokys lete it be syngle: & therwyth frette thycke the lyne the
re as the one ende of your hoke shal sytte a strawe brede. Theñ
sette there your hoke: & frette hym wyth the same threde ÿ two
partes of the lengthe that shall be frette in all. And whan ye co
me to the thyrde parte thenne torne the ende of your lyne aga
yn vpon the frette dowble. & frette it so dowble that other thyr
de parte. Thenne put your threde in at the hose twys or thries
& lete it goo at eche tyme rounde abowte the yerde of your hoke. Thenne wete the hose & drawe it tyll that it be faste. And lo
ke that your lyne lye euermore wythin your hokys: & not with
out. Thenne kytte of the lynys ende & the threde as nyghe as
ye maye: sauynge the frette.

Now ye knowe wyth how grete hokys ye shall angle to
euery fysshe: now I woll tell you wyth how many heeres ye shall to euery manere of fisshe. ¶ For the menow
wyth a lyne of one heere. For the waxyng roche: the bleke & the

of shomakers nalles in especyall the beste for grete fysshe. and that they bende atte the poynt whan they ben assayed/ for elles they ben not good Whan the hoke is bendyd bete the hynder ende abrode: & fyle it smothe for fretynge of thy lyne. Thenne put it in the fyre agayn: and yeue it an easy redde hete. Thenne sodaynly quenche it in water: and it woll be harde & stronge. And for to haue knowlege of your Instrumentes: lo theym he-re in fygure portrayd.

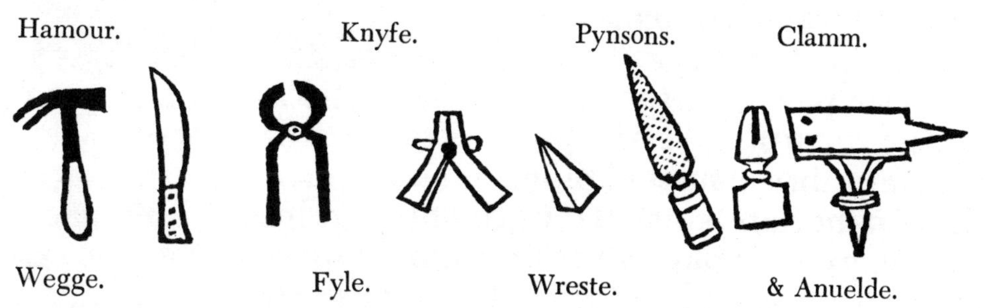

Whan ye haue made thus your hokis: thenne must ye set theym on your lynes acordynge in gretnesse & strength in this wyse. Ye shall take smalle redde silke. & yf it be for a grete hoke thenne double it: not twynyd. And elles for sma le hokys lete it be syngle: & therwyth frette thycke the lyne the re as the one ende of your hoke shal sytte a strawe brede. Thenn sette there your hoke: & frette hym wyth the same threde þe two partes of the lengthe that shall be frette in all. And whan ye co me to the thyrde parte thenne torne the ende of your lyne aga yn vpon the frette dowble. & frette it so dowble that other thyr de parte. Thenne put your threde in at the hose[9] twys or thries & lete it goo at eche tyme rounde abowte the yerde of your ho-ke. Thenne wete the hose[9] & drawe it tyll that it be faste. And lo ke that your lyne lye euermore wythin your hokys: & not with out. Thenne kytte of the lynys ende & the threde as nyghe as ye maye: sauynge the frette.

Now ye knowe wyth how grete hokys ye shall angle to euery fysshe: now I woll tell you wyth how many hee-res ye shall to euery manere of fisshe. For the menow wyth a lyne of one heere. For the waxyng roche: the bleke & the

[9] R: hole.

gogyñ & the ruffe wyᵗ a lyne of two heeris. For the darse & the grete roche wyth a lyne of thre heeres. For the perche: the flou der & bremet with foure heeres. For the cheuen chubbe: the bre me: the tenche & the ele wyth. vj. heeres. For the troughte: grap lynge: barbyll & the grete cheuyn wyth. ix. heeres. For the grete troughte wyth. xij. heeres: For the samon wyth. xv. heeres. And for the pyke wyth a chalke lyne made browne with your brow ne colour aforsayd: armyd with a wyre. as ye shal here herafter whan I speke of the pyke.

¶Your lynes must be plumbid wyth lede. And ye shall wyte yᵗ the nexte plūbe vnto the hoke shall be therfro a large fote & mo re. And euery plumbe of a quantyte to the gretnes of the lyne. There be thre manere of plūbis for a grounde lyne rennynge. And for the flote set vpon the grounde lyne lyenge. x. plumbes Joynynge all togider. On the grounde lyne rennynge. ix or. x. smalle. The flote plūbe shall be so heuy yᵗ the leest plucke of o ny fysshe maye pull it downe in to yᵉ water. And make your plū bis rounde & smothe yᵗ they stycke not on stonys or on wedys. And for the more vnderstondynge lo theym here in fygure.

The grounde lyne rennynge

The grounde lyne lyenge.

The flote lyne

The lyne for perche or tenche.

The lyne for a pyke: ¶Plūbe: Corke armyd wyth wyre

Thenne shall ye make your flotys in this wyse. Take a fayr corke that is clene without many holes. and bore it gogyn & the ruffe wyt a lyne of two heeris. For the darse & the grete roche wyth a lyne of thre heeres. For the perche: the floun der & bremet with foure heeres. For the cheuen chubbe: the bre me: the tenche & the ele wyth .vj. heeres. For the troughte: gray lynge: barbyll & the grete cheuyn wyth .ix. heeres. For the grete troughte wyth .xij. heeres: For the samon wyth .xv. heeres. And for the pyke wyth a chalke lyne made browne with your brow ne colour aforsayd: armyd with a wyre. as ye shal here herafter whan I speke of the pyke.

Facsimile, with Transcript, of the First Printed Text of the Treatise

Your lynes must be plumbid wyth lede. And ye shall wyte þ*at* the nexte pumbe[10] vnto the hoke shall be therfro a large fote & mo re/ And euery plumbe of a quantyte to the gretnes of the lyne. There be thre manere of plumbis for a grounde lyne rennynge. And for the flote set vpon the grounde lyne lyenge .x. plumbes Ioynynge all togider. On the grounde lyne rennynge .ix or .x. smalle. The flote plumbe shall be so heuy þ*at* the leest plucke of o-ny fysshe maye pull it downe in to þe water. And make your plum bis rounde & smothe þ*at* they stycke not on stonys or on wedys. And for the more vnderstondynge lo theym here in fygure.

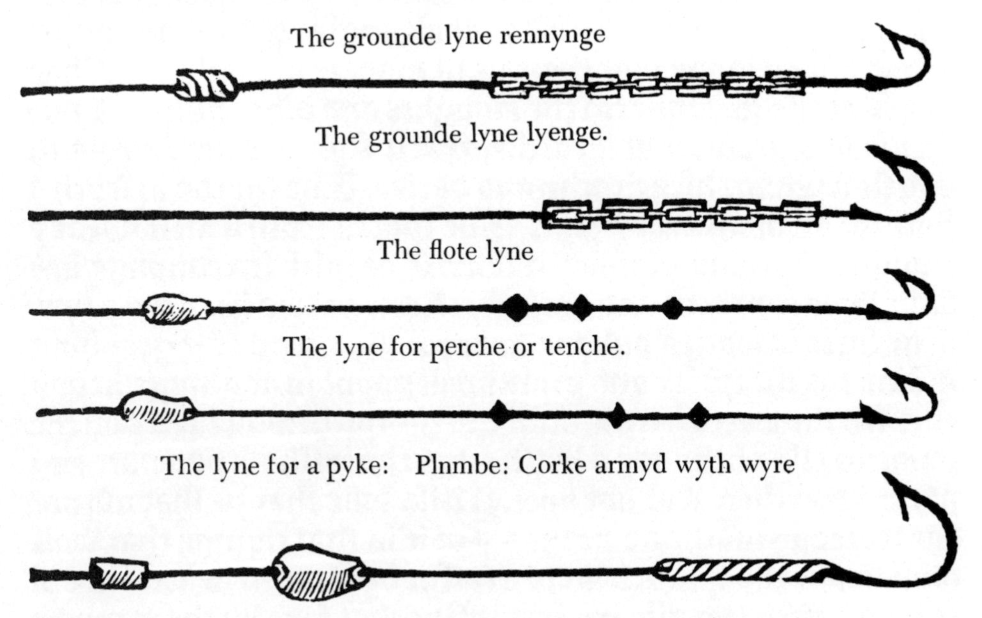

Thenne shall ye make your flotys in this wyse. Take a fayr corke that is clene without many holes. and bore it

[10] R: plumbe.

thrugh wyth a smalle hote yren: And putt therin a penne iuste and streyghte. Euer the more flote the gretter penne & the grete hole. Thenne shape it grete in the myddis and smalle at bo the endys. and specyally sharpe in the nether ende; and lyke vn to the fygures folowynge. And make theym smothe on a gryn dyng stone: or on a tyle stone. ¶ And loke that the flote for one heer be nomore than a pese. For two heeres: as a beene. for twel ue heeres: as a walnot. And soo euery lyne after the proporcōn. ¶ All manere lynes that ben not for the groūde must haue flo tes. And the rennynge grounde lyne must haue a flote. The ly enge grounde lyne wythout flote.

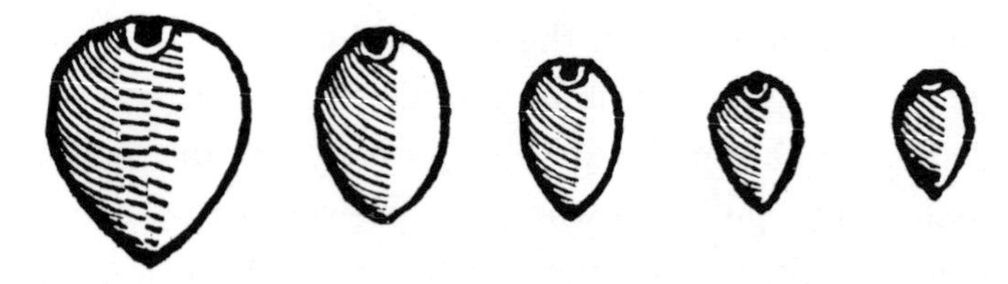

Now I haue lerned you to make all your harnays. Here I woll tell you how ye shall angle. ¶ Ye shall angle: vnderstonde that there is. vj. manere of anglyng. That one is at the grounde for the troughte and other fisshe. A nother is at ẏ grounde at an arche; or at a stange where it ebbyth and flowyth: for bleke: roche. and darse. The thyrde is wyth a flote for all manere of fysshe. The fourth wyth a menow for ẏ troughte wythout plumbe or flote. The fyfth is rennynge in ẏ same wyse for roche and darse wyth one or two heeres & a flye. The syxte is wyth a dubbyd hoke for the troughte & graylyng ¶ And for the fyrste and pryncypall poynt in anglynge: kepe ẏ euer fro the water fro the syghte of the fysshe: other ferre on the londe: or ellys behynde a busshe that the fysshe se you not. For yf they doo they wol not byte. ¶ Also loke that ye shadow not the water as moche as ye may. For it is that thynge that woll soone frayе the fysshe. And yf a fysshe be afrayed he woll not bi te longe after. For alle manere fysshe that fede by the grounde ye shall angle for theim to the botom. soo that your hokys shall renne or lye on the grounde. And for alle other fysshe that fede

thrugh wyth a smalle hote yren: And putt therin a penne iuste
and streyghte. Euer the more flote the gretter penne & the gre
ter hole. Thenne shape it grete in the myddis and smalle at bo
the endys. and specyally sharpe in the nether ende/ and lyke vn
to the fygures folowynge. And make theym smothe on a gryn
dyng stone: or on a tyle stone. And loke that the flote for one
heer be nomore than a pese. For two heeres: as a beene. for twel
ue heeres: as a walnot. And soo euery lyne after the proporcion.
All manere lynes that ben not for the grounde must haue flo
tes. And the rennynge grounde lyne must haue a flote. The ly
enge grounde lyne wythout flote.

Facsimile, with Transcript, of the First Printed Text of the Treatise

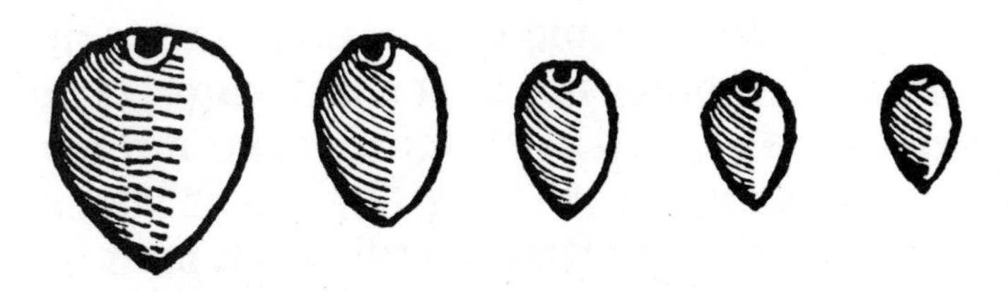

Now I haue lernyd you to make all your harnays. Here I woll tell you how ye shall angle. Ye shall angle:
vnderstonde that there is .vj. manere of anglyng. That
one is at the grounde for the troughte and other fisshe. A nother is at þe grounde at an arche/ or at a stange where it ebbyth
and flowyth: for bleke: roche. and darse. The thyrde is wyth a
flote for all manere of fysshe. The fourth wyth a menow for þe
troughte wythout plumbe or flote. The fyfth is rennynge in þe
same wyse for roche and darse wyth one or two heeres & a flye.
The syxte is wyth a dubbyd hoke for the troughte & graylyng
And for the fyrste and pryncypall poynt in anglynge: kepe þe
euer fro the water fro the sighte of the fysshe: other ferre on the
londe: or ellys behynde a busshe that the fysshe se you not. For
yf they doo they wol not byte. Also loke that ye shadow not
the water as moche as ye may. For it is that thynge that woll
soone fraye the fysshe. And yf a fysshe be afrayed he woll not bi
te longe after. For alle manere fysshe that fede by the grounde
ye shall angle for theim to the botom. soo that your hokys shall
renne or lye on the grounde. And for alle other fysshe that fede

aboue ye shall angle to theym in the myddes of the water or
somdeale bynethe or somdeale aboue. For euer the gretter fisshe
the nerer he lyeth the botom of the water. And euer the smaller
fysshe the more he swymmyth aboue. ¶ The thyrde good poynt is whan the fysshe bytyth that ye be not to hasty to smyte
nor to late; For ye must abide tyll ye suppose that the bayte be
ferre in the mouth of the fysshe; and thenne abyde noo longer.
And this is for the grou͂de. ¶ And for the flote whan ye se it pul
lyd softly vnder the water: or elles carryed vpon the water softly: thenne smyte. And loke that ye neuer ouersmyte the strengthe of your lyne for brekynge. ¶ And yf it fortune you to smyte a grete fysshe wyth a smalle harnays: thenne ye must lede
hym in the water and labour him there tyll he be drownyd and
ouercome. Thenne take hym as well as ye can or maye. and e-
uer bewaar that ye holde not ouer the strengthe of your lyne.
And as moche as ye may lete hym not come out of your lynes
ende streyghte from you; But kepe hym euer vnder the rodde;
and euermore holde hym streyghte: soo that your lyne may sus
teyne and beere his leppys and his plungys wyth the helpe of
your croppe & of your honde.

Here I woll declare vnto you in what place of the water
ye shall angle. Ye shall angle in a pole or in a stondinge
water in euery place where it is ony thynge depe. The
re is not grete choyse of ony places where it is ony thynge de
pe in a pole. For it is but a pryson to fysshe. and they lyue for ye
more parte in hungre lyke prisoners: and therfore it is the lesse
maystry to take theym. But in a ryuer ye shall angle in euery
place where it is depe and clere by the grounde: as grauell or
claye wythout mudde or wedys. And in especyall yf that there
be a manere whyrlynge of water or a couert. As an holow ban
ke: or grete rotys of trees: or longe wedes fletyng aboue in the
water where the fysshe maye couere and hyde theymself at cer-
tayn tymes whan they lyste Also it is good for to angle in depe styffe stremys and also in fallys of waters and weares: and
in floode gatys and mylle pyttes. And it is good for to angle
where as the water restyth by the banke: and where the streme
rennyth nyghe there by: and is depe and clere by the grounde

aboue ye shall angle to theym in the myddes of the water or
somdeale byneth or somdeale aboue. For euer the gretter fisshe
the nerer he lyeth the botom of the water. And euer the smaller
fysshe the more he smymmyth[11] aboue. The thyrde good poynt is whan the fysshe bytyth that ye be not to hasty to smyte
nor to late/ For ye must abide tyll ye suppose that the bayte be
ferre in the mouth of the fysshe/ and thenne abyde noo longer.
And this is for the grounde. And for the flote whan ye se it pul
lyd softly vnder the water: or elles caryed vpon the water softly: thenne smyte. And loke that ye neuer ouersmyte the strengthe of your lyne for brekynge. And yf it fortune you to smyte a grete fysshe wyth a smalle harnays: thenne ye must lede
hym in the water and labour him there tyll he be drownyd and
ouercome. Thenne take hym as well as ye can or maye. and e-
uer bewaar that ye holde not ouer the strengthe of your lyne.
And as moche as ye may lete hym not come out of your lynes
ende streyghte from you: But kepe hym euer vnder the rodde/
and euermore holde hym streyghte: soo that your lyne may sus
teyne and beere his lepys and his plungys wyth the helpe of
your croppe & of your honde.

Facsimile, with Transcript, of the First Printed Text of the Treatise

Here I woll declare vnto you in what place of the water
ye shall angle. Ye shall angle in a pole or in a stondinge
water in euery place where it is ony thynge depe. The
re is not grete choyse of ony places where it is ony thynge de
pe in a pole. For it is but a pryson to fysshe. and they lyue for þe
more parte in hungre lyke prisoners: and therfore it is the lesse
maystry to take theym. But in a ryuer ye shall angle in euery
place where it is depe and clere by the grounde: as grauell or
claye wythout mudde or wedys. And in especyall yf that there
be a manere whyrlynge of water or a couert. As an holow ban
ke: or grete rotys of trees: or longe wedes fletyng aboue in the
water where the fysshe maye couere and hyde theymself at cer-
tayn tymes whan they lyste Also it is good for to angle in depe styffe stremys and also in fallys of waters and weares: and
in floode gatys and mylle pyttes. And it is good for to angle
where as the water restyth by the banke: and where the streme
rennyth nyghe there by: and is depe and clere by the grounde

[11] R: swymmyth.

and inony other placys where ye may se ony fyssh houe or ha
ue ony fedynge.

NOw ye shall wyte what tyme of the daye ye shall angle
¶From the begynnynge of May vntyll it be Septem
bre the bytynge tyme is erly by the morowe from fou=
re of ÿ clocke vnto eyghte of the clocke. And at after none from
foure of the clocke vnto eyghte of the clocke : but not soo good
as is in the mornynge. And yf it be a colde whystelyng wynde
and a derke lowrynge daye . For a derke daye is moche better
to angle in than a clere daye. ¶From the begynnynge of Sep
tembre vnto the ende of Apryll spare noo tyme of the daye:
¶Also many pole fysshes woll byte beste in the none tyde.
¶And yf ye se ony tyme of the daye the trought or graylynge
lepe:angle to hym wyth a dubbe acordynge to the same month
And where the water ebbyth and flowyth the fysshe woll byte
in some place at the ebbe:and in some place at the flood. After ÿ
they haue restynge behynde stangnys and archys of brydgys
and other suche manere places.

HEre ye shall wyte in what weder ye shall angle. as I sa
yd before in a derke lowrynge daye whanne the wynde
blowyth softly. And in somer season whan it is brennyn
ge hote thenne it is nought . ¶From Septembre vnto Apryll
in a fayr sonny daye is ryght good to angle. And yf the wynde
in that season haue ony parte of the Oryent:the wedyr thenne
is nought. And whan it is a grete wynde. And whan it snowith
reynyth or haylyth. or is a grete tempeste;as thondyr or ligh
tenynge:or a swoly hote weder:thenne it is noughte for to an=
gle.

NOw shall ye wyte that there ben twelue manere of ym=
pedymentes whyche cause a man to take noo fysshe. wt
out other comyn that maye casuelly happe. ¶The fyrst
is yf your harnays be not mete nor fetly made. The seconde is
yf your baytes be not good nor fyne. The thyrde is yf that ye
angle not in bytynge tyme. The fourth is yf that the fysshe be
frayed wt the syghte of a man. The fyfth yf the water be very
thycke:whyte or redde of ony floode late fallen. The syxte yf
the fysshe styre not for colde . The seuenth yf that the wedyr

and in ony other placys where ye may se ony fyssh houe or ha
ue ony fedynge.

Now ye shall wyte what tyme of the daye ye shall angle
From the begynnynge of May vntyll it be Septem
bre the bytynge tyme is erly by the morowe from foure of þe clocke vnto eyghte of the clocke. And at after none from
foure of the clocke vnto eyghte of the clocke: but not soo good
as is in the mornynge. And yf it be a colde whystelyng wynde
and a derke lowrynge daye. For a derke daye is moche better
to angle in than a clere daye. From the begynnynge of Sep
tembre vnto the ende of Apryll spare noo tyme of the daye:
Also many pole fysshes woll byte beste in the none tyde.
And yf ye se ony tyme of the daye the trought or graylynge
lepe: angle to hym wyth a dubbe acordynge to the same month
And where the water ebbyth and flowyth the fysshe woll byte
in some place at the ebbe: and in some place at the flood. After þ*a*t
they haue restynge behynde stangnys and archys of brydgys
and other suche manere places.

Facsimile, with Transcript, of the First Printed Text of the Treatise

Here ye shall wyte in what weder ye shall angle. as I sa
yd before in a derke lowrynge daye whanne the wynde
blowyth softly. And in somer season whan it is brennyn
ge hote thenne it is nought. From Septembre vnto Apryll
in a fayr sonny daye is ryght good to angle. And yf the wynde
in that season haue ony parte of the Oryent: the wedyr thenne
is nought. And whan it is a grete wynde. And whan it snowith
reynyth or hayllyth. or is a grete tempeste/ as thondyr or ligh
tenynge: or a swoly hote weder: thenne it is noughte for to angle.

Now shall ye wyte that there ben twelue manere of ym-
pedymentes whyche cause a man to take noo fysshe. Wt
out other comyn that maye casuelly happe. The fyrst
is yf your harnays be not mete nor fetly made. The seconde is
yf your baytes be not good nor fyne. The thyrde is yf that ye
angle not in bytynge tyme. The fourth is yf that the fysshe be
frayed wt the syghte of a man. The fyfth yf the water be very
thycke: whyte or redde of ony floode late fallen. The syxte yf
the fysshe styre not for colde. The seuenth yf that the wedyr

be hote. The eyght yf it rayne. The nynthe yf it hayll or snow falle. The tenth is yf it be a tempeste. The enleuenth is yf it be a grete wynde. The twelfyfth yf the wynde be in the Eest; and that is worste For comynly neyther wynter nor somer ye fysshe woll not byte thenne. The weste and northe wyndes ben good but the south is beste.

And now I haue tolde you how to make your harnays: and how ye shall fysshe therwyth in al poyntes. Reason woll that ye knowe wyth what baytes ye shall angle to euery manere of fysshe in euery moneth of the yere / whyche is all the effecte of the crafte. And wythout whyche baytes knowen well by you all your other crafte here toforn auayllyth you not to purpose. For ye can not brynge an hoke in to a fyssh mouth wythout a bayte. Whiche baytes for euery manere of fyssh and for euery moneth here folowyth in this wyse.

For by cause that the Samon is the moost stately fyssh that ony man maye angle to in fresshe water. Therfore I purpose to begyn̄ at hym. ¶ The samon is a gentyll fysshe: but he is comborous for to take. For comynly he is but in depe places of grete ryuers. And for the more parte he holdyth the myddys of it: that a man maye not come at hym. And he is in season from Marche vnto Myghelmas. ¶ In whyche season ye shall angle to hym wyth thyse baytes whan ye maye gete theym. Fyrste wyth a redde worme in the begynnynge & endynge of the season. And also wyth a bobbe that bredyth in a dunghyll. And specyally wyth a souerayn bayte that bredyth on a water docke. ¶ And he bytith not at the grounde: but at ye flote. Also ye may take hym: but it is seldom seen with a dubbe at suche tyme as whan he lepith in lyke fourme & manere as ye doo take a troughte or a gryalynge. And thyse baytes ben well prouyd baytes for the samon.

The Troughte for by cause he is a right deyntous fyssh and also a ryght feruente byter we shall speke nexte of hym. He is in season fro Marche vnto Myghelmas. He is on clene grauely groūde & in a streme. Ye may angle to hym be hote. The eyght yf it rayne. The nynthe yf it hayll or snow falle. The tenth is yf it be a tempeste. The enleuenth is yf it be a grete wynde. The twelfyfth[12] yf the wynde be in the Eest/ and that is worste For comynly neyther wynter nor somer þe fysshe woll not byte thenne. The weste and northe wyndes ben good but the south is beste.

And now I haue tolde you how to make your harnays: and how ye shall fysshe therwyth in al poyntes Reason woll that ye knowe wyth what baytes ye shall angle to euery manere of fysshe in euery moneth of the yere/ whyche is all the effecte of the crafte. And wythout whyche baytes know en well by you all your other crafte here toforn auayllyth you not to purpose. For ye can not brynge an hoke in to a fyssh mo uth wythout a bayte. Whiche baytes for euery manere of fyssh and for euery moneth here folowyth in this wyse.

For by cause that the Samon is the moost stately fyssh that ony man maye angle to in fresshe water. Therfore I purpose to begynn at hym. The samon is a gentyll fysshe: but he is comborous for to take. For comynly he is but in depe places of grete ryuers. And for the more parte he hol- dyth the myddys of it: that a man maye not come at hym. And he is in season from Marche vnto Myghelmas. In whyche season ye shall angle to hym wyth thyse baytes whan ye maye gete theym. Fyrste wyth a redde worme in the begynnynge & endynge of the season. And also wyth a bobbe that bredyth in a dunghyll. And specyally wyth a souerayn bayte that bredyth on a water docke. And he bytith not at the grounde: but at þe flote. Also ye may take hym: but it is seldom seen with a dubbe at suche tyme as whan he lepith in lyke fourme & manere as ye doo take a troughte or a gryalynge.[13] And thyse baytes ben well prouyd baytes for the samon.

The Troughte for by cause he is a right deyntous fyssh and also a ryght feruente byter we shall speke nexte of hym. He is in season fro Marche vnto Myghelmas. He is on clene grauely grounde & in a streme. Ye may angle to hym

[12] R: twelfth. [13] R: graylynge.

all tymes wyth a grounde lyne lyenge or rennynge: sauyng in
leppynge tyme. and thenne wyth a dubbe. And erly wyth a ren=
nynge grounde lyne. and forth in the daye wyth a flote lyne.
¶ Ye shall angle to hym in Marche wyth a menew hangyd on
your hoke by the nether nesse wythout flote or plumbe: draw=
ynge vp & downe in the streme tyll ye fele hym faste. ¶ In the
same tyme angle to hym wyth a grou̅de lyne with a redde wor
me for the moost sure. ¶ In Aprill take the same baytes: & also
Jnneba other wyse namyd. vij. eyes. Also the canker that bre=
dyth in a grete tree and the redde snayll. ¶ In May take ẏ sto
ne flye and the bobbe vnder the cowe torde and the sylke wor=
me: and the bayte that bredyth on a fern̄ leyf. ¶ In Juyn take a
redde worme & nyppe of the heed: and put on thyn hoke a cod=
worme byforn. ¶ In Juyll take the grete redde worme and the
codworme togyder. ¶ In August take a flesshe flye & the grete
redde worme and the fatte of the bakon: and bynde abowte thy
hoke. ¶ In Septembre take the redde worme and the menew. ¶
In Octobre take the same: for they ben specyall for the tro=
ught all tymes of the yere. From Aprill tyll Septembre ẏ tro=
ugh leppyth. thenne angle to hym wyth a dubbyd hoke acordyn
ge to the moneth/ whyche dubbyd hokys ye shall fynde in then
de of this treatyse: and the monethys wyth theym.:

The graylynge by a nother name callyd vmbre is a de=
lycyous fysshe to mannys mouthe. And ye maye take
hym lyke as ye doo the trought. And thyse ben his bay
tes. ¶ In Marche & in Apryll the redde worme. ¶ In May the
grene worme: a lytyll breyled worme: the docke canker. and the
hawthorn worme. ¶ In June the bayte that bredyth betwene
the tree & the barke of an oke. ¶ In Juyll a bayte that bredyth
on a fern̄ leyf: and the grete redde worme. And nyppe of the he
de: and put on your hoke a codworme before. ¶ In August the
redde worme: and a docke worme. And al the yere after a redde
worme.

The barbyll is a swete fysshe/ but it is a quasy meete & a
peryllous for mannys body. For comynly he yeuyth
an introduccion to ẏ Febres. And yf he be eten rawe: he
maye be cause of mannys dethe: whyche hath oft be seen. Thy=

all tymes wyth a grounde lyne lyenge or rennynge: sauyng in
lepynge tyme. and thenne wyth a dubbe. And erly wyth a rennynge grounde lyne. and forth in the daye wyth a flote lyne.
Ye shall angle to hym in Marche wyth a menew hangyd on
your hoke by the nether nesse wythout flote or plumbe: draw-
ynge vp & downe in the streme tyll ye fele hym faste. In the
same tyme angle to hym wyth a grounde lyne with a redde wor
me for the moost sure. In Aprill take the same baytes: & also
Inneba other wyse namyd .vij. eyes. Also the canker that bredyth in a grete tree and the redde snayll. In May take þe sto
ne flye and the bobbe vnder the cowe torde and the sylke worme: and the bayte that bredyth on a fernn leyf. In Iuyn take a
redde worme & nyppe of the heed: and put on thyn hoke a codworme byforn. In Iuyll take the grete redde worme and the
codworme togyder. In August take a flesshe flye & the grete
redde worme and the fatte of the bakon: and bynde abowte thy
hoke. In Septembre take the redde worme and the menew.
In Octobre take the same: for they ben specyall for the trought all tymes of the yere. From Aprill tyll Septembre þe tro-
ugh[14] lepyth. thenne angle to hym wyth a dubbyd hoke acordyn
ge to the moneth/ whyche dubbyd hokys ye shall fynde in then
de of this treatyse: and the monethys wyth theym.:

Facsimile, with Transcript, of the First Printed Text of the Treatise

The grayllynge by a nother name callyd vmbre is a de-
lycyous fysshe to mannys mouthe. And ye maye take
hym lyke as ye doo the trought. And thyse ben his bay
tes. In Marche & in Apryll the redde worme. In May the
grene worme: a lytyll breyled worme: the docke canker. and the
hawthorn worme. In Iune the bayte that bredyth betwene
the tree & the barke of an oke. In Iuyll a bayte that bredyth
on a fernn leyf: and the grete redde worme. And nyppe of the he
de: and put on your hoke a codworme before. In August the
redde worme: and a docke worme. And al the yere after a redde
worme.

The barbyll is a swete fysshe/ but it is a quasy meete & a
peryllous for mannys body. For comynly he yeuyth
an introduxion to þe Febres. And yf he be eten rawe: he
maye be cause of mannys dethe: whyche hath oft be seen. Thy-

[14] R: trought.

se be his baytes. ¶ In Marche & in Apryll take fayr fresshe che
se : and laye it on a borde & kytte it in small square pecys of the
lengthe of your hoke. Take thenne a candyl & brenne it on the
ende at the poynt of your hoke tyll it be yelow. And theñe byn
de it on your hoke with fletchers sylke: a nd make it rough lyke
a welbede. This bayte is good all the somer season. ¶ In May
& June take ÿ hawthorñ worme & the grete redde worme. and
nyppe of the heed. And put on your hoke a codworme before. &
that is a good bayte. In Juyll take the redde worme for cheyf & the hawthorñ worme togyd. Also the water docke lef wor
me & the hornet worme togyder. ¶ In August & for all the yere take the talowe of a shepe & softe chese: of eche ylyke moche:
and a lytyll hony & grynde or stampe theym togyd longe. and
tempre it tyll it be tough. And put therto floure a lytyll & make it on smalle pellettys. And ÿ is a good bayte to angle wyth
at the grounde And loke that it synke in the water. or ellys it is
not good to this purpoos.

The carpe is a deyntous fysshe: but there ben but fewe in
Englonde. And therfore I wryte the lasse of hym. He is
an euyll fysshe to take. For he is soo stronge enarmyd
in the mouthe that there maye noo weke harnays holde hym.
And as touchynge his baytes I haue but lytyll knowlege of it
And me were loth to wryte more than I knowe & haue prouyd
But well I wote that the redde worme & the menow ben good
baytys for hym at all tymes as I haue herde saye of persones
credyble & also founde wryten in bokes of credence.

The cheuyn is a stately fysshe: & his heed is a deyty mor-
sell. There is noo fysshe soo strongly enarmyd wyth sca
lys on the body. And bi cause he is a stronge byter he ha
the the more baytes which ben thyse. ¶ In Marche the redde
worme at the grounde: For comynly thenne he woll byte there
at all tymes of ÿ yere yf he be ony thinge hungry. ¶ In Apryll
the dyche canker that bredith in the tree. A worme that bredith
betwene the rynde & the tree of an oke The redde worme: and
the yonge frosshys whan the fete ben kyt of. Also the stone flye
the bobbe vnder the cowe torde: the redde snaylle. ¶ In May ÿ
i j

se be his baytes. In Marche & in Apryll take fayr fresshe che
se: and laye it on a borde & kytte it in small square pecys of the
lengthe of your hoke. Take thenne a candyl & brenne it on the
ende at the poynt of your hoke tyll it be yelow. And thenne byn
de it on your hoke with fletchers sylke: and make it rough lyke
a welbede. This bayte is good all the somer season. In May
& Iune take þe hawthornn worme & the grete redde worme. and
nyppe of the heed. And put on your hoke a codworme before. &
that is a good bayte. In Iuyll take the redde worme for cheyf & the hawthornn worme togyder. Also the water docke leyf wor
me & the hornet worme togyder. In August & for all the yere take the talowe of a shepe & softe chese: of eche ylyke moche:
and a lytyll hony & grynde or stampe theym togyder longe. and
tempre it tyll it be tough. And put therto floure a lytyll & make it on smalle pellettys. And þ*at* is a good bayte to angle wyth
at the grounde And loke that it synke in the water. or ellys it is
not good to this purpoos.

Facsimile, with Transcript, of the First Printed Text of the Treatise

The carpe is a deyntous fysshe: but there ben but fewe in
Englonde. And therfore I wryte the lasse of hym. He is
an euyll fysshe to take. For he is soo stronge enarmyd
in the mouthe that there maye noo weke harnays holde hym.
And as touchynge his baytes I haue but lytyll knowlege of it
And me were loth to wryte more than I knowe & haue prouyd
But well I wote that the redde worme & the menow ben good
baytys for hym at all tymes as I haue herde saye of persones
credyble & also founde wryten in bokes of credence.

The cheuyn is a stately fysshe: & his heed is a deyty[15] mor-
sell. There is noo fysshe soo strongly enarmyd wyth sca
lys on the body. And bi cause he is a stronge byter he ha
the the more baytes/ whiche ben thyse. In Marche the redde
worme at the grounde: For comynly thenne he woll byte there
at all tymes of þe yere yf he be ony thinge hungry. In Apryll
the dyche canker that bredith in the tree. A worme that bredith
betwene the rynde & the tree of an oke The redde worme: and
the yonge frosshys whan the fete ben kyt of: Also the stone flye
the bobbe vnder the cowe torde: the redde snaylle. In May þe

[15] R: deynty.

bayte that breedyth on the osyer leyf & the docke canker togyd'
upon your hoke. Also a bayte that bredyth on a fern leyf: ẏ cod
worme. and a bayte that bredyth on an hawthorn. And a bayte
that bredyth on an oke leyf & a sylke worme & a codworme togyder. ¶ In June take the creket & the dorre & also a red worme: the heed kytte of & a codworme before: and put theym on ẏ
hoke. Also a bayte in the osyer leyf: yonge froisshys the thre fete
kitte of by the body: & the fourth by the knee. The bayte on the
hawthorn & the codworme togyder & a grubbe that bredyth in
a dunghyll: and a grete greshop. ¶ In Juyll the greshop & the
humbylbee in the medow. Also yonge bees & yonge hornettes.
Also a grete brended flye that bredith in pathes of medowes &
the flye that is amonge pysmeers hyllys. ¶ In August take
wortwormes & magotes unto Myghelmas. ¶ In Septembre
the redde worme: & also take the baytes whan ye may gete the
ym: that is to wyte, Cheryes: yonge myce not heeryd: & the hou
se combe.

The breeme is a noble fysshe & a deyntous. And ye shall
angle for hym from Marche unto August wyth a redde
worme: & thenne wyth a butter flye & a grene flye. & with
a bayte that bredyth amonge grene rede: and a bayte that bre
dyth in the barke of a deed tree. ¶ And for bremettis: take mag
gotes. ¶ And fro that tyme forth all the yere after take the red
worme: and in the ryuer browne breede. Moo baytes there ben
but they ben not easy & therfore I lete theym passe ouer.

A Tenche is a good fyssh: and heelith all manere of other
fysshe that ben hurte yf they maye come to hym. He is
the most parte of the yere in the mudde. And he styryth
moost in June & July: and in other seasons but lytyll. He is an
euyll byter. his baytes ben thyse. For all the yere browne bree
de tostyd wyth hony in lyknesse of a butteryd loof: and the gre
te redde worme. And as for cheyf take the blacke blood in ẏ her
te of a shepe & floure and hony. And tempre theym all togyder
somdeale softer than paast: & anoynt therwyth the redde worme: bothe for this fysshe & for other. And they woll byte moche
the better therat at all tymes.

¶ The perche is a daynteuous fysshe & passynge holsom and

bayte that bredyth on the osyer leyf & the docke canker togyder vpon your hoke. Also a bayte that bredyth on a fernn leyf: þe cod worme. and a bayte that bredyth on an hawthornn. And a bayte that bredyth on an oke leyf & a sylke worme & a codworme to-gyder. Inn Iune take the creket & the dorre & also a red wor-me: the heed kytte of & a codworme before: and put theym on þe hoke. Also a bayte in the osyer leyf: yonge frosshys the thre fete kitte of by the body: & the fourth by the knee. The bayte on the hawthornn & the codworme togyder & a grubbe that bredyth in a dunghyll: and a grete greshop. In Iuyll the greshop & the humbylbee in the medow. Also yonge bees & yonge hornettes. Also a grete brended flye that bredith in pathes of medowes & the flye that is amonge pysmeers hyllys. In August take wortwormes & magotes vnto Myghelmas. In Septembre the redde worme: & also take the baytes whan ye may gete the ym: that is to wyte/ Cheryes: yonge myce not heeryd: & the hou se[16] combe.

Facsimile, with Transcript, of the First Printed Text of the Treatise

The breeme is a noble fysshe & a deyntous. And ye shall angle for hym from Marche vnto August wyth a redde worme: & thenne wyth a butter flye & a grene flye. & with a bayte that bredyth amonge grene rede: and a bayte that bre dyth in the barke of a deed tree. And for bremettis: take mag gotes. And fro that tyme forth all the yere after take the red worme: and in the ryuer browne breede. Moo baytes there ben but they ben not easy & therfore I lete theym passe ouer.

A Tenche is a good fyssh: and heelith all manere of other fysshe that ben hurte yf they maye come to hym. He is the most parte of the yere in the mudde. And he styryth moost in Iune & Iuly: and in other seasons but lytyll. He is an euyll byter. his baytes ben thyse. For all the yere browne bree de tostyd wyth hony in lyknesse of a butteryd loof: and the gre te redde worme. And as for cheyf take the blacke blood in þe her te of a shepe & floure and hony. And tempre theym all togyder somdeale softer than paast: & anoynt therwyth the redde wor-me: bothe for this fysshe & for other. And they woll byte moche the better therat at all tymes.

The perche is a daynteuous fysshe & passynge holsom and

[16] R: honye.

a free bytyng. Thise ben his baytes. In Marche the redde wor
me. In Aprill the bobbe vnder the cowe torde. In May the slo
thorn worme & the codworme. In Iune the bayte that bredith
in an olde fallen oke & the grene canker. In Iuyll the bayte that
bredyth on the osyer leyf & the bobbe that bredeth on the dung
hyll: and the hawthorn worme & the codworme. In August the
redde worme & maggotes. All the yere after the red worme as
for the beste.

¶ The roche is an easy fysshe to take: And yf he be fatte & pen
nyd thenne is he good meete. & thyse ben his baytes. In Marche the most redy bayte is the red worme. In Aprill the bobbe
vnder the cowe torde. In May the bayte ẏ bredyth on the oke
leyf & the bobbe in the dunghyll. In Iune the bayte that bredith on the osyer & the codworme. In Iuyll hous flyes. & the
bayte that bredith on an oke. and the notworme & mathewes &
maggotes tyll Myghelmas. And after ẏ the fatte of bakon.

¶ The dace is a gentyll fysshe to take. & yf it be well refet then
is it good meete. In Marche his bayte is a redde worme. In
Aprill the bobbe vnder the cowe torde. In May the docke can
ker & the bayte on ẏ slothorn and on the oken leyf. In Iune the
codworme & the bayte on the osyer and the whyte grubbe in ẏ
dunghyll. In Iuyll take hous flyes & flyes that brede in pys-
mer hylles: the codworme & maggotes vnto Mighelmas. And
yf the water be clere ye shall take fysshe whan other take none
And fro that tyme forth doo as ye do for the roche. For comyn
ly theyr bytynge & theyr baytes ben lyke

¶ The bleke is but a feble fysshe. yet he is holsom His baytes
from Marche to Myghelmas be the same that I haue wryten
before. For the roche & darse sauynge all the somer season asmo
che as ye maye angle for hym wyth an house flye: & in wynter
season wt bakon & other bayte made as ye herafter may know.

¶ The ruf is ryght an holsom fysshe: And ye shall angle to him
wyth the same baytes in al seasons of the yere & in the same wi
se as I haue tolde you of the perche: for they ben lyke in fysshe
& fedinge/ sauynge the ruf is lesse. And therfore he must haue ẏ
smaller bayte.

¶ The flounder is an holsom fisshe & a free. and a subtyll byter
in his manere: For comynly whan he soukyth his meete he fe-

i ij

a free bytyng. Thise ben his baytes. In Marche the redde wor
me. In Aprill the bobbe vnder the cowe torde. In May the slo
thornn worme & the codworme. In Iune the bayte that bredith
in an olde fallen oke & the grete canker. In Iuyll the bayte that
bredyth on the osyer leyf & the bobbe that bredeth on the dung
hyll: and the hawthornn worme & the codworme. In August the
redde worme & maggotes. All the yere after the red worme as
for the beste.

The roche is an easy fysshe to take: And yf he be fatte & pen
nyd thenne is he good meete. & thyse ben his baytes. In Marche the most redy bayte is the red worme. In Apryll the bobbe
vnder the cowe torde. In May the bayte þ*a*t bredyth on the oke
leyf & the bobbe in the dunghyll. In Iune the bayte that bredith on the osyer & the codworme. In Iuyll hous flyes. & the
bayte that bredith on an oke. and the notworme & mathewes &
maggot es tyll Myghelmas. And after þ*a*t the fatte of bakon.

The dace is a gentyll fysshe to take. & yf it be well refet thenn
is it good meete. In Marche his bayte is a redde worme. In
Apryll the bobbe vnder the cowe torde. In May the docke can
ker & the bayte on þe slothornn and on the oken leyf. In Iune the
codworme & the bayte on the osyer and the whyte grubbe in þe
dunghyll. In Iuyll take hous flyes & flyes that brede in pys-
mer hylles: the codworme & maggotes vnto Mighelmas. And
yf the water be clere ye shall take fysshe whan other take none
And fro that tyme forth doo as ye do for the roche. For comyn
ly theyr bytynge & theyr baytes ben lyke.

The bleke is but a feble fysshe. yet he is holsom His baytes
from Marche to Myghelmas be the same that I haue wryten
before. For the roche & darse sauynge all the somer season asmo
che as ye maye angle for hym wyth an house flye: & in wynter
season wt bakon & other bayte made as ye herafter may know.

The ruf is ryght an holsom fysshe: And ye shall angle to him
wyth the same baytes in al seasons of the yere & in the same wi
se as I haue tolde you of the perche: for they ben lyke in fysshe
& fedinge/ sauynge the ruf is lesse. And therfore he must haue þe
smaller bayte.

The flounder is an holsom fisshe & a free. and a subtyll byter
in his manere: For comynly whan he soukyth his meete he fe-

wyth at grounde. ⁊ therfore ye must angle to hym wyth a gro
unde lyne lyenge. And he hath but one manere of bayte. ⁊ that
is a red worme. Whiche is moost cheyf for all manere of fysshe.
¶ The gogen is a good fisshe of the mochenes: ⁊ he byteth wel
at the grounde And his baytes for all the yere ben thyse. ẏ red
worme: codworme: ⁊ maggotes. And ye must angle to him wᵗ
a flote. ⁊ lete your bayte be nere ẏ botom or ellis on ẏ groñde.
¶ The menow whan he shynith in the water theñ is he bytter
And though his body be lytyll yet he is a rauenous biter ⁊ an
egre. And ye shall angle to hym wyth the same baytes that ye
doo for the gogyn: sauynge they must be smalle.
¶ The ele is a quasy fysshe a rauenour ⁊ a deuourer of the bro
de of fysshe. And for the pyke also is a deuourer of fysshe I put
them bothe behynde all other to angle. For this ele ye shall fyn
de an hole in the grounde of the water. ⁊ it is blewe blackysshe
there put in your hoke tyll that it be a fote wythin ẏ hole. and
your bayte shall be a grete angyll twytch or a menow.
¶ The pyke is a good fysshe: but for he deuouryth so many as
well of his owne kynde as of other: I loue hym the lesse. ⁊ for
to take hym ye shall doo thus. Take a codlynge hoke: ⁊ take a
roche or a fresshe heeryng ⁊ a wyre wyth an hole in the ende: ⁊
put it in at the mouth ⁊ out at the taylle downe by the ridge of
the fresshe heeryng. And thenne put the lyne of your hoke in af
ter. ⁊ drawe the hoke in to the cheke of ẏ fresshe heeryng. Theñ
put a plumbe of lede vpon your lyne a yerde longe from youre
hoke ⁊ a flote in mydwaye betwene: ⁊ caste it in a pytte where
the pyke vsyth. And this is the beste ⁊ moost surest crafte of ta
kynge the pyke. ¶ A nother manere takynge of hym there is.
Take a frosshe ⁊ put it on your hoke at the necke bytwene the
skynne ⁊ the body on ẏ backe half: ⁊ put on a flote a yerde ther
fro: ⁊ caste it where the pyke hauntyth and ye shall haue hym.
¶ A nother manere. Take the same bayte ⁊ put it in Asa fetida
⁊ cast it in the water wyth a corde ⁊ a corke: ⁊ ye shall not fayll
of hym. And yf ye lyst to haue a good sporte: thenne tye the cor
de to a gose fote: ⁊ ye shall se god halynge whether the gose or
the pyke shall haue the better.

Now ye wote with what baytes ⁊ how ye shall angle to
euery manere fysshe. Now I woll tell you how ye shall

dyth at grounde. & therfore ye must angle to hym wyth a gro
unde lyne lyenge. And he hath but one manere of bayte. & that
is a red worme. whiche is moost cheyf for all manere of fysshe.

The gogen is a good fisshe of the mochenes: & he byteth wel
at the grounde And his baytes for all the yere ben thyse. þe red
worme: codworme: & maggotes. And ye must angle to him wt
a flote. & lete your bayte be nere þe botom or ellis on þe grounde.

The menow whan he shynith in the water thenn is he byttyr
And though his body be lytyll yet he is a rauenous biter & an
egre. And ye shall angle to hym wyth the same baytes that ye
doo for the gogyn: sauynge they must be smalle.

The ele is a quasy fysshe a rauenour & a deuourer of the bro
de of fysshe. And for the pyke also is a deuourer of fysshe I put
them bothe behynde all other to angle. For this ele ye shall fyn
de an hole in the grounde of the water. & it is blewe blackysshe
there put in your hoke tyll that it be a fote wythin þe hole. and
pour[17] bayte shall be a grete angyll twytch or a menow.

The pyke is a good fysshe: but for he deuouryth so many as
well of his own kynde as of other: I loue hym the lesse. & for
to take hym ye shall doo thus. Take a codlynge hoke: & take a
roche or a fresshe heering & a wyre wyth an hole in the ende: &
put it in at the mouth & out at the taylle downe by the ridge of
the fresshe heeryng. And thenne put the lyne of your hoke in af
ter. & drawe the hoke in to the cheke of þe fresshe heeryng. Thenn
put a plumbe of lede vpon your lyne a yerde longe from youre
hoke & a flote in mydwaye betwene: & caste it in a pytte where
the pyke vsyth. And this is the beste & moost surest crafte of ta
kynge the pyke. A nother manere takynge of hym there is.
Take a frosshe & put it on your hoke at the necke bytwene the
skynne & the body on þe backe half: & put on a flote a yerde ther
fro: & caste it where the pyke hauntyth and ye shall haue hym.
A nother manere. Take the same bayte & put it in Asa fetida
& cast it in the water wyth a corde & a corke: & ye shall not fayll
of hym. And yf ye lyst to haue a good sporte: thenne tye the cor
de to a gose fote: & ye shall se god halynge whether the gose or
the pyke shall haue the better.

Now ye wote with what baytes & how ye shall angle to
euery manere fysshe. Now I woll tell you how ye shall

[17] R: your.

kepe and fede your quycke baytes. Ye shall fede and kepe them
all in generall: but euery manere by hymself wyth suche thyngis
in and on whiche they brede. And as longe as they ben quycke
& newe they ben fyne. But whan they ben in a slough or elles
deed thenne ben they nought. Oute of thyse ben excepted thre
brodes: That is to wyte of hornettys: humblylbees. & waspys.
whom ye shall bake in breede & after dyppe theyr heedes in blo
de & lete them drye. Also excepte maggotes: whyche whan thei
ben bredde grete wyth theyr naturell fedynge: ye shall fede the
ym ferthermore wyth shepes talow & wyth a cake made of flou
re & hony. thenne woll they be more grete. And whan ye haue
clensyd theym wyth sonde in a bagge of blanket kepte hote vn
der your gowne or other warm thyng two houres or thre. then
ben they beste & redy to angle wyth. And of the frosshe kytte þ
legge by the knee. of the grasshop the leggys & wynges by the
body.

¶Thyse ben baytes made to laste all the yere. Fyrste been flou
re & lene flesshe of the hepis of a cony or of a catte: virgyn wexe
& sheppys talowe: and braye theym in a morter: And thenne tem
pre it at the fyre wyth a lytyll puryfyed hony: & soo make it vp
in lytyll ballys & bayte therwyth your hokys after theyr quan
tyte. & this is a good bayte for all manere fresshe fysshe.

¶A nother. take the sewet of a shepe & chese in lyke quantyte: &
braye theim togider longe in a mortere: And take thenne floure
& tempre it therwyth. and after that alaye it wyth hony & ma
ke ballys therof. and that is for the barbyll in especyall.

¶A nother for darse. & roche & bleke. take whete & sethe it well
& thenne put it in blood all a daye & a nyghte. and it is a good
bayte.

¶For baytes for grete fyssh kepe specyally this rule. Whan ye
haue take a grete fysshe: vndo the mawe. & what ye fynde ther
in make that your bayte: for it is beste.

¶Thyse ben the. xii. flyes wyth whyche ye shall angle to þ tro
ught & grayllyng: and dubbe lyke as ye shall now here me tell.

¶Marche.

kepe and fede your quycke baytes. Ye shall fede and kepe them all in generall: but euery manere by hymself wyth suche thyng in and on whiche they brede. And as longe as they ben quycke & newe they ben fyne. But whan they ben in a slough or elles deed thenne ben they nought. Oute of thyse ben excepted thre brodes: That is to wyte of hornettys: humbylbees. & waspys. whom ye shall bake in breede & after dyppe theyr heedes in blo de & lete them drye. Also excepte maggotes: whyche whan thei ben bredde grete wyth theyr naturell fedynge: ye shall fede the ym ferthermore wyth shepes talow & wyth a cake made of flou re & hony. thenne woll they be more grete. And whan ye haue clensyd theym wyth sonde in a bagge of blanket kepte hote vn der your gowne or other warmm thyng two houres or thre. thenn ben they beste & redy to angle wyth. And of the frosshe kytte þe legge by the knee. of the grasshop the leggys & wynges by the body.

Thyse ben baytes made to laste all the yere. Fyrste been flou re & lene flesshe of the hepis of a cony or of a catte: virgyn wexe & shepys talowe: and braye theym in a morter: And thenne tem pre it at the fyre wyth a lytyll puryfyed hony: & soo make it vp in lytyll ballys & bayte therwyth your hokys after theyr quan tyte. & this is a good bayte for all manere fresshe fysshe.
A nother. take the sewet of a shepe & chese in lyke quantyte: & braye theim togider longe in a mortere: And take thenne floure & tempre it therwyth. and after that alaye it wyth hony & ma- ke ballys therof. and that is for the barbyll in especyall.
A nother for darse. & roche & bleke. take whete & sethe it well & thenne put it in blood all a daye & a nyghte. and it is a good bayte.

For baytes for grete fyssh kepe specyally this rule. Whan ye haue take a grete fysshe: vndo the mawe. & what ye fynde ther- in make that your bayte: for it is beste.

Thyse ben the .xij. flyes wyth whyche ye shall angle to þe tro ught & grayllyng/ and dubbe lyke as ye shall now here me tell.

Marche.

The donne flye the body of the donne woll & the wyngis of the pertryche. A nother doone flye. the body of blacke woll: the wynges of the blackyst drake: and the Jay vnd the wynge & vnder the tayle. ¶ Apryll.

¶ The stone flye. the body of blacke wull: & yelowe vnder the wynge. and vnder the tayle & the wynges of the drake. In the begynnynge of May a good flye. the body of roddyd wull and lappid abowte wyth blacke sylke: the wynges of the drake & of the redde capons hakyll. ¶ May.

¶ The yelow flye. the body of yelow wull: the wynges of the redde cocke hakyll & of the drake lyttyd yelow. The blacke lou per. the body of blacke wull & lappyd abowte wyth the herle of ye pecok tayle: & the wynges of ye redde capon wt a blewe heed.

¶ June. ¶ The donne cutte: the body of blacke wull & a ye-low lyste after eyther syde: the wynges of the bosarde bounde on with barkyd hempe. The maure flye. the body of doske wull the wynges of the blackest mayle of the wylde drake. The tan dy flye at saynt Wyllyams daye. the body of tandy wull & the wynges contrary eyther ayenst other of the whitest mayle of ye wylde drake. ¶ Juyll.

¶ The waspe flye. the body of blacke wull & lappid abowte wt yelow threde: the winges of the bosarde. The shell flye at saynt Thomas daye. the body of grene wull & lappyd abowte wyth the herle of the pecoks tayle: wynges of the bosarde.

¶ August. ¶ The drake flye. the body of blacke wull & lap-pyd abowte wyth blacke sylke: wynges of the mayle of the blac ke drake wyth a blacke heed.

¶ Thyse fygures are put here in ensample of your hokes.

The donne flye the body of the donne woll & the wyngis of the pertryche. A nother doone flye. the body of blacke woll: the wynges of the blackyst drake: and the Iay vnder the wynge & vnder the tayle. Apryll.

The stone flye. the body of blacke wull: & yelowe vnder the wynge. and vnder the tayle & the wynges of the drake. In the begynnynge of May a good flye. the body of roddyd wull and lappid abowte wyth blacke sylke: the wynges of the drake & of the redde capons hakyll. May.

The yelow flye. the body of yelow wull: the wynges of the redde cocke hakyll & of the drake lyttyd yelow. The blacke lou per. the body of blacke wull & lappyd abowte wyth the herle of þe pecok tayle: & the wynges of þe redde capon wt a blewe heed.

Iune. The donne cutte: the body of blacke wull & a ye-low lyste after eyther syde: the wynges of the bosarde bounde on wyth barkyd hempe. The maure flye. the body of dolke[18] wull the wynges of the blackest mayle of the wylde drake. The tan dy flye at saynt Wyllyams daye. the body of tandy wull & the wynges contrary eyther ayenst other of the whitest mayle of þe wylde drake. Iuyll.

The waspe flye. the body of blacke wull & lappid abowte wt yelow threde: the winges of the bosarde. The shell flye at saynt Thomas daye. the body of grene wull & lappyd abowte wyth the herle of the pecoks tayle: wynges of the bosarde.
August. The drake flye. the body of blacke wull & lap-pyd abowte wyth blacke sylke: wynges of the mayle of the blac ke drake wyth a blacke heed.

Thyse fygures are put here in ensample of your hokes.

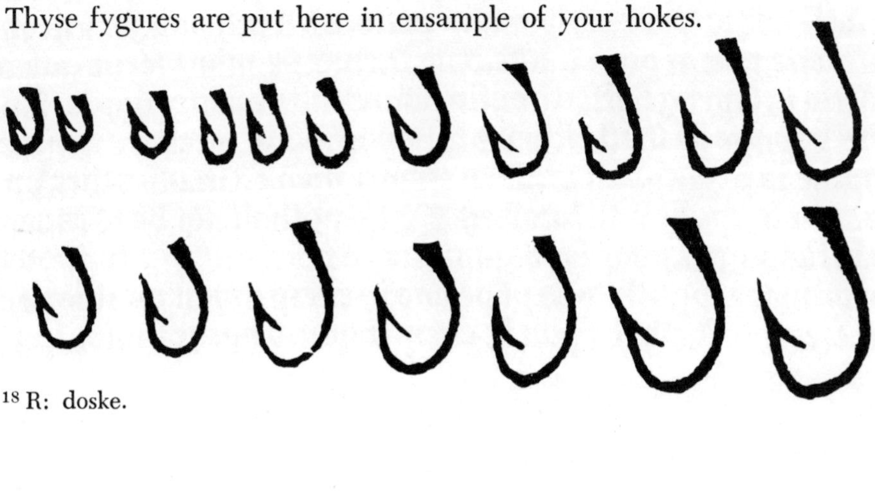

Facsimile, with Transcript, of the First Printed Text of the Treatise

[18] R: doske.

¶Here folowyth the order made to all those whiche shall haue the vnderstondynge of this forsayde treatyse & vse it for theyr pleasures.

Ye that can angle & take fysshe to your plesures as this forsayd treatyse techyth & shewyth you: I charge & requyre you in the name of alle noble men that ye fysshe not in noo poore mannes seuerall water: as his ponde: stewe: or other necessary thynges to kepe fysshe in wythout his lycence & good wyll. ¶Nor that ye vse not to breke noo mannys gynnys lyenge in theyr weares & in other places due vnto theym. Ne to take the fysshe awaye that is taken in theym. For after a fysshe is taken in a mannys gynne yf the gynne be layed in the comyn waters: or elles in suche waters as he hireth, it is his owne propre goodes. And yf ye take it awaye ye robbe hym: whyche is a ryght shamfull dede to ony noble man to do ye that theuys & brybours done: whyche are punysshed for theyr euyll dedes by the necke & otherwyse whan they maye be aspyed & taken. And also yf ye doo in lyke manere as this treatise shewyth you: ye shal haue no nede to take of other mennys: whiles ye shal haue ynough of your owne takyng yf ye lyste to labour therfore. Whyche shall be to you a very pleasure to se the fayr bryght shynynge scalyd fysshes dysceyued by your crafty meanes and drawen vpon londe. ¶Also that ye breke noo mannys heggys in goynge abowte your dysportes: ne opyn noo mannes gates but that ye shytte theym agayn. ¶Also ye shall not vse this forsayd crafty dysporte for no couetysenes to thencreasynge & sparynge of your money oonly, but pryncypally for your solace & to cause the helthe of your body. and specyally of your soule. For whanne ye purpoos to goo on your disportes in fysshyng ye woll not desyre gretly many persones wyth you. whiche myghte lette you of your game. And thenne ye maye serue god deuowtly in sayenge affectuously youre custumable prayer. And thus doynge ye shall eschewe & voyde many vices. as ydylnes whyche is pryncypall cause to enduce man to many other vyces. as it is ryght well knowen. ¶Also ye shall not be to rauenous in takyng of your sayd game as to moche at one tyme: whiche ye maye lyghtly doo yf ye doo in euery poynt as this present treatyse shewyth you in euery poynt. whyche sholde lyght

Here folowyth the order made to all those whiche shall haue the vnderstondynge of this forsayde treatyse & vse it for theyr pleasures.

Ye that can angle & take fysshe to your plesures as this forsayd treatyse techyth & shewyth you: I charge & requyre you in the name of alle noble men that ye fysshe not in noo poore mannes seuerall water: as his ponde: stewe: or other necessary thynges to kepe fysshe in wythout his lycence & good wyll. Nor that ye vse not to breke noo mannys gynnys lyenge in theyr weares & in other places due vnto theym. Ne to take the fysshe awaye that is taken in theym. For after a fysshe is taken in a mannys gynne yf the gynne be layed in the comyn waters: or elles in suche waters as he hireth/ it is his ow ne propre goodes. And yf ye take it awaye ye robbe hym: whyche is a ryght shamfull dede to ony noble man to do þ*a*t that theuys & brybours done: whyche are punysshed for theyr euyll de des by the necke & otherwyse whan they maye be aspyed & taken. And also yf ye doo in lyke manere as this treatise shewyth you: ye shal haue no nede to take of other mennys: whiles ye shal haue ynough of your owne takyng yf ye lyste to labour therfo re. whyche shall be to you a very pleasure to se the fayr bryght shynynge scalyd fysshes dysceyued by your crafty meanes and drawen vpon londe. Also that ye breke noo mannys heggys in goynge abowte your dysportes: ne opyn noo mannes gates but that ye shytte theym agayn. Also ye shall not vse this for sayd crafty dysporte for no couetysenes to thencreasynge & spa rynge of your money oonly/ but pryncypally for your solace & to cause the helthe of your body. and specyally of your soule. For whan ye purpoos to goo on your disportes in fysshyng ye woll not desyre gretly many persones wyth you. whiche my ghte lette you of your game. And thenne ye maye serue god de uowtly in sayenge affectuously youre custumable prayer. And this doynge ye shall eschewe & voyde many vices. as ydylnes whyche is pryncypall cause to enduce man to many other vyces. as it is ryght well knowen. Also ye shall not be too raueno us in takyng of your sayd game as to moche at one tyme: whi che ye maye lyghtly doo yf ye doo in euery poynt as this present treatyse shewyth you in euery poynt. whyche sholde lyght ly be occasyon to dystroye your owne dysportes & other mennys also. As whan ye haue a suffycyent mese ye sholde coueyte nomore as at that tyme. ¶Also ye shall besye yourselfe to nouryssh the game in all that ye maye: & to dystroye all suche thynges as ben deuourers of it. ¶And all those that done after this rule shall haue the blessynge of god & saynt Petyr/ whyche he theym graunte that wyth his precyous blood vs boughte.

¶And for by cause that this present treatyse sholde not come to the hondys of eche ydle persone whyche wolde desire it yf it were enpryntyd allone by itself & put in a lytyll plaunflet therfore I haue compylyd it in a greter volume of dyuerse bokys concernynge to gentyll & noble men. to the entent that the forsayd ydle persones whyche sholde haue but lytyll mesure in the sayd dysporte of fysshyng sholde not by this meane utterly dystroye it.

ly be occasyon to dystroye your owne dysportes & other mennys also. As whan ye haue a suffycyent mese ye sholde coueyte
nomore as at that tyme. Also ye shall helpe yourselfe to nouryssh the game in all that ye maye: & to dystroye all suche thyn
ges as ben deuourers of it. And all those that done after this
rule shall haue the blessynge of god & saynt Petyr/ whyche he
theym graunte that wyth his precyous blood vs boughte.

And for by cause that this present treatyse sholde not come
to the hondys of eche ydle persone whyche wolde desire it yf it
were enpryntyd allone by itself & put in a lytyll plaunflet ther
fore I haue compylyd it in a greter volume of dyuerse bokys
concernynge to gentyll & noble men. to the entent that the for
sayd ydle persones whyche sholde haue but lytyll mesure in the
sayd dysporte of fysshyng sholde not by this meane vtterly dys
troye it.

CHAPTER 9

Comparison of Manuscript and First Printed Version of the Treatise

A comparison of the Yale Wagstaff Manuscript of the *Treatise of Fishing* with its somewhat later form in Wynkyn de Worde's print of 1496 reveals many differences, of varying degrees of importance. We think that we can safely conclude, from its nonconformity to the conventional standards as well as from its earlier date, that the manuscript more nearly represents the language and style of the original author than does the 1496 print. Some of the differences in the versions are undoubtedly due to changes made by the printer; for a parallel case, one may compare the manuscript of Malory's *Morte d' Arthur* with Caxton's printed version. Other differences may be due to alterations made by fifteenth-century scribes in copying the manuscript used by the printer (or its ancestors) or in copying the Yale Wagstaff Manuscript (or its ancestors). It is even possible that in some instances both the reading of the Yale Wagstaff Manuscript and that of the print may go back to the original author. We are seldom able to assign a specific item to any specific source or cause; but an examination of the differences observed, with a few examples, may reveal something about the history and development of the text.

There are many differences in spelling, grammar, and diction, most of them minor but interesting. In general, the printed version tends to eliminate the archaic, the dialectal, the individualistic, the strange or unusual; it tends to normalize the language and style in the direction of the southeastern English affected by the printers of the fifteenth and sixteenth centuries.

Other differences involve errors found in one version but not in the other, omissions in one which can be supplied from the other, and additions or amplifications appearing in only one version. From these, we can frequently draw fairly reliable inferences as to how the text was developed and transmitted. We take up the latter group first.

ERRORS IN THE MANUSCRIPT

The Yale Wagstaff Manuscript of the *Treatise of Fishing* is a rough copy, very different from some of the luxury manuscripts of its age. It was written hurriedly and with little regard for scribal niceties. At the same time it is reasonably accurate as manuscripts go, and the copyist seems to have been anxious to produce a faithful copy. In a number of instances he has written the wrong word, made a false start, written something twice, or copied from the wrong line of his exemplar. These errors were usually corrected immediately, the copyist merely starting afresh at the point of the mistake and rewriting the text correctly. There are no signs of erasure; sometimes the redundant portions of the text are deleted by a stroke of the pen, sometimes not. These faults do not appear in the printed text, probably because they were made by the copyist of the Yale Wagstaff Manuscript himself and were not found in the manuscript from which the printer worked. Of course, the printer might have had in the shop an editor who made corrections. Three examples should suffice to illustrate the typical situations:

Manuscript	*Print*
2, 1. spry spryt	spyryte
2, 6. ocupocon occupacion	occupacyon
8, 23 to 9, 1. Then schaue the stafe wel at bothe endes and make hyt	Then shaue your staffe & make hym

The first of these is certainly not a "spry spirit." The files of the *Middle English Dictionary* contain no example of *spry* other than this one, and the earliest example cited by the *Oxford English Dictionary* is of the eighteenth century. Moreover, this use of the word would have to be figurative and of a sort unlikely to occur unless the word in its ordinary meanings were well established. What we have here is merely an instance of double copying in the manuscript. In the second example, the copyist made an error and immediately corrected it; *ocupocon* is crossed out. In the last example, the copyist skipped a line and began to copy at "wel at bothe endys" (9, 2); seeing his error, he went back to "and make hyt" and copied from there on; the redundant words are crossed out. If we needed evidence that the Yale Wagstaff Manuscript is a copy rather than the author's original, an error like the last would be sufficient to prove that the manuscript was copied from something. Of course, it might be the author copying a rough draft. In that case the author should have been familiar enough with the composition not to make mistakes of this sort very often.

Comparison of the Manuscript and the First Printed Version of the Treatise

There are a few careless errors—not many—of which the following are typical:

Manuscript	*Print*
2, 10. to a place (altered to: to a places)	to places
2, 13. send (for "find")	fynde
3, 1. clothes tornes	clothes torne

The first may stem from an author's alteration; i.e., in changing *place* to *places,* he forgot (as one often does in revisions of this sort) to delete the article.[1] (There are several other ways of accounting for this error, however, and we should not want to build any theories on it.) The second is careless writing; one form of fifteenth-century *s* is very similar to an *f*, and the confusion of *e* and *i* (or *y*) is treated below. In the third example the copyist unthinkingly repeated the ending of *clothes* when he wrote the adjective.

More significant than the rest are two apparent errors which involve winds favorable or unfavorable to angling. In each case the print has a correct reading, or at any rate a reading which is consistent with what is said elsewhere in the treatise.

Manuscript	*Print*
17, 4–6. And yf the wynde þat sesan [September–April] haue any parte of þe oriente, þe wetur þen ys good	And yf the wynde in that season haue ony parte of the Oryent, the wedyr thenne is nought

The manuscript must be in error here, for a few lines farther on both the manuscript and the print agree in stating that a wind from an easterly

[1] See Chapter 7.

direction is unfavorable to angling in any season. Perhaps a negative was omitted in the manuscript from which the Yale Wagstaff copy was transcribed. In any case, the copyist tried to correct the mistake by writing *northe* above *oriente*. He can hardly have meant to substitute *oriente-northe* (i.e., northeast), for this wind was invariably bad (cf. 18, 3). Very likely, he meant to substitute *northe* for *oriente*, to indicate that a north wind might be favorable in some circumstances; this would at least be consistent with what the print has a little farther on: "The Weste and northe Wyndes ben good, but the south is beste." If this is the correct interpretation of the first reading, we may have a clue to an error in these lines:

Manuscript	*Print*
18, 3–6. yf hyt [the wind] be by the northe or northe Est or sowthe est . . . the fysche wyll not commynly byte ne styre	yf the wynde be in the Eest, and that is worste, For comynly . . . þe fysshe woll not byte thenne

The statement of the manuscript would certainly appear more logical if the first *northe* were changed to *Est*. We should not go so far as to emend the text, but this point deserves careful thought, for it has a bearing on the locality in and for which the treatise was written.

ERRORS IN THE PRINT

There are relatively few careless errors in the printed version, but there are several which appear to be due to misreading of archaic or dialectal terms in the manuscript from which the printer worked. These seem to be probable instances:

Manuscript	*Print*
3, 14. [The hawk obstinately refuses to fly at the game.] The[n] wyl sche baythe	thenne woll she bathe
7, 22. Ye schall kytte . . . a feyr staf . . . and beke hem in a ovyn	Ye shall kytte . . . a fayr staffe . . . And bethe hym in an hote ouyn

In the first, the author used the rare verb *baythe*, "to consent, agree," etc.; but because of the author's tendency to write *ay* or *ai* for *a* (noted below), the printer assumed that this must be *bathe*, "to take a bath." The ordinary sense of *bathe* is inapplicable here; hawks were bathed with great care and many precautions against sickness, and would never be bathed while out hawking. Thomas Satchell, in his glossary, compares this passage with the "Nun's Priest's Tale," where Chaucer figuratively refers to the hens as bathing in the sand; he suggested that the hawk would "grovel in the dust." This is hard to take seriously. In the Chaucerian passage the sand is overtly mentioned in the context; and there is no reason to suppose that a fifteenth-century reader would understand *bathe* all by itself to mean "bathe in sand," or dust, or what have you. In the second example, *beke* means "to heat," while *bethe* is "to soak." A hot oven of the fifteenth-century sort seems a poor place in which to put a piece of wood to soak. No doubt the printer mistook an original *beke,* a rare word in this treatise, for *bethe,* which is used a number of times.

There are other places in which we think that the reading of the printed version is due to misunderstanding, but we are speculating.

Manuscript	*Print*
2, 16–17. lyke as y thynke to scrywe, of it and all þe other, þe greuys	lyke as I thynke to dyscryue of it and of alle the other.
5, 22 to 6, 1. And yf þe angler take þe fysche hardly, þen ys þer no man meryer þen he is in hys sprit*es*	And yf the angler take fysshe, surely thenne is there noo man merier than he is in his spyryte.

In the first instance, the angler has just referred to the Master of Game and how he describes the joys of hunting. The angler will show the reverse of the coin, describe the griefs of hunting as well as of hawking and fowling. Unpunctuated, the construction is certainly a bit difficult; most people must read it twice to get the meaning. The printer (or one of the scribes who preceded him) missed the point entirely and relieved the awkwardness of the construction by changing its sense. We realize that a bright copyist could have changed the sentence in the Yale Wagstaff Manuscript, adding the griefs, but we prefer to attribute a touch like this to the author. In the second instance, obviously an angler is pleased when he catches fish, but we suspect that—even in the fifteenth century—anglers got more pleasure when the fish was taken *hardly,* "with difficulty." The printer, taking *hardly* in another of its Middle English senses, changed it to *surely.* It is possible that this is the meaning of *hardly* which the author intended, but it seems to us more likely that the meaning lies in the pleasure of winning against a hard-fighting trout, and that the printer has again missed the point.

OMISSIONS IN THE MANUSCRIPT

The copyist of the Yale Wagstaff Manuscript (or one of his predecessors) evidently omitted some things in the original text, and occasionally the print enables us to supply the missing portions. A common situation in copying occurs when a scribe encounters the same phrase twice, the situation being especially hazardous if the expression occurs at the beginnings of two different lines. Here is an instance:

13, 19–22. ffor all man*er* of fyche þat fedyt by the grounde, *ye schall angle* to hym in the myddes of the watur, & som deyl moyr be-neythe þen a-boue.

The print reads thus (the line-lengths are revised to suggest a possible arrangement of the original):

For alle manere fysshe that fede by the grounde,
ye shall angle for theim to the botom soo that
your hokys shall renne or lye on the grounde.
And for alle other fysshe that fede aboue,
ye shall angle to theym in the myddes of the water,
or somdeale byneth or somdeale aboue.

What happened here should be obvious to anyone. The passage is significant, in that it proves that the manuscript from which Wynkyn de Worde worked was independent of the Yale Wagstaff Manuscript, and descended from a different copy of the original text.

Other omissions are less obvious and less revealing, but an additional example or two may be of interest:

Manuscript	*Print*
17, 2. [It is good to fish] yn som*ur* seasen when hyt ys brennyng hote	in somer season whan it is brennynge hote, thenne it [fishing] is nought.
17, 12 to 18, 6. [Of the twelve impediments, only eleven are given in the manuscript; the second is missing.]	The seconde is yf your baytes be not good nor fyne.

The fact of the omission is rather obvious in the second example, although the reason is not. In the first example there is no evidence of omission, except that the statement as given in the manuscript will seem to most anglers a manifest absurdity.

OMISSIONS IN THE PRINT

Comparison of the Manuscript and the First Printed Version of the Treatise

If the omissions in the Yale Wagstaff Manuscript prove that the print is derived from an independent copy of the original, omissions in the print are of equal force in proving that the Yale Wagstaff Manuscript is not derived from the print or from the manuscript that the printer used. The clearest example, with line-lengths rearranged as above, is the following:

6, 1–6. Also whoso wol vse þe game and disporte of angleyng,
he muste take hede to thys sentence of the olde
pr*o*u*er*be, þ*at* is, thise v*er*sus: Surge, miser,
mane *set* noli surger*e* vane; Sanctificat, sanat,
ditat quoq*ue* surger*e* mane. This is to sey,
he must ryse erly . . .

The printed version skips from the first *he must* to the second: "Also who soo woll vse the game of anglynge, he must ryse erly." In both versions, an exposition of the quotation follows; and although differences appear in the wording, the substance is the same. It seems rather odd in the print to have the text expounded in detail when it has not even been announced. Apparently this anomaly struck the printer also, for at the end he adds: "As the olde englysshe prouerbe sayth in this wyse. Who soo woll ryse erly shall be holy, helthy & zely." The fact that he used an English version, rather than the more learned and impressive Latin, suggests that the omission is not due to the printer but to the manuscript from which he worked; i.e., the Latin form of the proverb was not available to him.

Another probable omission is in the discussion of baits for the salmon:

Manuscript	*Print*
19, 8–9. Fyrst, w*ith* a bleke, like as ye do to þe trowt w*ith* a menows, and w*ith* a red worme	Fyrste, wyth a redde worme.

In another place, it seems probable that the printer found an obvious omission in his manuscript and patched up the text as best he could:

Manuscript	Print
4, 3–7. Yn þe mornyng he walket yn the dew; he goyth also wetschode and soyr a-colde to dyner by the morow, and sum tyme to bed, or he haue wyl sowpud for any thynge þat he may geyt by fowlyng	At morn tyde in the dewe he is weete shode vnto his taylle.

It is hard to believe that the crude and colorless version of the print could be a deliberate substitution for the circumstantial and vivid account in the manuscript.

ADDITIONS IN THE MANUSCRIPT

Some things which appear in the Yale Wagstaff Manuscript but not in the print cannot be characterized with any certainty as omissions in the latter. Of this sort are most of the section headings:

3, 6. Hawkynge
3, 19. ffowlyng
4, 14. ffyschynge
7, 16–17. How ȝe schall make ȝowr rode
14, 22–23. In wat place is best angleyng
15, 22–23. Wat tyme of þe day is best to angleyng

From their appearance in the manuscript these would seem to have been a scribe's (perhaps the author's) afterthoughts. The first two given here are not on separate lines but added at the ends of lines, as if inserted from the margin of the manuscript being copied. It is of interest to note that "hunting" has no heading of its own and that "fishing" is the first to be spaced out on a separate line. It is possible, of course, that some of these headings were added by the copyist of the Yale Wagstaff Manuscript, but that is an unlikely explanation for some of the others, for example, the last two given. These are placed at the foot of the page, the section itself beginning in each case at the top of the next page. A scribe might arrange his work in this manner in order not to waste writing materials, but it is more likely that he would stop at the end of a section, leaving a line or two blank, and put his fresh heading at the top of the next page—unless he were copying the headings from another manuscript, rather hurriedly and without thinking too much about the logic of the arrangement. It would appear that the manuscript from which the Yale Wagstaff Manuscript was copied had some of these headings, perhaps all, and that the size of the leaves in that manuscript differed from the size in the Yale Wagstaff Manuscript, so that the spacing did not always come out right.

Two other additions in the Yale Wagstaff Manuscript may be of interest:

Manuscript	*Print*
3, 8–9. [Hawking is a very annoying sport], & it is ver[y] trowthe.	
18, 11–12. eu*er*y man*er* freche watur fyche	euery manere of fysshe.

The second is an alteration in the manuscript, which without it would have read like the print. Possibly this is an author's afterthought, which was inserted in one manuscript of the treatise but not in another; or it could be due to a reader or a copyist, for anyone could have noted that the treatise is concerned with fresh-water fishing. The first example looks like a marginal comment by a reader ("Ain't that the truth!") copied into the body of the text by mistake; but it could also be an author's addition.

ADDITIONS IN THE PRINT

There are also some apparent additions or amplifications in the print, of which the following are most notable:

Manuscript	*Print*
1, 11. and fyschyng, namely anglyng	fysshynge . . . The beste to my symple dyscrec*ion* whyche is fysshynge, callyd Anglynge.
12, 12–14. Then schap hem [the floats] yn maner of a dove egge, lesse and mor as ȝe wylle	Thenne shape it [the float] grete in the myddis and smalle at bothe endys, and specyally sharpe in the nether ende and lyke vnto the fygures folowynge.
19, 16. [The manuscript finishes baits for salmon, proceeds immediately to the trout.]	And thyse baytes ben well prouyd baytes for the samon.

In the first instance both manuscript and print read rather awkwardly. Perhaps something has been omitted in the former, but it is equally possible that something has been added in the latter. The second looks like an attempt to make the simple directions of the manuscript version more precise. It seems unlikely that a copyist would substitute a dove's egg for the complicated (and rather confusing) directions found in the printed version—even if he had the temerity, he would probably lack the imagination. We are inclined to attribute the dove's egg to the author, and the printed version to a scribe or to the printer himself. The third example suggests the *probatum est*, etc., of the medical books of the Middle Ages; and since the author has already shown an interest in the *Regimen Sanitatis Salernitanum*, it may well be that this is another author's addition, preserved in the manuscript from which the print is descended but not in the manuscript which was the ancestor of the Yale Wagstaff Manuscript.

It will be noted that, if our interpretation of the data is correct, the author possessed more than one manuscript of the treatise. Revisions were made in both but not always transferred from one manuscript to the other.

This leads to the problem of the illustrations in the printed text. The skill with which medieval artists decorated manuscripts is well known, and the works on medicine and surgery were often illustrated. Drawings or diagrams of surgical instruments appear in the Middle English translation of Guy de Chauliac's *Grande Chirurgie*, and sketches of medicinal plants are common in some of the herbals. Usually, there was a division of labor, for a good scribe was not necessarily an artist, and vice versa. The scribe would leave spaces at the appropriate points, and the artist would then fill them in with his work. The Yale Wagstaff Manuscript contains no illustrations, although it contains one remark which may suggest that it was intended to have illustrations (or, more likely, that it was copied from an illustrated original). After enumerating the items of fishing gear which are described later, the author says (7, 14–15): "All þese ȝe schall fynd expressed openly to your ye" (i.e., to your eye). This is not conclusive, for in Middle English *expressed* may mean "depicted, portrayed," or merely "expressed" in the modern sense. Again, after describing the floats to be used on different types of lines, the author says (12, 20–21): "The lying ground lyne *with*-ovte floyte." This may be merely a verbless sentence, or it may have been the heading which accompanied an illustration in the original manuscript. The illustrations and their headings as found in the print have no counterpart in the Yale Wagstaff Manuscript. It is possible that they originated with the printer, but there is one circumstance which suggests that he was imitating the drawings of a manuscript. On signature H.3, his text promises pictures of the water knot and the duchess knot, and space is left for woodcuts. The space is vacant, very likely because the drawings were too difficult to reproduce. This situation would be unlikely to arise unless the printer were setting type from a manuscript containing illustrations at this point.

Comparison of the Manuscript and the First Printed Version of the Treatise

There is nothing in the description of the twelve artificial flies, as it appears in the print, to indicate whether it was supposed to be accompanied by illustrations. In the light of what has been said above, it is not unreasonable to suppose that illustrations of the flies appeared in the manuscript but were too difficult for Wynkyn de Worde to reproduce with woodcuts. The description of the flies opens with something of a fanfare, but the description itself shows signs of having been reduced as far as space is concerned; e.g., the months, except for the first, are crowded into the lines rather than given lines to themselves. It is possible that the manuscript had a more spacious and elaborate treatment of the flies, in which much of the space was devoted to pictures.

The following discussion of spelling, grammar, and diction is rather technical. It forms part of our argument that the manuscript more nearly represents the work of the original author. It is for those who are interested in the language aspect of the *Treatise of Fishing;* others may pass over it without great loss.

SPELLING

The Yale Wagstaff Manuscript tends to use "diphthongal" spellings for simple vowels (usually, but not always, long vowels), and the reverse: *ai* (or *ay*) for *a*, a for *ai*, etc.[2] The spellings of the print usually adhere rather closely to the conventions of late fifteenth-century London English, as in the following selected instances:

[2] The diphthongal spellings, however, were not always diphthongs in pronunciation.

Manuscript	*Print*	*Manuscript*	*Print*
1, 8. far, "fair"	fayr	4, 2. snayr, "snare"	snare
1, 12. treyt, "treat"	treate	4, 9. leyf, "leave"	leue
1, 13. boith, "both"	both	5, 2. hayf, "have"	haue
1, 19. neyd, "need"	nede	5, 19. þer, "their"	theyr
2, 4. orden, "ordain"	ordeyne	6, 15. meyn, "means"	meane
2, 10. sweyt, "sweet"	swete	8, 19. shoyt, "shoot"	shote
2, 20. soyr, "sore"	sore	13, 12. gralyng, "grayling"	graylyng
2, 22. heyghoge, "hedgehog"	hegge hogge	14, 12. smayl, "small"	smalle

Since *grayling* could be spelled with either *ay* or *ey* in the fifteenth century, we also find the form *grelyng* in the manuscript (11, 11).

A tendency to confuse *e* with *i* (or *y*) is present in the manuscript to a lesser degree, both long and short vowels being affected; this tendency is less noticeable in the print:

Manuscript	*Print*	*Manuscript*	*Print*
1, 3. bynne, "be" (present plural)	ben	15, 7. a presoner	prisoners
1, 8. by, "be" (present plural)	ben	16, 1. wete, "know"	wyte
4, 6. wyl, "well"	[omitted]	16, 6. westeling	whystelyng
7, 22. hem, "him"	hym		
14, 15. strynght	strengthe		

An archaic *-e* instead of *-y* occurs as an adjectival ending in the manuscript; e.g.:

Manuscript	*Print*	*Manuscript*	*Print*
2, 11. hungre, "hungry"	hungry	17, 3. sonne, "sunny"	sonny

The manuscript is rather unusual for the middle of the fifteenth century in its spelling of unaccented vowels, especially in its tendency to use *u* where other vowels might be expected:

Manuscript	*Print*	*Manuscript*	*Print*
2, 5. plesens	pleasaunce	4, 18. laburs	laborous
2, 14. nobul, "noble"	noble	7, 3. colers, "colors"	colours
2, 23. prykud, "pricked"	pryckyd	9, 3. laten, "latten"	laton
3, 3. displesons	dyspleysaunce	17, 2. seasen	season
4, 22. angur, "anger"	angre	19, 2. cumburs	comborous

A few other vowel differences may be noted. In *age* (1, 2), the manuscript had a normal English form; *aege* in the print looks like one of the pedantries of the Renaissance, with an *ae* imported from Latin *aetas*. In 7, 1, *furst* and *lurne* reflect the uncertainty of vowel pronunciation before *r* which existed in the fifteenth century; the print uses more conventional *fyrste, lerne,* although the pronunciation of the printer was no doubt the same as that of the writer of the manuscript.

Comparison of the Manuscript and the First Printed Version of the Treatise

There are several notable features of consonantal usage in the manuscript, although some of them affect relatively few words: *ch* for *sh, ff* for capital *F*, ȝ for *y* or for *gh, a* instead of *an* before initial *h, sch* for *sh, t* for final *th,* more rarely *th* for final *t, þ* for initial *th, v* for *w, w* for *v* (or *u*), and *w* for *wh.* We shall not attempt at this time to distinguish between usages which were probably phonetic and those which were purely orthographic. The manner in which these features tended to be normalized in the print may be seen below:

Manuscript	*Print*	*Manuscript*	*Print*
13, 20. fyche	fysshe	1, 1. maket	makyth
18, 16. fyche	fyssh	2, 21. wenyt	wenyth
1, 22. ffyrst	Fyrste	4, 19. weyth, "wet"	wete
11, 5. ffor	For	7, 6. wath	what
2, 14. ȝorke	Yorke	1, 1. þat	that
7, 9. ȝer	yere	7, 12. þyng	thynge
2, 14. ryȝght	ryght	11, 5. vith, "with"	wyth
17, 16. syȝt	syghte	18, 2. veþer, "weather"	[omitted]

Manuscript	*Print*	*Manuscript*	*Print*
1, 12. a hoke	an hoke	2, 16. scrywe, "describe"	dyscryue
2, 21. a hare	an hare	17, 17. wery	very
1, 19. schall	shall	18, 15. awaileth	auayllyth
4, 16. fyschyng	fysshynge	2, 21. wen, "when"	whan
5, 6. fysche	fisshe	4, 19. wyche	whyche
12, 13. schap	shape	9, 18. wyht	whyte

The normalizing process is not carried out completely in all cases; e.g., the print has initial *þ* several times in *þe* (the), *þt* (that), etc.

The print uses *v* initially for both the consonant *v* and the vowel *u;* and *u* medially for both consonant and vowel. In the manuscript there is a tendency to use *v* medially, especially for the consonant:

Manuscript	*Print*	*Manuscript*	*Print*
2, 12. dyscryve	dyscryue	12, 3. hevy, "heavy"	heuy
3, 2. grevys, "griefs"	greues	12, 21. with-ovte	wythout

A few further differences in the treatment of consonants may be noted. Generally, the manuscript has archaic, phonetic, or unconventional forms, which are normalized in the print; however, the *gh* which the print inserts in *trout* fits none of these categories.

Manuscript	*Print*	*Manuscript*	*Print*
9, 5. honful	handfull	13, 9. troute	troughte
9, 14. nemyll, "nimble"	nymbyll	18, 19. samond, "salmon"	Samon
11, 5. Dare, "dace"	darse	19, 12. souerent, "sovereign"	souerayn
11, 16. plomed	plumbid		
12, 1. plumys	plumbes	19, 18. trowyt	Troughte

GRAMMAR

Grammatical forms, allowing for differences in spelling, are pretty much alike in the two versions. Most of the differences are due to retention of archaic pronoun forms in the manuscript and its preference for forms of the verb *will* which have since become standard in English. The following may be noted here:

Manuscript	*Print*
1, 6. jn wyche (neuter antecedent)	in whom
1, 9. will, "will" (manuscript also has *wol* occasionally)	woll
2, 21. hyt (manuscript usually preserves the *h*)	it
3, 4. hem, "them" (manuscript also has *them*)	theym
3, 4. louyth, "love" (present plural, archaic and dialectal)	loue
13, 20. fedyt, "feed" (same as above, with *t* for *th*)	fede
13, 21. hym, "them" (cf. confusion of *e* and *i* noted above)	theym
13, 23. ner, "nearer" (archaic comparative of adverb)	nerer
20, 2. a, "and" (archaic or dialectal)	and

In syntax the two versions frequently differ as to details of phrasing and word order, but it is hard to see any definite pattern in the differences. It would be hard to say that either version is more archaic, dialectal, or unconventional than the other. The printer (or the person who copied the manuscript from which he worked) may have had a slight preference for the verb-subject word order; while the original writer of the treatise (or some intervening copyist) may have had a predilection for *shall*-phrases with a vaguely future sense. Here are a few examples, which may or may not be very significant:

Comparison of the Manuscript and the First Printed Version of the Treatise

Manuscript	*Print*
1, 7. Than þis folowythe, þat . . . disportes by cause	Thenne folowyth it þat . . . games ben cause
2, 12. Y wyl now dyscryve	Now thenne woll I dyscryue
3, 2–3. suche grevys . . . to the hunter hapeth	Suche greues . . . hapyth vnto the hunter
3, 10–11. þen all hys dispor[tes] ben gon	Thenne is his game & his dysporte goon
3, 15. With mysfedyng þen schall sche haue the frounce	With mys fedynge she shall haue the Fronse
5, 14–15. þat schall make hyt ryght hongre	that makyth hym hungry
5, 17. He schall se	He seeth

DICTION

Variations in wording between the Yale Wagstaff Manuscript and the printed version are numerous and frequently seem unimportant. Many are undoubtedly due to capricious changes by scribes or the printer. In general, the manuscript is more archaic and individualistic in its diction, as a few examples will show:

Manuscript	*Print*
1, 4. reduse, "bring to or into" (a rare sense)	enduce
2, 5. pensifulnes, "pensiveness" (a rare formation)	pensyfnesse
3, 1. fulw[y], "foul, dirty" (rare, possibly corrupt)	all myry
4, 22. ne, "not, nor" (archaic)	nor
6, 18. þo, "those" (archaic)	you (due to misreading *þ* as *y*?)

15, 12. a Wherly pyt of watur (dialectal)	a manere whyrlynge of water
16, 3. iiij at cloke (rather rare idiom)	foure of þe clocke
19, 12. watur sokul (local dialect)	water docke (i.e., the plant)
19, 18. deyntet, "dainty" (rare and archaic)	deyntous

It is true, of course, that the expressions used in the print look rather archaic to us today, but generally they are in keeping with the usages of the late fifteenth century in the neighborhood of London.

Many of the differences, as I have suggested above, are purely stylistic matters. A few of these may have some interest:

Manuscript	*Print*
1, 2. That ys to sey	that is
1, 10. þat ys to sey	that is to wyte
1, 17. That ys to sey	Ye shall vnderstonde that this is for to saye
1, 5–6. good & honest dysportes and games	good dysportes & honest gamys
1, 7. good & honeste disportes	gode dysportes & honest games
1, 9–10. good disportes and honest gamys	good disportes & honeste gamys
2, 2. debates and stryves	debate
2, 5. plesens	ease and pleasaunce
1, 21. good dyet of cleyn metes & drynkes sesonable	dyete mesurable
1, 22. be mery	euer more be in mery thoughtes
2, 14. þe ryȝght nobul duke of ȝorke	the ryght noble and full worthy prynce the duke of Yorke

On the basis of such examples it would be hard to say which version is characterized by elegant variation and amplification, or which is addicted to the laconic style, or which to unimaginative repetition. It is our impression, however, that the printed version is expanded, that it shows a greater tendency to couple synonyms and insert explanatory phrases which may or may not be necessary.

In one instance the printed version has a phrase which has caught the fancy of modern anglers; the manuscript describes the trout (19, 18) as "a deyntet fyche & a fre bytyng," which is not bad, but the print calls him "a right deyntous fyssh and also *a ryght feruente byter*."

In two instances early in the text, the manuscript shows greater exactness in translating from the Latin:

Manuscript	Print
1, 1. glad (Latin *gaudens*)	good
1, 17. leches or medicens (Latin *medici,* plural)	leche or medicyne

Comparison of the Manuscript and the First Printed Version of the Treatise

If we assume that the original writer, being closer to the Latin works quoted as authority, would be more careful in Englishing them, we would infer from these examples that the manuscript preserves the original diction better than the print.

APPENDIXES

APPENDIX A

Prologue to Master of Game *(c. 1406), Modernized*

The *Treatise of Fishing* acknowledges as its model a hunting treatise, *Master of Game,* the earliest treatise on hunting in English. *Master of Game* is largely a translation of a French treatise, *Livre de Chasse* (c. 1387), the most celebrated book on the chase in history. The translation with additions was made by Edward, Duke of York, in 1406. He followed both the content and the form of the French original. That form, consisting of a prologue followed by instruction, was adopted in the *Treatise of Fishing.* The prologue sets forth the attitude of sport.

We have here modernized the Duke of York's text, using—as will be indicated—portions of two manuscripts of *Master of Game,* one in the British Museum, the other in the Yale Library.

PROLOGUE
TO
THE MASTER OF GAME

To the honor and reverence of you, my right worshipful and dread Lord Henry,[1] by the grace of God eldest son and heir of the high, excellent, and Christian prince Henry the Fourth (by the aforesaid grace, King of England and of France), Prince of Wales, Duke of Guienne, of Lancaster, and of Cornwall, and Earl of Chester:

[1] Prince Hal, later Henry V.

I,[2] your own in every humble way, have ventured to make this little, simple book, which I commend and submit to your noble and wise correction; the which book, if it please your aforesaid Lordship, shall be named and called *Master of Game*. And for this reason; namely, that the matters which this book treats of are most lasting in every season and, to my thinking, are oftenest the most entertaining of all sports to every nobleman's heart; that is to say, it treats of Hunting. For, although hawking with noble hawks for the heron and for waterfowl is noble and commendable, yet it seldom lasts, at the most, over half the year. And even if men found enough game to hawk at between May and Lammas,[3] no one could find any hawks to hawk with. But as for hunting, there is no season of all the year that game cannot right well be found in every good region, and also hounds ready to pursue it. And since this book will be entirely of hunting, which is so noble a sport and also so lasting throughout all the year (for different animals, according as the season requires, for the delight of man), it seems to me that I may well call it "Master of Sports."

And although it is true, my dear lord, that many a one could have dealt with this matter better and more intelligently than I, yet there are two things that chiefly have emboldened me and caused me to take this work in hand. The first is confidence in your noble correction, to which, as I said before, I submit this little and simple book. The second is that, although I am unworthy, I am master of this sport with that noble prince your father, the aforesaid sovereign and liege lord of us all. And because I would not want his hunters or yours that now are, or those that come hereafter, to be ignorant of this art in all its perfection, I wish therefore to leave this simple record. For as Chaucer says in his prologue of the twenty-five good women,[4] "By writing, men often have memory of things past, for writing is the key of all good remembrance."

And first I will begin to describe the nature of the hare; secondly, the nature of the hart; third, the buck and his nature; fourth, the roe and his nature; fifth, the wild boar and his nature; sixth, the wolf and his nature; seventh, the fox and his nature; eighth, the badger and his nature; ninth,

[2] Edward of Norwich, cousin of the prince, and second Duke of York, who held the office of Master of Game, 1406–13.

[3] August 1. During this period the hawks would be molting.

[4] *The Legend of Good Women.* The duke may have heard rather than read the poem, for he overestimates the number of the ladies, and he quotes very loosely.

the wildcat and his nature; tenth, the marten and his nature; eleventh, the otter and his nature. Now I have related how I will describe, in this little book, the nature of these aforesaid beasts of venery and of chase;[5] and therefore I will now name the dogs which I will describe hereafter, both as to nature and as to characteristics. And first I will begin with raches and their nature; after that, with greyhounds and their nature; after that, with alans and their nature; after that, with spaniels and their nature; after that, with mastiffs, which men call curs, and their nature; and after that, with small dogs that happen to be terriers and their nature. And afterward I will describe and tell the diseases and infirmities of hounds. And beyond that, I will describe what qualities and habits a good hunter should have, and what his bearing should be like. Afterward I will describe the manner and shape of the kennel, what sort of surroundings and arrangement it should have. And moreover, I will describe in what fashion a hunter's horn should be made; and afterward, how the leashes should be made for the raches, and of what length. And furthermore I will prove by various arguments in this little prologue that there is no man's life, of those that engage in noble games and sports, that is less displeasing to God than is the life of a fully trained and skillful hunter, nor any such life that more good comes from. The first argument is that the sport often causes a man to avoid the Seven Deadly Sins. Secondly, men are better horsemen, more just and intelligent, more accomplished, more gracious, more enterprising, and better acquainted with all districts and all routes, both short and long. All good habits and manners come from it, as well as the health of a man and of his soul. For whoever escapes the Seven Deadly Sins will, as we believe, be saved; then a good hunter will be saved, and in this world have joy enough and gladness and pleasure, provided he guards against two things. The first is that he does not give up the knowledge or the service of God, from whom all good comes, on account of his hunting. The second, that he does not fail in the service of his master or in his own duties,[6] which might profit him most.

Now I will prove to you how a hunter cannot under any circumstances

[5] Some animals, like the hare and the hart, were beasts of venery; others, like the badger, were beasts of chase. The number in each group and the animals listed vary with different medieval writers.

[6] The Yale *Master of Game* manuscript begins here. The authority to this point has been British Museum manuscript Cotton Vespasian B.12.

fall into any of the Seven Deadly Sins. For when a man is idle and careless, without toil, and men are not occupied in doing anything and remain either in their beds or in their chambers, that is a thing which draws men to imagination of fleshly lust and pleasure. For such men have no desire except to stay always in one place, and they think about Pride or about Avarice or about Wrath or about Sloth or about Gluttony or about Lechery or about Envy. For the imaginations of men turn more readily to evil than to good, because of the three enemies which mankind has, that is, the Devil, the World, and the Flesh. Then is this proven sufficiently. Nevertheless there are many other arguments, which would be too long to tell, and moreover every man who has good sense knows well that idleness is the source of all wicked imaginations.

Now I will prove to you how Imagination is lord and master of all works, good or evil, that a man's body or his limbs do. You know well that good works or evil, great or small, never were done unless first they were imagined or thought of. Therefore, Imagination is mistress of all deeds, for according as Imagination bids, men do good deeds or evil ones, whichever it may be, as I said before. And if a man, notwithstanding that he were wise, should imagine always that he were a fool or that he had some other sickness, he would be even so. For since he would suppose steadfastly that he was a fool, he would do a fool's deeds, as his imaginings would command, provided that he believed it steadfastly. Therefore it seems to me that I have proved enough about Imagination, although there are many other arguments, which I omit to avoid writing at great length and because every man that has good sense knows well that what I say is true.

Now I will prove how the good hunter cannot be idle or dreaming or have evil imaginings or, afterward, any evil works. For the night immediately before he is to go to perform his task, he will lay himself down in his bed and will have no thought but to sleep and to do his task well and diligently as a good hunter should do. And he will not have any concern for, nor think of, anything except the necessary things that he is appointed to do. He is not idle, for he has enough to do to think about arising early and doing his task well, without thinking either of sins or of other evil deeds. And early in the dawning of the day, he must be up to go to his quest—which in English is called searching—well and diligently, just as I shall explain more clearly when I speak of how men should quest or search in order to track the hart to his resting place. And in such activity he will not be idle, for he will always be busy. And when he has come back to the assembly or meeting, then he has most to do, in order to arrange his finders and relays and set the hart in motion and uncouple his hounds. With all that, he cannot be idle, and he will not have occasion to think of anything but doing his task. And when he has uncoupled, he is even less idle and will think even less about any sins, for he will have enough to do to ride or foot it well with his hounds and be always near them, and to shout or call to the hounds well, and to blow well, and to see what he is pursuing, and to observe which hounds are the vanchasers[7] and which the perfecters,[8] and to bring back his hounds and set them right when they have followed the wrong scent or happened upon inferior beasts. And when the hart is dead, or whatever other game that he hunts, he is even less idle and less likely to think about doing evil, for he will have enough to do and think about in cutting up his hart well according to its nature, and in raising well what pertains to him,[9] and in rewarding the hounds well, and in seeing how many of his hounds are missing of those that he brought to the wood in the morning, and in seeking them out and coupling them again. And when he has come home, he should think even less of doing evil, for he will have enough to think about in getting his supper and refreshing himself and his horse and sleeping and taking his rest, because he is weary, and drying himself out from the dew or perhaps from the rain. And therefore I say that all the time of the hunter is without idleness and without evil thoughts and without evil deeds of sin, for I have said that idleness is the source of all vices and sins. And the hunter cannot be idle if he will do his task properly. And also he can have no other thoughts, for he has enough to do to imagine and to think about his task, which is no small responsibility for those who will do it well and diligently—especially those that love the hounds and their task. Therefore I say, since a hunter is never idle, he cannot have any evil thoughts, nor can he do any evil deeds. Consequently, he must go into paradise. I could prove these things by many other arguments, which

[7] The hounds that lead the chase.

[8] The finishers, who come in last and bring the hart to bay.

[9] Laying claim to those parts of the deer which, by custom, were allotted to the hunters. The above passage is an awkward translation of the French *"et lever les droitz qu'ils apartiennent."*

would be tedious, but this will suffice me, for every man that has good sense knows well that I tell you the high truth.

Now I will prove how hunters live in this world more joyfully than any other men. For when the hunter rises in the morning, he sees the sweet and fair morning and the weather clear and bright, and he hears the song of the small birds, which sing sweetly with great melody and full of love, each in his own language in the best way that he can, according to what he has derived from his nature. And when the sun is arisen, he will see the fresh dew upon the small twigs and grass and the sun which, by its power, will make them sparkle; and that is a great pleasure and joy to the hunter's heart. Afterward, when he is on his quest or searching, if he sees or meets the hart soon, without any great looking, and he tracks him to his lair well and readily within a short time, it is a great joy and pleasure to the hunter. Afterward, when he comes to the assembly or gathering, and he reports before the lord and his company, either as he has seen with his eyes or by the measurement of the tracks (which he ought rightly to take anyway) or by the droppings that he has in his horn or in his lap, and every man says, "Lo, here is a great hart and a deer of high meating,[10] or pasturing; let us go and move[11] him" (I will declare hereafter what these terms mean), then the hunter has great joy. Afterward, when he begins to pursue and has pursued but a little, and he hears or sees the hart start up before him, and he knows well that it is the right one, and his hounds that are the finders that day come to the lair or to the spoor and are there uncoupled without any going coupled, and they all run well and pursue, then the hunter has great joy and great pleasure. Afterward he leaps on a horse's back (if he is of that rank, and otherwise he goes afoot) in great haste to follow his hounds. And because his hounds may, by chance, have gone far from where he uncoupled them, he seeks some advantage to get in front of his hounds. And then he sees the hart pass before him, and he halloos and calls to the hounds mightily, and he sees which hounds come in the vanchase[12] and which are in the middle and which are the perfecters, according to the order in which they come. And then, when his hounds have passed before him, then he rides after them, and

[10] Well-grown, well-fed.
[11] Rouse him, start him moving.
[12] The first group of hounds, the leaders.

he shouts and blows as loud as he can with great joy and great pleasure. (And I assure you that he does not think of any other sin or any other evil.) Afterward, when the hart is overtaken and is at bay, he will have great pleasure. And afterward, when the hart is run through and dead, he carves him up and makes his quarry,[13] and inquires, or rewards, his hounds, and so he has great pleasure. And when he comes home, he comes joyfully, for his lord has given him to drink of his good wine at the quarry. And when he has come home, he will take off his clothes and take off his shoes and his hose; and he will wash his thighs and his legs and possibly all his body. And in the meanwhile, he will have his supper well prepared with soups made from the neck of the hart and with other good foods and with good wine or ale. And when he has eaten and drunk well, he will be all glad and well at his ease. Then he will go to take the air in the evening of the night because of the great heat that he has had. And then he will go drink and then lie in his bed in fair, fresh clothes; and he will sleep well and soundly all the night without any evil thought of any sin. Wherefore I say that hunters go into paradise when they die, and they live in this world most joyfully of any men.

Prologue to Master of Game, *Modernized*

Yet I will prove to you how hunters live longer than any other men, for as Hippocrates [14] says, full repletions of food kill more men than any sword or knife. But hunters eat and drink less than any other men of this world. For in the morning at the assembly, they eat but a little, and even if they eat well at the supper, at least they have resisted their nature.[15] For they have eaten but a little, and their nature[16] will not be hindered in accomplishing digestion; whereby no wicked humors or other superfluities can be engendered. And always, when a man is sick, men put him on a diet and have him drink water made with sugar or barley water and such things for two or three days to put down the evil humors and superfluities; and moreover men purge him. But it is not necessary to do so for a hunter, for he can have no repletion with the little food and with the great toil that he has. But let us suppose that which cannot be; namely, that he were full of wicked humors. Men know well that the greatest terminator of sickness that may be is sweat. And when the hunters perform their function,

[13] The pile formed of part of the entrails and other parts of the deer, with bread, etc., which is given to the hounds. The making of the quarry, like everything else in the chase, is done with great flourish and ceremony.

[14] Regarded in the fifteenth century as one of the highest authorities in medicine.

[15] Probably their natural appetites, the human tendency to overeat.

[16] Probably the natural forces governing their bodily functions.

either on horseback or afoot, they sweat often. Then if they have any evil, it must go away in the sweating, provided they keep [from][17] cold after the heat. And therefore it seems to me that I have proved it sufficiently. For the physicians order little food to the sick men to heal them, and sweat to cure and heal them entirely. And since hunters eat little and [sweat] often, they should always live long and be healthy.

Men desire to live long in this world in health and in joy, and have health of the soul after death. And hunters have all these things. Therefore be you all hunters, and you will do as wise men; and therefore I counsel all manner of folk, of whatever rank or condition they may be, that they love the hounds and the huntings and the delight of animals—one or another of them, or else hawking—to avoid idleness. For to be idle and have no pleasure either in hounds or in hawks is a bad sign. For as Phoebus, the Earl of Foix,[18] that noble hunter, says in his book, he never saw a good man, were he never so great and rich, that did not have joy in some of these. For if he were in need or at war, he would not know what to do, for he would not be used nor accustomed to toil, and so another man would have to do what he ought to do. For men have said in old sayings, "A lord is worth as much as he can make his lands prosper." And also he says in the aforesaid book that he never saw a man that loved toil and the joy of hounds and of hawks who did not have many good habits. For that[19] comes to him from great nobility and gentleness of heart, of whatever rank the man may be, whether a great lord or a small one, a poor one or a rich.

[17] The two bracketed readings in this paragraph do not correspond to anything in the manuscript but seem to be demanded by the context.

[18] Count Gaston (Phoebus) de Foix (1331–91), author of *Livre de Chasse*, from which most of the *Master of Game* is translated.

[19] That is, his love of hunting(?).

APPENDIX B

Prologue to The Art of Falconry *(c. 1245), Translated from the Latin*

The art of writing about sport was first given complete expression in the Middle Ages by Frederick II in his 589-page treatise of falconry. A claim can be made for this treatise as the first modern writing on sport. It is itself the first modern scientific work on ornithology and a superlative sporting work, as well as the model of the sporting treatise. Its fusion of the elements of chivalry and learning expresses the tradition of hunting treatises to the present. The *Treatise of Fishing* derived from this tradition and in turn gave rise to the literature of sport fishing.

Frederick's biographers are invariably staggered by his performance, calling him the "scholar emperor," the "sporting emperor," the "infidel emperor" and the like. His court at Palermo, Sicily, was the center of a cosmopolitan Mediterranean culture, and full of writers. Having grown up in Sicily, he was friends with Jews and Mohammedans, and familiar with their culture and that of Byzantium. The revival of ancient learning, begun in earnest in the previous century, had reached a high point in his time; at his court, translators put a good deal of Greek and Arabic into Medieval Latin. Great scholars were invited there, among them the celebrated Michael Scot, astrologer and translator of the ancients. Troubadour love poets were there. There, Dante says, Italian poetry began. Frederick was not only a patron of the arts; he was also a participant as scholar, poet, and prose writer. Oriental fashion, he kept a harem with eunuchs, for which he has been complimented by a lady biographer on the ground that this proved his lack of hypocrisy as it kept him from courtly love affairs. He was excommunicated twice, though not for his private life, and lest his character seem uncomplicated, it should be mentioned that he persecuted heretics. Dante put him in hell, with heretics (Canto X).

For the treatise on falconry, Frederick studied Aristotle and Arab writings, consulted master falconers, and made direct observations.

The treatise consists of a prologue and instruction. We print here the prologue, and the introductory material in Book I, which define the attitude of sport.

GENERAL PROLOGUE
TO THE
DE ARTE VENANDI CUM AVIBUS
by the
Most Noble and Learned Emperor
Frederick II[1]

Your urgent requests to undertake this present work, O most illustrious of men, M. E.,[2] prompts us to correct the many errors made by our predecessors who, when writing on the subject, degraded the noble art of falconry by slavishly copying the misleading and often insufficient statements to be found in the works of certain hackneyed authors. With the object of bequeathing it to posterity we now offer a true and careful account of these matters between the covers of this monograph.

We had proposed for a long time to present our theories in a work such as this, but deferred the task for nearly thirty years because we felt our insufficient experience and need of continued preparation. However, as time passed and we heard no report that any other writer had anticipated us and donated to the world a full account of such material as we have

[1] *The Art of Falconry*, by Frederick II of Hohenstaufen. Translated from the Latin and edited by Casey A. Wood and F. Marjorie Fyfe. Stanford University Press. Copyright 1943 by Board of Trustees, Leland Stanford Junior University. Reprinted 1961.

[2] This dedication is obscure. One conjecture, discussed by the editors, is that it was made in an early draft and directed to Malik El-Kamil (or Elkamil), Sultan of Egypt (d. 1238), who, as the text indicates, may have suggested to Frederick II that he write the treatise of falconry. Later versions have "M.S.," probably El-Kamil's son, Malik-Es Salih. The Stanford editors used chiefly the Bologna and Vatican texts for their translation which appears here.

been enabled to gather for the work, we finally decided to publish our own account of falconry. Certain branches of the art have, it is true, been explored by various other persons in the practice alone, and accounts thereof have been published, but with a lamentable want of mastery of the general topic.

Prologue to
Art of Falconry,
Translated from the Latin

We have investigated and studied with the greatest solicitude and in minute detail all that relates to this art, exercising both mind and body so that we might eventually be qualified to describe and interpret the fruits of knowledge acquired from our own experiences or gleaned from others. For example, we, at great expense, summoned from the four quarters of the earth masters in the practice of the art of falconry. We entertained these experts in our own domains, meantime seeking their opinions, weighing the importance of their knowledge, and endeavoring to retain in memory the more valuable of their words and deeds.

As the ruler of a large kingdom and an extensive empire we were very often hampered by arduous and intricate governmental duties, but despite these handicaps we did not lay aside our self-imposed task and were successful in committing to writing at the proper time the elements of the art. *Inter alia,* we discovered by hard-won experience that the deductions of Aristotle, whom we followed when they appealed to our reason, were not entirely to be relied upon, more particularly in his descriptions of the characters of certain birds.

There is another reason why we do not follow implicitly the Prince of Philosophers: he was ignorant of the practice of falconry—an art which to us has ever been a pleasing occupation, and with the details of which we are well acquainted. In his work, the *Liber Animalium,* we find many quotations from other authors whose statements he did not verify and who, in their turn, were not speaking from experience. Entire conviction of the truth never follows mere hearsay.

The fact that many writers [on natural history] have written numerous works on diverse subjects with only a few scant references to falconry is, in our opinion, proof that the topic presents many phases that are difficult to discuss. We now offer the suggestion that those of our peers who have more leisure than we at their command and who are devotees of the art and find the present work an aid to its successful practice might well give us a complementary work clarifying such new and puzzling aspects of the subject as are continually arising in the practice of this gentle art.

We beg every nobleman who by reason of his rank should be interested in the contents of this work to order it read and explained to him by some master of the science. At the same time we crave indulgence for any ambiguity in our presentation of the subject. This art, like all other avocations, has its own peculiar vocabulary; and, inasmuch as the exact terms we require cannot be found in Latin grammars, we have substituted for them the terms that in our opinion best express our meaning.

Our main thesis, then, is *The Art of Falconry;* and this we have divided into two cardinal sections. The first contains the argument, by which we mean contemplative thought, or theory; the second illustrates practice, which portrays experimental action. In addition, a third subsection contains a part of the argument and includes certain data pertaining to both theory and practice. Our purpose is to present the facts as we find them. Up to the present time the subject of falconry has been devoid of both artistic and scientific treatment.

The medium we have chosen for this monograph is prose, with prologue and text. The latter has many ramifications and analyses; among them will be found much descriptive matter, comparisons indicating similarities and differences, inquiries into causes, and numerous other lines of reasoning, all of which will be obvious to the reader.

The author of this treatise, the august Frederick II, Emperor of the Romans, King of Jerusalem and of Sicily, is a lover of wisdom with a philosophic and speculative mind.

The work called *The Art of Falconry* has manifold and far-reaching uses. The pursuit of falconry enables nobles and rulers disturbed and worried by the cares of state to find relief in the pleasures of the chase. The poor, as well as the less noble, by following this avocation may earn some of the necessities of life; and both classes will find in bird life attractive manifestations of the processes of nature. The whole subject of falconry falls within the realm of natural science, for it deals with the nature of bird life. It will be apparent, however, that certain theories derived from written sources are modified by the experiences set forth in this book.

The title of our work is: "The Book of the Divine Augustus, Frederick II, Emperor of the Romans, King of Jerusalem and Sicily, *De Arte Venandi cum Avibus,* an Analytical Inquiry into the Natural Phenomena Manifest in Hawking."

The subdivisions of the theme are clearly indicated; the Introduction precedes the text; generalities are discussed before taking up particulars, and natural phenomena are debated in their logical sequence.

BOOK I

THE STRUCTURE AND HABITS OF BIRDS

Prologue to Art of Falconry, *Translated from the Latin*

CHAPTER I

Falconry Is an Art More Noble than Other Forms of Hunting

Since falconry is undoubtedly a variety of the chase, and as the art of hunting has numerous branches, each with its peculiar practices, we might consider in what both the art of venery, with all its subdivisions, and the actual practice of hunting consist. Setting aside all else, we shall at the present time discourse mainly on falconry.

The art of hunting is the sum total of experience by which men have learned to capture wild creatures of all sorts for their use by means either of force or of skill.

Hunting itself is nothing else but a form of bodily exercise and practices employed to capture animals. There are, in fact, three kinds of venery: that in which inanimate instruments are employed; that in which live animals are trained to catch other live animals; and that in which combinations of the first two are used.

The art of hunting with inanimate objects is a greatly diversified one and includes the employment of nets, snares, slings, bows, arrows, and numerous other instruments.

Examples of venery of the second class are seen in the use of such living animals as dogs, leopards, and other four-footed beasts, as well as birds of prey. What birds are to be considered rapacious and what nonrapacious we shall shortly determine.

As we intend to confine the present work to hunting by means of birds, we shall now take up the employment for that purpose of trained raptores and in this chapter give our reasons for believing it to be an occupation more worthy than other forms of hunting and explain why we select it for discussion.

There are many arguments that can be advanced to demonstrate the noble character of falconry, as the discriminating reader of this book will soon discover; and he will in this way learn more about the secrets of nature than if he followed other kinds of venery. It is true that the latter are more popular, because their technique is crude and easier to learn; falconry, on the other hand, is less familiar and does not commend itself to the majority because skill in it is difficult to acquire and because it is more refined.

Moreover, as regards other forms of hunting, which so many follow with enthusiasm, they are less noble because they depend merely upon the use of artificial implements, such as nets, snares, traps, hunting spears, javelins, bows, and slings, or they are carried on by means of four-footed animals, both tame and wild, such as various sorts of leopards, dogs, lynx (male and female), ferrets, and other beasts.

On the other hand, the art of falconry is not dependent upon such auxiliaries as artificial tools or four-footed animals but is almost entirely conducted with the aid of birds of prey that are indeed more noble instruments of the chase than inanimate objects or trained quadrupeds.

It is also true that it is far more difficult and requires more ingenuity to teach raptorial birds the stratagems of hawking than to instruct dogs or wild quadrupeds to hunt, because birds of prey are more afraid of man than are other birds or such four-footed animals as are used in the chase.

Moreover, raptorial species do not eat grain or similar food cultivated by man as do many other birds. As a result they do not associate with men and do not easily become domesticated. It is also well known that raptorials avoid man more than do other avian species and certain quadrupeds. Again, birds of prey frequent localities inhabited by man less than do the last-named animals. It may be added that wild and shy quadrupeds that shun mankind are difficult to tame and train for hunting and these difficulties are still more marked in the case of birds of prey. It is to be remembered, also, that the habitat of quadrupeds is limited to the earth's surface, their movements are not very rapid, and they generally run along in an upright position, whereas birds fly quickly through the air. Consequently the former are more easily brought under human subjection than are the latter, and they are readily caught by the use of force or are trapped by other means because they remain on the ground. Fully fledged birds, on the other hand, can be captured and trained only by finesse.

It is thus evident not only that the art of falconry presents greater difficulties but requires more unusual skill than do other forms of venery.

By means of this noble art most raptorial birds can be taught to hunt and capture even such birds as cranes, bustards, geese, and other large game birds that are bigger and heavier than those they capture alone in their wild state, as well as to take smaller quarry not only in their natural fashion but more often than is effected by other methods.

Although it is true that birds of prey display an inborn antipathy to the presence and company of mankind, yet by means of this noble art one may learn how to overcome this natural aversion, to win their confidence, and to induce them even to seek those they previously avoided.

Prologue to Art of Falconry, *Translated from the Latin*

By the proper exercise of falconry, raptorial birds are taught to tolerate the society of human individuals and their associates for hunting purposes, to fly after quarry, and to behave (without control) just as they would in their wild state. Any dabbler in venery can readily hold in leash or let loose dogs or other quadrupeds; but in the pursuit of falconry no tyro can so easily join in the chase, either to carry his birds or to throw them off at the quarry. Falcons and other hawks are rendered clumsy or entirely unmanageable if placed under control of an ignorant interloper. By using his hearing and eyesight alone an ignoramus may learn something about other kinds of hunting in a short time; but without an experienced teacher and frequent exercise of the art properly directed no one, noble or ignoble, can hope to gain in a short time an expert or even an ordinary knowledge of falconry.

Here it may again be claimed that, since many nobles and but few of the lower rank learn and carefully pursue this art, one may properly conclude that it is intrinsically an aristocratic sport; and one may once more add that it is nobler, more worthy than, and superior to other kinds of venery.

Let it then be the first one discussed. To other forms of venery, especially those patronized by the nobility, we shall return (our life being spared) when we have completed this present treatise.

APPENDIX C

Text of William Burton in Which Dame Juliana Was First Identified as a Nun and Noblewoman

The earliest statement that Dame Juliana was a nun and noblewoman was made by the antiquary William Burton (1575–1645), elder brother of Robert Burton, and author of the *Description of Leicestershire.* The text of the statement, and evidence that the writing is in Burton's hand, are reproduced here in facsimile. These are the basic documents of the legend which is described in Chapter 4.

The legend of Dame Juliana Berners rests mainly on handwritten notes on blank pages in a copy of the first *Book of St. Albans* (1486), This copy, now in the Cambridge University Library, is believed to have once belonged to Burton. From Burton it found its way into a famous library belonging to John Moore, Bishop of Ely, and from there went to Cambridge.

The notes in Burton's copy of the *Book of St. Albans* state that the book was written by Lady Juliana Berners, Prioress of the Sopwell Nunnery at St. Albans, where, they say, the book was first printed. Because of William Burton's reputation as an antiquary and his connections, these few statements carried force enough to launch the legend of the noble nun and sportswoman. A century after they were written, that is, in the early eighteenth century, they were taken at face value and publicized by several eminent antiquaries. As we have been interested in tracing the legend, one simple question remained: Are these notes actually in William Burton's hand? We think they are.

Evidence that William Burton wrote the notes is as follows:

We obtained from the University Library, Cambridge, England, photostats of the handwritten notes in the *Book of St. Albans* which came from Bishop Moore's library (No. 4214 in the published *Catalogue of the Fifteenth-Century Printed Books in the University Library, Cambridge*). A facsimile of these notes follows this discussion.

For comparison, we obtained from the Bodleian Library, Oxford, photostats of a portion of a transcript of Leland's *Itinerary* in William Burton's hand (MS. Gough, Gen. Top. 2). A facsimile of several lines of this manuscript follows this discussion.

Proof that this Leland transcript is in Burton's hand we take from Lucy Toulmin Smith's introduction (in Vol. 1) to her edition of Leland's *Itinerary* (1907–10). The relevant text, on page xxv, is as follows:

> Burton, who was fully alive to their value, made a copy of seven "parts," as he calls them, of the "Itinerary," in an interesting folio of 252 leaves [the footnote to this reads "MS. Gough, Gen. Top. 2, in the Bodleian. Hereafter referred to as Burton a."], closely written in a crabbed hand and yellowed ink, which has been much injured by mice and is only badly repaired. Fifty-nine of these leaves are filled with extracts from Leland's "Collectanea."
>
> Some years elapsed before this volume, begun in 1628, added to in 1641, was filled. The second flyleaf bears the following note: "The itinerarye of John Leiland the famous Antiquarie. Begunne before or about an. do. 1538, an. 30 H.8. The first part copied out of the originall, 1628, by me William Burton." He begins with Leland's letter to Henry VIII (out of the "Collectanea," vol. iii, p. 281). Five "parts" (including the first) follow consecutively, answering to the parts in Hearne's printed vols. i, ii, iii, vol. iv, part 2, and vol. v (of Leland's MS., vols. i, ii, iii, and v, the part answering to vol. iv, part 2 is now lost).

Librarians at the Bodleian kindly checked the statement on the second flyleaf and it does indeed say, ". . . by me William Burton."

We compare this transcript, known to be Burton's, with the notes in the *Book of St. Albans* from Moore's library.

First, however, we observe that all three notes in Burton's copy of the *Book of St. Albans* appear to have been written by the same person. There are differences in general appearance, which could be accounted for on the supposition that they were not all written at the same time or with the same pen. But the basic forms of the letters and the manner of combining them are the same in all three notes.

The problem is complicated by the fact that the writer had two or more distinct ways of writing several of the letters. This is best seen in *d, e, r,* and *y,* each of which has two basically different shapes. There are very noticeable, although less basic, differences in the forms of *b, f, h,* and *p.* There are three distinct forms of *s.* The ligatures, or combinations, *sh, st,* and *th,* have two different shapes each. There are also minor differences in the forms of *c, w,* and some other letters. (The different forms referred to here do not include the capitals.)

In the first note (blank leaf at beginning of the book) the writer uses one set of letter-forms (a) in the body of the note, another set (b) in the proper names and the dates. It is as though he were using roman and italic type. Set (a) has one of his two varieties of *b, d, e, f, h, p, r,* and *y;* set (b) has the other variety of each of these. One of the three varieties of *s* does not occur in set (a); all three occur in (b). We can indicate how he used the two sets by italicizing set (b) in the note, thus:

> This booke was made by the *Lady Julian Berners* daughter of *Sr James Berners* of *Berners Roding* in *Essex* knight & sister to *Richard Lord Berners* she was *Lady Prioresse* of *Sopwell Nunnery* neere *St Albons,* in which Abbey *of St Albons* this was first printed *:1486:2:H.7:* she was living *1460:39: H 6:* according to *John Bale: Centur 8: fol:611:*

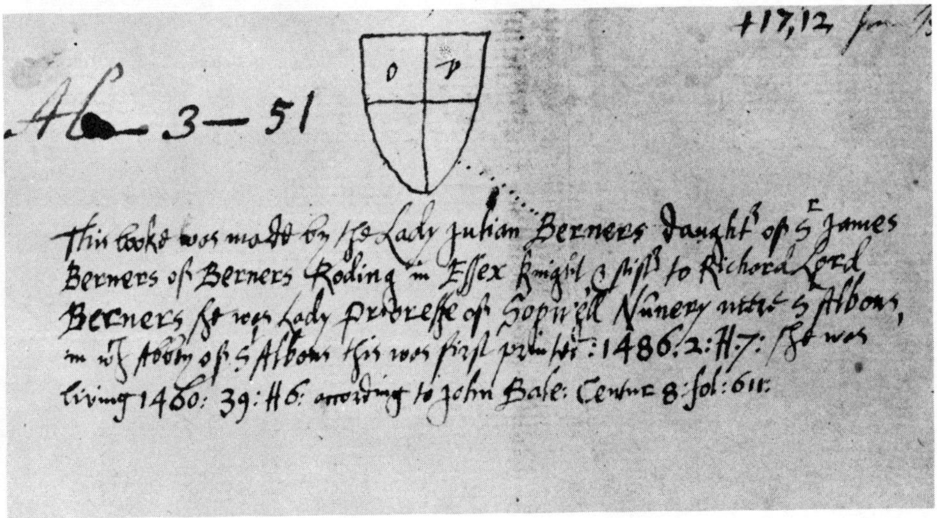
Al 3—51
+17,12
This booke was made by the Lady Julian Berners daughter of Sr James
Berners of Berners Roding in Essex knight & sister to Richard Lord
Berners she was Lady Prioresse of Sopwell Nunnery neere St Albons,
in which Abbey of St Albons this was first printed :1486:2:H.7: she was
living 1460: 39: H6: according to John Bale: Centur 8: fol:611:

Text of William Burton in Which Dame Juliana Was First Identified as a Nun and Noblewoman

The second note (leaf f4 recto of the first alphabet) shows a similar use of the two sets of letter-forms, but set (b) is used for more than proper names and dates, thus:

Ex Lelando et Bale:
Juliana Barnes, fæmina illustris, corporis et animi dotibus abundans, et formæ elegantia spectabilis, claruit author huius operis *:1460:j:E4:*

(*Bale* has been altered to *Baleo,* perhaps by a later writer.)

Explicit Dam Julyans Barnes in her boke of huntyng.

Ex Lelando et Baleo:
Juliana Barnes, fæmina illustris, corporis et animi dotibus abundans, et formæ elegantia spectabilis, claruit author huius operis: 1460: j: E4:

f iiij

The third note (leaf f9 verso of the second alphabet) seems to be written entirely in set (b). It contains forms of *c, t, w,* and the suprascript *er* that may belong to set (a), but there is insufficient material in these notes to permit a decision on that point. The doubtful letters are in roman type here:

*Liber Willmi Burton Lindliaci Leicestrensis, morantis apud Fold com Staff: ex dono consanguinei mei charissimi Thomæ Purefey de Barwell iuxto Lindley in com: Leiceste*r*: Arming: 1612:*

gedyr at Seynt albons the yere from thincarnacion of oure lorde Jhu Crist. M. CCCC. lxxx vi. 2: H.7:

Liber Willmi Burton Lindliaci Leicestrensis moratis apud Fold co Staff. ex dono consanguinei mei charissimi Thomæ Purefey de Barwell iuxta Lindley in com: Leicest: armig: 1612:

Text of William Burton in Which Dame Juliana Was First Identified as a Nun and Noblewoman

On the following pages are samples of handwriting known to be William Burton's own transcript of a Leland text.

We are satisfied that the writer of the Leland transcript on folios 56^{v} and 57^{r} could be, and very likely is, the same as the writer of the Burton notes. All significant letter-forms and ligatures of the Burton notes can be matched in the transcript, including those of both set (a) and set (b). In general, the two sets are used much as in Burton note 1; that is, set (b) for the proper names in the margin and in the body of the transcript, set (a) for the rest of the body.

There are occasional inconsistencies such as one might expect of a writer making a rapid transcription. The name *Selwode* (56^{v} line 3) has its final *e* from set (a). *Newton castle* (56^{v} left margin) is written in set (a). *From* (56^{v} line 1) has the *r* of set (b); the same *r* occurs in *From* several times at beginnings of new paragraphs and may be intentional. Several other instances of inconsistency could be cited, but they are not enough to obscure the writer's general scheme.

In short, since we know that Burton wrote folios 56^{v} and 57^{r} (MS. Gough, Gen. Top. 2, in the Bodleian) of the Leland transcript, he probably wrote the three notes in his copy of the *Book of St. Albans.*

This conclusion was surmised by a Cambridge antiquary, Thomas Baker, in 1733, and conveyed in a letter to Thomas Hearne. The evidence presented here is the first effort, we believe, to establish the fact.

A comparison of these established samples with the hand that wrote the Dame Juliana legend in Bishop Moore's copy of the *Book of St. Albans,* proves them to be the same hand.

56

Nunney Delamare. From Melles to Nunney Delamare a 2 miles by hilly and enclosid ground, thens about a m[ile]
by like hille unto Tut .... a long village wher peroche chirch is to Nunney Delamare, thens [a]
a mile farther, and so to the marche forest of Selwood, and so passing half a mile farther I left
Witham — straight hand Witham the late Priory of Carthusians, not in the forest but joyning ...
on the edge of it, thens partly by forest ground and partly by champayne a 4 miles to Stourt[on].

Stourton — The village of Stourton standeth in the bottom of an hill in leva ripa Stoure. The Lo[rd]
Stourtons place standeth on a meane hill, the soyle therof being stony. This manor place hat[h]
2 courtes, the front of the inner court is magnificent, and high embatelid castle like, ther[e is]
a park emonge hilles joyning on the manor place. The river of Stoure risith there of [6]
fontaines or springes, wherof 3 be on the northe syde of the park hard by within the pale, the other
be north also, but without the park, the L. Stourton givith these 6 fontaines in his armes, the
name of the Stourtons be very auncient in those partes.

There be 4 campes that served men of warre about Stourton, one toward the north[e]
within the park double dikid, I reckon that here stode manor place or castle my lord Stour[ton]
... There is another campe a mile di. of Stourton double dichid in the toppe of a
high hill, this is called comonly Whiteshete hill. the other 2 campes be abroade in the Lordshippe.

There is on an hill a litle without Stourton a grove, and in it is a very praty plac[e]
Bonhome — callid Bonhomes builded of late by my L. Stourton. Bonhome of Wilshire of the ...
house the Bonhomes there is lord of it.

From Stourton unto .... a 4 miles much by woody ground, for I passi[d]
Colewater at a great ford, a mile beyond I left
Stapleford — on the left hand, and thens a mile farther I came to Stapleford a praty uplandish towne
and standith meately well builded, where at the north end of the towne ....
[illegible] Thornehulle of Thornehull hath buried on
a fa .... owne builded. The lordship and townlett of Stapleford in Bla[k]more hath longid of auncient tyme to the abbay of Shirburne.

Dorsett R. — Cale water cummith downe from Moreland unto Stapleford leving it on the right ...
Stapleford is by estimation a 7 miles north from Wikehampton from whens Cale ...

Thornehull — From Stapleford unto Thornehull a mile by good ground, here dwellith Mr. Thorne[hull]
an auncient gent. From Thornehulle to Stourminster a 2 miles by enclosid and woody ground, and
Lidden bridge. — the middle way I passed over a stone bridge of 5 arches under the which runneth a broke callid ..
then I passid over a woden bridge .... a litle above the towne.

Stourminster — The townelet of Stourminster standeth in a valley, and is no great thing, and the buildin[g]
of it is meane, there is a very good market, it standeth in ripa sinistra of Stoure, there [is]
a very faire stone bridge of 6 arches at the townes end made of late tymes chiefly by the
vicar of Stourminster, and the parsone of Shillington agayne Eyford bridge in ripa dextra
Sturi in the waye to Blandford. Eyford bridge is a 2 miles beneth Stourminster. At the end
of the bridge in ripa dextra Sturi flu: is a faire manor place of an hill made ste[pe]
Newton castle: — round by mans hand callid in olde writinge Newton castle.

King .... gave this Stourminster and Newton unto the abbey of Glassenbur[y].
the castle was clerely decayed, and abbot of Glastenbury made there a faire manor pla[ce]
and used to resort unto it. the parsonage of the towne was impropriate unto Glass[en]
bury, and the revenues of the lordship mounted to an 80li. by the yere.

From Stourminster over the bridge, I kept thens a mile farther I passid over
a bridge of 4 arches that standith on a water callid Devilles broke, and thens about ...

Cornwal. Wadebridge.

om Wadebridge I rode a mile and there I passid a broke. This broke risith a 2 miles by [illegible] est above S. Esse, and so cumming by S. Esse cummith a 5 miles to this bridge, and so goith [illegible] Wadebridge into the streame of Alane. This broke is caullid [illegible]. There cummith [illegible] broke from Carnsew's house, and goith into Alane by the est side a mile above Padstow.

From Wadebridge to Dunmere bridge of 3 arches a 2 miles, under the which Alane runnith. [illegible] litle beyond is a bridge of one arche under the which the broke that cummith from Bodmin rennith [illegible] litle beneth Dunmere bridge goith into Alane.

There is another broke cumming from south west [illegible] a 2 miles beneth the confluence [illegible] to Alane on the same side above Wadebridge. From Dunmere bridge to Bodmin a mile.

Bodmin.

The towne of Bodmin lyith almost in length by west and est, there is a chapel [illegible] . . . . . . end of the towne and another at the . . . . The paroche [illegible] at . . . . [illegible] of the towne. A Carnarie chapel in the [illegible].

The Priory stood at the est side [illegible] of the paroche churchyard. There lyith buried before [illegible] on high tombe of very darkish gray marble one Tho: Vivian Prior of [B]odmin and Suffragan [illegible] episcopatus, he dyed not long sins.

There was a place of Gray Friars by south on the market place of Bodmin, one John of [Lo]ndon a merchant began it. Edmund E[arl] of Cornwal was after a good benefactor unto it. [illegible] Hugh Peverel and S. Tho: Peverel benefactors to the house. A river [illegible]. [Th]is river cummith fro south est and goith into Alane a 2 miles above Padstow, by the west [si]de, and it ebbith and flowith fro Alane up into the creke of this river.

S. Lawrence.

From Bodmin to S. Columbes 8 miles. From Bodmin to S. Laurence, where there is a [p]oore hospital or lazarhouse, about a mile, and of the Peverels gave a litle annuity to this [illegible], there I passid over a stone bridge and under it runnith a praty broke, the which cummith out of the [illegible] [s]outh est and goith into Alane a 2 miles above Padstow by the west side, and by the [illegible] the [illegible] crekes, it ebbith and flowith up into the creke of this river.

From S. Laurence I passid by morish ground al barren of wood a 6 miles, leving about [illegible] 6 miles and S. Columbes, about a 2 miles of on the right hand, and thereabout I left [illegible] on the same hand a good mile of, but I saw no building on it, but [illegible] bering the name. Thens to S. Michael a litle thoroughfare a 2 or 3 miles [by] moorish ground, al barren of wood. Thens a 5 miles to a litle . . . . . . paroche church . . . . and thereabout the . . . . very good corne.

. . . . This Arundell cummith not of the house of great Ar[un]del of Lanheron by S. Columbes, but a cumming [illegible] thought, the name of the Arundels in [illegible] Normandy, the which were lordes of Ewly castel, that is now descended to one [illegible] de la Fontaine [a] Frenchman by heire general. This Arundale is callid of Trerise for difference fro him of [La]nheron. Trerise is a lordship of his 4 miles fro [illegible]. Arundale of Tre[r]ise had to his first wife one of the 2 doughters and heires of Boivile alias Bevile, and Grenevile [ha]d the other, and they had betwixt them litle lakke of 400 markes of land by yere in partition.

Trerise.

The house that Jo: Arundel of Trerise dwellith in, was Beviles, who bare for his armes an [illegible] gules in or. There is yet one of the name of Bevile a man of an [illegible] land purchasid by his grand[fa]ther . . . . . . Bevile now living [illegible] Bevile hath . . . . [illegible] . . . . [illegible]

[illegible] Jo: Arundel of Trerise. [illegible] Arundel a man of [illegible]